CRIMINAL MISCONDUCT IN OFFICE

OXFORD MONOGRAPHS ON CRIMINAL LAW AND JUSTICE

Series Editor: Andrew Ashworth CBE QC, Emeritus Vinerian Professor of English Law, All Souls College, Oxford

This series aims to cover all aspects of criminal law and procedure including criminal evidence. The scope of this series is wide, encompassing both practical and theoretical works.

OTHER TITLES IN THIS SERIES

The Preventive Turn in Criminal Law
Henrique Carvalho

Criminal Justice and Taxation
Peter Alldridge

In Search of Criminal Responsibility
Ideas, Interests, and Institutions
Nicola Lacey

Character in the Criminal Trial
Mike Redmayne

Preventive Justice
Andrew Ashworth and Lucia Zedner

Homicide and the Politics of Law Reform
Jeremy Horder

The Insecurity State
Vulnerable Autonomy and the Right to Security in the Criminal Law
Peter Ramsay

Manifest Madness
Mental Incapacity in the Criminal Law
Arlie Loughnan

The Ethics of Plea Bargaining
Richard L. Lippke

Punishment and Freedom
Alan Brudner

Prosecuting Domestic Violence
A Philosophical Analysis
Michelle Madden Dempsey

Abuse of Process and Judicial Stays of Criminal Proceedings
Andrew L.-T. Choo

A Philosophy of Evidence Law
Justice in the Search for Truth
Hock Lai Ho

The Criminal Justice System and Healthcare
Edited by Charles A. Erin and Suzanne Ost

Rethinking Imprisonment
Richard Lippke

Killing in Self-Defence
Fiona Leverick

Delayed Prosecution for Childhood Sexual Abuse
Penney Lewis

Lying, Cheating, and Stealing
A Moral Theory of White Collar Crime
Stuart P. Green

Defining Crimes
The Special Part of Criminal Law
Edited by Anthony Duff and Stuart P. Green

Criminal Responsibility
Victor Tadros

Proportionate Sentencing
Exploring the Principles
Andrew von Hirsch and Andrew Ashworth

Appraising Strict Liability
Edited by Andrew Simester

Criminal Misconduct in Office

Law and Politics

JEREMY HORDER

OXFORD
UNIVERSITY PRESS

OXFORD
UNIVERSITY PRESS

Great Clarendon Street, Oxford, OX2 6DP,
United Kingdom

Oxford University Press is a department of the University of Oxford.
It furthers the University's objective of excellence in research, scholarship,
and education by publishing worldwide. Oxford is a registered trade mark of
Oxford University Press in the UK and in certain other countries

First Edition published in 2018

British Library Cataloguing in Publication Data
Data available

Library of Congress Control Number: 2018930537

ISBN 978–0–19–882370–4

General Editor's Preface

This monograph opens up the (until recently) somewhat neglected topics of misconduct in a public office and corruption. It is a volume that combines research in history, in political theory, and in law—not just criminal law, but also regulatory and constitutional law. Jeremy Horder interweaves these approaches to scholarship with the events of the twenty-first century, notably the exposure of self-serving practices among members of parliament in the first decade and the subsequent institutional response to those practices. The arresting term 'corruption' is used advisedly, with reference not only to abuse of a public office for self-serving or dishonest ends but also to other practices that are dishonest, on either a political or a personal level. The author argues that there are degrees of misconduct and corruption, and that the response to them should be sensitive and proportionate. The most egregious forms of corruption should still be the subject of criminal prosecution, using forms of an offence such as misconduct in a public office: the criminal law would thereby discharge the function of protecting constitutional values. But there may be lesser forms of corruption and misconduct that justify a lesser response, such as what the author calls 'negation' (taking away a gain or benefit) and other regulatory penalties. In the monograph's final chapter, Professor Horder ranges over a variety of recent political events in order to illustrate the application of the definitions of corruption and misconduct, and in so doing he demonstrates the way in which scholarship of this depth and breadth succeeds in placing the criminal law in its proper constitutional context.

Andrew Ashworth

Preface

In some respects, the research and writing for this book has taken me back thirty years, to the time of writing my doctoral thesis. I was inspired to write on an area of law about which I knew little, facing persistent uncertainty about the direction in which to head (dead ends and red herrings aplenty), but also maintaining a clear belief that I could make a worthwhile scholarly difference if I could reach the end.

Having done so, this time, I am left with the firm conviction that, risky though it may be, criminal lawyers have something to contribute by leaving the comfort zone of offences against the person and property, general defences or principles, and the other bread-and-butter issues germane to textbooks, and applying their learning to very different fields of activity. My focus has been corruption in high places, but there are many other fields where a similar approach could be taken.

That I have indeed reached the end this time is in no small measure due to the help and assistance of others. I would like to thank Professor Alan Ware for steering me away from a number of errors, as well as for his wise counsel more generally. I am also very grateful for the painstaking work of Gabriele Watts in reading and correcting the manuscript, as well as to Sharon Park for doing the same, in addition to compiling a table of cases and statutes.

Table of Contents

Table of Cases

NON-UK CASES

Hong Kong

Victoria, Australia

Canada

United States

Table of Statutes

UK STATUTES

NON-UK STATUTES

United States

Australia

International

Introduction

The initial driving force behind the decision to write this book was astonishment, and no little anger, at how few members of the UK Parliament faced criminal investigation following the expenses scandal of 2009. Barely more than a handful of Members of Parliament (MPs) faced charges. Those who did were blatant abusers, even of the lax scheme MPs had themselves set down (initially keeping the details of expenditure secret from the public) to govern expense claims. Many expense abusers were not investigated for criminal wrongdoing. This was not owing to evidential difficulties. It was the result of a failure of nerve on the part of a prosecution service reluctant to be seen taking large numbers of elected politicians through the criminal courts. This reluctance was accompanied by an unwillingness to see MPs' closely guarded spending privileges and practices judged at the bar of public (jury) opinion, in the way that they would have been, had the offence of misconduct in a public office been deployed against MPs indulging in those practices.

Here is an example. In his Report following the 2009 scandal, Sir Thomas Legg said that:

> a particular challenge has proved to be the widespread lack of proper evidence on the record from MPs to support substantial payments, especially of mortgage interest, even though this was expressly required by the rules.[1]

Yet, it has been clear for 250 years or more that the undue destruction of public records constitutes misconduct in a public office. For Sir Matthew Hale:

> at the common law the undue razure or embezzling of a record was a great offence, for which even a judge himself was punishable by fine and imprisonment.[2]

Why were MPs who disposed of the evidence of mortgage interest payments they were required to retain not prosecuted on this basis for misconduct in public office? If there were widespread failures amongst MPs to obtain such evidence, why were there no prosecutions on the straightforward basis that such a failure, in knowing breach of the rules, amounts in itself to an abuse of the public's trust and hence constitutes criminal misconduct? Further, those in positions of authority, responsible for allowing widespread abuse of the system to flourish, escaped the attention of the prosecution authorities altogether. They escaped prosecution, even though

[1] Sir Thomas Legg (2010), at para 9.

[2] Sir Matthew Hale (1736), at 646.

the misconduct offence, focused on abuse of public trust, is perfectly capable of applying to those guilty of management failures.[3] Constitutionally, parliamentarians have historically been insulated from legal challenge, when they devise expense schemes favourable to themselves and their families, by reliance on parliamentary privilege. In Chapter 4, the breadth of this doctrine—the rationale of which is freedom of speech, not freedom to spend—is challenged, in so far as it can protect corrupt practices from legal action.

There is, however, a broader story that I seek to relate. This concerns the constitutional significance of the offence of misconduct in a public office. This offence should be seen as a constitutional fundamental. It provides an essential way in which, as a last resort, prosecutors and courts can deter and punish (with an appropriate label) corrupt conduct on the part of legislators and other officials, and thereby make the use of power accountable by reference to the standards of ordinary people. When other—civil law or regulatory—means prove insufficient, it should ultimately be possible for ordinary members of a jury, and not for parliamentarians, to decide whether and when the expenditure of public money on legislators' private income and benefits amounts to a criminal abuse of the public's trust. This is what I call the 'bottom-up' (jury standards-led) as opposed to the 'top-down' (officials applying their own standards) view of the role and limits of the use of the criminal law in constitutional contexts.

Although MPs' misconduct provided the motivation for writing this book, an important intellectual challenge has been to provide a history, philosophy, and politics of the offence of misconduct in office, an offence hitherto little considered by mainstream criminal law theorists in the UK (with some honourable exceptions). This challenge is pursued in Chapters 1–3, in a way that I hope will make this book of relevance to anyone interested in the constitutional role of the misconduct offence. In Chapter 1, I provide reasons to regard to courts' power to apply the misconduct offence to MPs' conduct as a vital measure of last resort to deter and punish corruption at the highest level. In Chapter 2, I turn my attention to the justification for the offence more broadly. Is misconduct in office an offence clearly supported by the harm principle, like other offences, or is it best explained by reference to some other principle of criminalization? What kinds of misconduct does the offence legitimately cover? In that regard, we will see that codes of conduct that govern officials—a vital written element to the UK's constitution—play a role not merely in setting boundaries but also in minimizing rule of law uncertainty about the kind of misconduct that may be found to fall within the scope of the offence. In Chapter 3, I explore the development of the offence principally during the eighteenth century. I see in that development an emerging contrast between the bottom-up and top-down understandings of the role of the misconduct offence in holding officials to account in criminal law. I also explain the way in which the offence came to be regarded as one edge of a two-edged sword (the other edge being judicial review) in the hands of

[3] There were many egregious and well-documented failures of this kind leading up to and during the so-called 'rotten' Parliament of 2005–2010: Sir Thomas Legg (n 1) para 2.

the courts, to deter and punish official misconduct. I find in Sir William Blackstone's work an important constitutional theoretical justification for the offence.

No analysis of the misconduct offence would be complete, in its bearing on MPs, without a broader understanding of corruption, and of the weaknesses in the UK's political system that make it prone to corrupt influences. A definition of 'corruption' is provided in Chapter 4, distinguishing personal and political corruption. Political corruption is then the focus of Chapter 5. In Chapter 5, I explore the important point that prosecution for a serious common law offence such as misconduct in a public office can hardly be the sole, or even the main, way in which officials are held to account for corrupt conduct. So, I consider the most important—indeed, primary—remedy for corruption in politics, which I call 'negation': the setting back at naught of corrupt (potential) gains. I then go on to consider efforts to address risks of corruption through regulation (including regulatory offences), especially in relation to elections, but also in relation to the practice of 'lobbying'. Discussion of lobbying provides an opportunity to discuss in Chapter 5 how 'republican' the UK constitution really is: how resistant it is to cheque-book influences, or more broadly to the influence of repeat players amongst the wealthy and powerful. I do not have detailed political prescriptions to apply in such contexts, but what I do offer is a view of the proper relationship and application of the civil law (the remedy of negation), regulatory criminal offences, and the offence of misconduct in a public office. In broad terms, whilst increased scrutiny of lobbyists would be highly desirable, there also needs to be a greater deterrent focus on the role of MPs and ministers who make themselves available to lobbyists (a matter addressed in Chapter 4).

Here follows a brief summary of some of the specific conclusions I reach, in relation to the law of misconduct in public office:

1. *Chapter 1*: in constitutional terms, corrupt custom and practice tolerated by MPs, to benefit themselves, is rightly challenged and deterred through use of the criminal law, and of the misconduct offence in particular.
2. *Chapter 2*: there should be two offences of misconduct:
    (a) Wilful neglect or misconduct (whether through act or omission), amounting to an abuse of a public position, power, or duty. In appropriate cases, it should be possible to deal with this offence through the imposition of an administrative penalty.
    (b) Misconduct (whether through act or omission), amounting to an abuse of a public position, power or duty, caused by gross negligence on the part of a public organization, in which negligence on the part of senior managers played a substantial role.
3. *Chapter 3*: The misconduct offence was understood historically, and should still be understood, as a dimension of public law, buttressing the power of judicial review respecting official errors. The offence has always been understood to be concerned with the deterrence and punishment of officials who have gone beyond mere error, and betrayed the trust placed in them, by acting in a self-serving or dishonest way.

4. *Chapter 4*: the use of public funds by MPs to employ their spouses or relatives should have been (and should still be) regarded as criminal corruption and hence misconduct in public office, notwithstanding its status as a widespread custom and practice.
5. *Chapter 4*: parliamentary privilege, excluding the jurisdiction of the courts, should apply only to speech or collective decisions made in the course of parliamentary proceedings. When such decisions introduce schemes for spending by MPs that would be regarded as corrupt by ordinary people of integrity, parliamentary privilege should not then extend to individual spending decisions outside parliamentary proceedings. Privilege should not extend that far, even if an individual spending decision is in conformity with the (privileged) collective decision in question.
6. *Chapter 4*: the misconduct offence should be regarded as covering a dishonest breach of the Ministerial Code of conduct, and the dishonest making of a false or misleading statement in relation to an obligation under that code. Alternatively, such conduct should be made the subject of specific criminal offences.
7. *Chapter 4*: the misconduct offence should be regarded as covering (a) a dishonest breach of the MPs' code of conduct as it relates to obligations, inter alia, respecting lobbying, and (b) the dishonest making of a false or misleading statement in relation to such an obligation under that code. Alternatively, such conduct should be made the subject of specific criminal offences.
8. *Chapter 4*: parliamentary parties should be regarded as unincorporated associations, meaning that they can be prosecuted for criminal offences such as misconduct.
9. *Chapter 5*: the misconduct offence should be used to target the toleration by senior officials of election spending abuses.

1

Criminal Misconduct and the Constitution

1.1 Corruption and the Offence of Misconduct in Constitutional Jurisprudence

> [Government] is therefore a trust, which ought to be bounded with many and strong restraints, because power renders men wanton, insolent to others, and fond of themselves. Every violation therefore of this trust, where such violation is considerable, ought to meet with proportionable punishment.[1]

The demand that public officials behave consistently in an ethical manner in the discharge of their duties ought to be recognized as one of the most significant of all constitutional requirements. The criminal law, and the offence of misconduct in a public office in particular, very obviously has the potential to be a powerful disincentive to—as well as an appropriate punishment for—the worst kinds of unethical behaviour perpetrated by public officials. Yet, few theorists have explored the properties of the criminal law and of the misconduct offence that make it part of constitutional law and protection in this respect.

Through the use of the criminal law to punish and deter culpable breaches of duty by those holding public office, the Crown Prosecution Service (CPS) and the courts may play a crucial role in ensuring that key constitutional principles do not yield to pernicious countervailing tendencies, such as corrupt customs and practice.[2] In that regard, the misconduct offence can come into its own, not simply because there may be no other more specific offence that applies to a public office holder's conduct, but because no other offence will label the wrongdoing in an appropriate way. As the Law Commission remarked about the misconduct offence:

> It may be argued that there may be a distinctive wrong inherent in a public office holder committing a serious breach of a determinative duty. If such an individual were simply to be charged with fraud, for example, this might not accurately convey the distinctive nature of the wrong inherent in the fact he or she committed a serious breach of the duties associated with his or her office.[3]

[1] John Trenchard and Thomas Gordon, letter of 22 July 1721, in John Trenchard and Thomas Gordon (1995), cited by Mark Knights (2016), at 13.
[2] Such as those sustained by MPs, considered in ch 4.
[3] Law Commission (2016a), at para 5.54.

When officials misconduct themselves in making decisions, the right remedy may be the quashing of the decision, as through judicial review; but clearly, not all forms of misconduct come in the form of a 'decision' that may be reviewed and quashed. For a police officer verbally or physically to abuse a suspect is not conduct with a character making it susceptible to judicial review. That is one of the reasons why, in cases of abuse of suspects by police officers (or by other public officials), general criminal offences are capable of providing a bulwark against state oppression.[4] In any event, the taking of some decisions involves by its nature such serious wrongdoing that the criminal law is rightly invoked to deter and punish those who took the decision, irrespective of the decision's legal validity. An example would be the decision by a police officer to disclose to a criminal gang the identity and whereabouts of the individual who reported the gang's activities to the police.

In such cases, the CPS and the courts can be understood as implementing the will of Parliament, either specifically or generally, in relation to the way in which society expects that its public office-holders will behave in accordance with the rule of law. Yet, there is more to what prosecutors and the courts do in such cases than see to the implementation of the will of Parliament: the 'top-down' justification for their role in controlling the (ab)use of public power. There is also a 'bottom-up' justification for this role.[5] For the citizen subject to an abuse of power, the enforcement of the criminal law against the abuser may be his or her last resort or line of defence against abuse.[6] It may also be the only way in which to secure public affirmation of the individual's status as someone who has been wronged, and wronged not just by anyone, but by an agent of the state whose responsibility it was to promote the public good rather than betray it. We could think of this as the 'republican' dimension to the role of prosecutors and the courts, in using the criminal law to deter and punish wrongdoing on the part of officials. As Philip Pettit puts it:

> The republican notion of freedom as citizenship has a second distinctive connotation ... Citizenship gives protection and constitutes freedom only so far as the law is appropriately framed, respected, and applied and only so far, therefore, as people can be relied upon to make themselves available for public office *and to behave properly while in office*.[7]

For that reason, action taken against state officials in the name of the Crown is, perhaps paradoxically, in an important sense a 'bottom-up' form of control or influence over state power. Prosecutors and judges can and do defend the interests of the *(re)public*, in their capacity as Crown officials. It is not only parliamentarians who represent the public in their capacity as elected representatives. Broadly, the same point was made by Lord Mansfield in his discussion of the offence of misconduct

[4] For an outstanding discussion of this point see John Gardner (2013a). For further discussion of this example see ch 2.5 and 2.9.

[5] See ch 3 on the historical background to the 'top-down' and 'bottom-up' roles of the courts in controlling corruption.

[6] On the importance of public officials as the 'last line of resort' see John Gardner (n 4) 113–16.

[7] Philip Pettit (1996), at 312 (my emphasis). For criticism of Pettit's understanding of the link between freedom and institutional guarantees of non-domination see Thomas W Simpson (2017). These criticisms do not affect the analysis given here.

in a public office when, in speaking of that offence as an offence against the king, he added: 'and when I say "the King", or "Public", I mean the same thing'.[8]

What is the position when the misconduct at issue is that of those holding the highest elected office, Members of Parliament (MPs)? The hallowed place of the doctrine of parliamentary supremacy, within the separation of powers, means that there is no place for prosecutors and courts in protecting people from misconduct in what can broadly be called parliamentary proceedings, even though the courts reserve the right to police the boundaries of what are treated as parliamentary 'proceedings'.[9] Article 9 of the Bill of Rights protects such proceedings from legal challenge.[10] So, the role of the courts in upholding principles of anti-corruption and the rule of law, when such proceedings are in issue, might seem to be only a highly attenuated one. In some respects, that is inevitable. We may sometimes have to trust Parliament itself to devise and follow procedures to ensure that its members do not abuse their privileges: for example, in relation to the exercise of freedom of speech within Parliament. We may, at least in some instances, have to do this because the intervention of the courts in such matters might exercise a 'chilling' effect on parliamentary speech more detrimental to good constitutional governance, in the long run, than any gains to be had from policing such speech with a view to providing legal remedies for wrongdoing.[11] We can think of such cases as cases where absolute trust must be placed in parliamentarians themselves to avoid and provide remedies for wrongdoing.

However, there is a great deal more parliamentary activity that is shielded from challenge or prosecution in the courts than intrinsically valued and constitutionally crucial activity, such as speaking in Parliament. Parliament's 'exclusive cognisance'—its freedom from challenge in the courts—extends to embrace, for example, multi-million pound decisions about spending on the parliamentary estate (enhancing the conditions in which MPs work).[12] Such decisions—which cover, say, a decision to refurbish a fully equipped gym within the estate[13]—carry a risk that they will be driven by self-interest, rather than being motivated by a desire to enhance the democratic vitality of the state. Yet, it seems that they are shielded from challenge just the same. We discuss this issue in depth in Chapter 4, but a brief examination of the more jurisprudential aspects of the courts' position is called for here.

There can be no 'top-down' justification—fidelity to the intention of Parliament—on which the courts can draw to challenge decisions within Parliament's exclusive cognizance. In a democracy, the argument is that there will be 'bottom-up' influence on such matters, not through prosecutions or litigation against government by citizens, but through the electoral process. In the next section, some reasons will be given to think that the electoral process is not in practice an effective or sensible way

[8] *Rex v Bembridge* (1783) XXII State Trials 29, at 152.

[9] See *R v Chaytor* [2010] UKSC 52, and the discussion in ch 4.9 and 4.10.

[10] See the discussion in ch 4. Article 9 reads: 'the freedom of speech and debates or proceedings in Parliament ought not to be impeached or questioned in any court or place out of Parliament'.

[11] See the discussion in ch 4.8. [12] ibid.

[13] See https://www.parliament.uk/site-information/foi/foi-and-eir/commons-foi-disclosures/estates-information/westminster-gym-refit-2014/.

in which to ensure that such influence is felt. Moreover, at a theoretical level, there is an alternative way of approaching the issue. First, we identify conduct on the part of MPs that is predominantly self-directed, as opposed to being part and parcel of the development of public policy. Then, we say that we repose only *conditional* as opposed to absolute trust in MPs to be entirely self-governing, with respect to the nature and limits of that self-directed conduct.[14] Having done that, we can say that the trust breaks down when the conduct in question is tainted by corruption, giving the courts (or other independent bodies) a legitimate basis for intervening through the use of the criminal law in appropriate cases. As Zephyr Teachout argues, albeit in an American constitutional context:

> [T]he 'anti-corruption' principle should be treated as a freestanding constitutional principle ... In cases ranging from campaign finance to gerrymandering, this deeply embedded idea should inform whether or not ... [official] efforts to reform political processes can be upheld.[15]

Anti-corruption principles already exercise constraints within the UK constitution, creating situations of conditional trust and even constraining the democratic process. Parliament has decreed that the electoral process may itself be questioned in a court on the grounds of corruption. In some instances, such as 'treating' (bribing) the electorate,[16] it is the criminal law that becomes involved. A broader example where a breach of (conditional) trust can lead to a legal remedy can be found in section 164 of the Representation of the People Act 1983. An election is void if, on an election 'petition',[17] it is found that:

> corrupt or illegal practices or illegal payments, employments or hirings committed in reference to the election for the purpose of promoting or procuring the election of any person at that election have so extensively prevailed that they may be reasonably supposed to have affected the result.

As will be seen in Chapter 5, there are many instances in which gains or appointments, made in the political sphere but tainted by corruption, may be negated and suspect political donations to parties compulsorily returned, if not through court processes then through the work of independent tribunals or similar bodies. It is not fanciful to suggest that the avoidance of corruption plays a constitutional role as important as the observance of the rule of law.[18] That is arguable, even if it is the (non-)observance of the rule of law that is most often litigated, and which has tended to hog the jurisprudential limelight in the post Diceyan period.[19] In all of the instances just mentioned, such as the offence under section 164 of the 1983 Act, what might broadly be called political actions are regarded as only conditionally matters to be 'punished' by no means other than the ballot box, and hence beyond the scrutiny

[14] An approach consistent with 'leveller' opinion, encountered in ch 3.1.

[15] Zephyr Teachout (2009), at 343.

[16] See the Representation of the People Act 1983, s 114. The 1983 Act contains a number of other corruption-related electoral offences, such as bribery and personation.

[17] On petitions see the Electoral Commission (2012), at paras 13–16.

[18] See Teachout (n 15).

[19] See Evan Fox-Decent (2011), at 172.

of the courts or other independent bodies. Where such political actions are tainted by corruption, the trust we place in the political actors who performed them breaks down. That breakdown of trust can and should expose the actors to legal proceedings (including, where appropriate, criminal prosecution) that are—as in the case of an election petition—themselves a kind of 'bottom-up' means of exercising influence or control in the political sphere.[20]

Let me pursue these points a little further, in relation to the subject of Chapter 4, the personal corruption of MPs. In recent times, much has been done through the introduction of regulation of different kinds to impose a measure of control, openness, and accountability in relation to the non-legislative (mis)use by MPs of their powers, individually and collectively. Two prominent examples are the establishment of the Independent Parliamentary Standards Authority (IPSA)[21] and of the Parliamentary Commissioner for Standards.[22] These regulatory efforts are largely concerned with the important tasks of preventing abuse, perhaps especially financial misconduct, with negating its effects (as through requiring repayment), or with invoking Parliament's internal disciplinary procedures to deal with offenders.[23] These bodies work *with* MPs, on rule-application,[24] something that the courts do not do. Inevitably, thus, there will be tension between the IPSA's and the Commissioner's dual roles in, on the one hand, advising MPs as to the correctness of their claims or their conduct[25] and, on the other hand, monitoring breaches of the rules.[26] The legitimacy of bodies such as the Parliamentary Standards Authority and the IPSA is ever-precarious, unlike the position of the courts. Senior MPs put formal pressure on the former to change decisions or proposals they do not like,[27] or call for their abolition in order to avoid scrutiny of expenditure[28] in a way they do not typically do where the courts are concerned. As Kelly and Hamlyn put it:

> [U]ltimately, Members still decide collectively how to deal with breaches of the Code of Conduct, in that the House as a whole can overturn recommendations from the Committee on Standards (which can itself decline to accept recommendations from the Commissioner).[29]

In Dawn Oliver's terms, in this respect, when challenged, parliamentarians may tend to exhibit 'groupish' or clannish behaviour, not only towards rival parties, but also towards bodies doing the challenging when they are perceived to be constitutionally inferior to themselves, even if those bodies are notionally independent:

[20] Dawn Oliver (2010), at 664.

[21] http://parliamentarystandards.org.uk/Pages/default.aspx.

[22] http://www.parliament.uk/mps-lords-and-offices/standards-and-interests/pcfs/.

[23] http://www.parliament.uk/mps-lords-and-offices/standards-and-financial-interests/parliamentary-commissioner-for-standards/complaints-and-investigations/.

[24] See eg http://parliamentarystandards.org.uk/IPSAMPs/Guidance/Pages/home.aspx.

[25] http://parliamentarystandards.org.uk/IPSAMPs/Guidance/Pages/home.aspx.

[26] Through the actions of IPSA's compliance officer: http://www.parliamentarycompliance.org.uk/Pages/default.aspx.

[27] http://www.theguardian.com/politics/2015/jun/04/david-cameron-to-write-to-ipsa-over-mps-pay-rise.

[28] http://www.theguardian.com/politics/2016/aug/30/corbyn-ally-calls-for-mps-expenses-to-be-paid-automatically.

[29] Richard Kelly and Matthew Hamlyn (2013), at 118.

> Commonly when relationships are conflictual in politics, groups and their members tend to put their own interests … before the public interest, which they are supposed to be prioritising.[30]

As Oliver rightly observes, when this happens parliamentarians may need reminding—by the courts, if need be—that 'their purpose is supposed to be a public interest'.[31] What this means is that bodies such as the IPSA cannot be systematically concerned with the development of law and policy in relation to the deterrence and punishment of serious corruption in the use of high office, other than when they refer an individual case—as any citizen might do—to the police. These regulatory bodies can develop rules that should be followed by MPs to avoid conflicts of interest or other ethically questionable behaviour. They would be nonetheless relatively powerless if MPs decided *en masse* to ignore or belittle those rules.[32] These bodies cannot, thus, deal adequately with culpability for unethical—corrupt—conduct if MPs feel relatively free simply to block the development of regulatory oversight when it goes in that direction.[33] In a broader context, this is a basic point about regulation. In regulatory contexts, one may expect to use the criminal law relatively rarely; but without a genuine threat that it may be used, in (say) cases of serious, highly culpable, or persistent wrongdoing, the force and legitimacy of the regulatory enterprise may be blunted or undermined.[34]

Following the seminal work of Antony Duff, criminal lawyers have learned to acknowledge that the criminal law is, beyond matters of deterrence and retribution, a system with the high moral purpose of calling people to account for their wrongs.[35] Even so, criminal lawyers are yet to explore fully the overlap that this creates with the high constitutional principle of calling political wrongdoers to account when they betray their office. This book begins that exploration. Speaking of judicial review, Paul Craig has explained that:

> The constitution assigns a role to the courts as well as the legislator … In a constitutional democracy it is both right and proper for the courts to impose limits on the way in which power is exercised. This was indeed the *traditional* approach to the constraints imposed on public power in the seminal case law which laid the foundations for judicial review. The courts imposed limits that were felt to be normatively justified. Coke, Heath, Holt and Mansfield based judicial review on the capacity of the common law to control public power.[36]

As we will see in Chapter 3, for Lord Mansfield, that traditional approach also involved the application of the offence of misconduct in public office. This offence constituted one edge of a two-edged sword with which the misuse of public power could be attacked, the other cutting edge being provided by judicial review. For that reason, we can categorize misconduct in a public office as a hybrid, public–criminal

[30] See Oliver (n 20) 656–57. [31] ibid 657.

[32] http://www.telegraph.co.uk/news/politics/12194972/MPs-break-the-rules-because-they-do-not-agree-with-them-says-standards-watchdog-Kathryn-Hudson.html.

[33] http://www.theguardian.com/politics/2014/jul/14/mps-standards-independent-watchdog-grave-concerns-blocked-debate-andrew-lansley.

[34] See more generally Law Commission (n 3). [35] See eg R A Duff (2007).

[36] Paul Craig, *Administrative Law* (2008), at 21 (Craig's emphasis). See further Paul Craig (2000).

law remedy. The misconduct offence should be reconceived as a key dimension of the 'sacred'[37] public law principle that *nemo iudex in sua causa*—'no one may be a judge in their own cause'—especially when what is at issue is the advancement of the personal (pecuniary; proprietary; family) interests of those who take decisions using their public powers.[38] As Justice Michael McHugh observed in the *Spycatcher* case: 'governments . . . are constitutionally required to act in the *public* interest'.[39]

1.2 Personal Corruption and MPs: Who Will Guard the Guards?

> Few are in a higher position of trust or have a duty to discharge in which the public have a greater interest, than Members of Parliament.[40]

Most systems of government carry the risk that they will be subject to so-called 'X inefficiency', that is, inefficiency stemming from uncritical self-evaluation in relation to the running of house administration.[41] X inefficiency is a problem rooted in a familiar rhetorical question: *quis custodies ipsos custodiet* ('who will guard the guards')? Consider a firm in which managers are judges not only of workers' effectiveness but also of their own (managerial) effectiveness. In such a firm, there will be a tendency for managers to act self-interestedly with regard to the assessment of managerial effectiveness, rather than in a way that maximizes managers' productivity, because managers are accountable only to themselves. To the extent that this occurs, 'X inefficiency' is liable to become endemic, unless kept at bay by the pressure of market forces. The analysis can be applied with equal effect to Parliament. Parliament does not performance-manage its MPs, and so there are no benchmarks against which to assess performance, and few accepted ways of testing whether MPs are working as opposed to shirking.[42] Parliamentarians are the judges of their own efficiency, as well as standards, in relation to 'house-keeping', and hence may be tempted to maximize benefits for themselves rather than for those in whose interests they govern. The World Bank has explained how this temptation should be understood in economic terms in relation to government and its agencies:

> Corruption will tend to emerge when an organization or person has monopoly power over a good or service which generates rent, has the discretion to decide who will receive it (thus on how rents will be allocated), and is not accountable.[43]

[37] See Craig, *Administrative Law* (n 36) 418.

[38] As a number of theorists have pointed out, the *nemo iudex* principle is of most constitutional significance in such cases—where personal interests clash with public responsibilities. In many other instances, the simple fact that one is a judge in one's own cause—for example, when a competent court or Parliament determines its own jurisdiction—is not necessarily even a prima facie wrong. For a helpful discussion see Adrian Vermeule (2012).

[39] *Attorney-General (UK) v Heinemann Publishers Australia Pty Ltd* (1987) 10 NSWLR 86, 191 (my emphasis).

[40] *R v Greenway* [1998] PL 356 at 358 (Buckley J).

[41] See generally Harvey Liebenstein (1966).

[42] For a benign view see Timothy Besley and Valentino Larcinese (2011).

[43] World Bank (2015).

In the parliamentary context, there is no doubt that X inefficiency (resulting in increased costs) has been assisted by information asymmetry facilitating a situation of moral hazard, arising from the way in which Parliament takes decisions in its collective capacity. For so long protected by the paucity of information about their expenditure on administrative matters, MPs were relatively free to increase costs and engage in rent-seeking, safe in the knowledge that the costs could simply be passed on to the public purse. As the IPSA's one-time chief executive remarked about MPs' remuneration:

> Once you begin to look at MPs' remuneration, you can't help but be struck at the peculiar benefits which have grown up over time ... Successive governments failed to address MPs' pay in a transparent way. Resettlement payments emerged—worth up to a year's salary. And MPs' pensions evolved into something quite unsustainable.[44]

The MPs' pension scheme came at a cost of 32.4 per cent of payroll, as compared with an average of 21.6 per cent of payroll for the other main public service schemes, with the Treasury contributing a further 9.5 per cent of payroll to cover deficit in the fund. Following its introduction in 2010, the new regulatory scheme for claiming expenses introduced by the IPSA had saved over £35 million by 2013.[45] In relation to resettlement payments, a consultation on MPs' pay and pensions remarked:

> We turn next to the consideration of resettlement payments: these have historically been paid when MPs leave Parliament ... the financial cushion awarded to them on their return [to the community] is generous: at the end of the last Parliament, some MPs were entitled to a full year's salary. This is no longer justifiable, if it ever was. Before IPSA was established, resettlement was paid to all MPs on leaving Parliament at an election whether or not they fought for their seat ...[46]

Linked to the problem of X inefficiency reinforced by the secrecy cloaking key elements of their work, as well as the broader unaccountability of Parliament's 'managers' (MPs themselves), is the connection between white-collar crime and the violation of norms of trust.[47] As long ago as 1940, in his famous article coining the term 'white-collar crime', Edwin Sutherland observed that: '[the] varied types of white-collar crimes ... consist principally of violations of delegated or implied trust ...'.[48] Such violations are made easier and more tempting in situations of moral hazard: where one party or group (MPs) feels free to pass on costs or risks to another party or group (the public), because of information asymmetries and a lack of accountability.[49] What Lord Rodger refers to, in the leading decision on the subject,[50] as the constitutionally untouchable 'deliberative processes' of the House[51] can be

[44] Andrew McDonald (2013).
[45] Independent Parliamentary Standards Authority (2013a) http://www.bbc.co.uk/news/uk-politics-24063954.
[46] Independent Parliamentary Standards Authority (2013b), at paras 33 and 88.
[47] See Susan Shapiro (1990).
[48] Edwin Sutherland (1940), cited by Shapiro (n 47) 347.
[49] With pure moral hazard, rent-taking incumbents are aided in their survival as such by the privacy of information: see J Ferejohn (1986).
[50] *R v Chaytor* (n 9).
[51] ibid para 122.

understood criminologically in a quite different way. Speaking not only of private organizations but also of government bodies, Shapiro observes that:

> These 'collective' agents ... remain insulated from the preferences, demands, incentives, or surveillance of each discrete principal [voter] and relatively unresponsive to them ... the complex social organisation of agency relationship affords ... safer and more lucrative forms of fiduciary theft—for example, the abuse of discretion to serve personal interests (self-dealing) or the sale of fiduciary loyalty (corruption).[52]

The abuses of the assisted costs allowance scheme and the employment of family members are two good examples of how this analysis has played out in UK politics. Individual MPs do not benefit from these abuses to the same extent as some of their eighteenth-century predecessors (although that is not saying much in their favour). Even so, what is notable is, first, how widespread the abuses have been[53] and, secondly, how little understanding MPs have that their conduct is widely regarded as corrupt. Whereas only 15 per cent of MPs regard the use of allowances to employ their own relatives as an example of personal corruption, over 54 per cent of the public regard the practice in just such a light.[54] The significance of MPs' majority attitude is two-fold. First, it reduces the moral stakes involved for any hitherto honest MP thinking of becoming a rent-seeker, and limits the exposure to political risk of any established rent-seeker. As economists have put it: 'rent-takers survive ... if the fraction of honest incumbents is sufficiently small (and patience is great enough)'.[55] Secondly, the cross-party basis for abuse[56] means that the traditional political remedy for wrongdoing—'throw the rascals out!'—is blunted. Whoever is elected will face the same low moral stakes involved in becoming a rent-seeker, because the level of the stakes is not influenced by party lines. This problem is exacerbated by the well-known tendency for electors and parties alike to be motivated more by ideological considerations than by candidate probity when making decisions about candidates.[57]

The creation of the Parliamentary Standards Authority and the IPSA are indications that parliamentarians accept that they cannot be trusted institutionally to manage parliamentary administration themselves, without undue risks of X inefficiency, and in some instances corruption and abuse. Even now, however, there is evidence from the Commissioner for Parliamentary Standards that a parliamentary culture is maintained in which many MPs simply fail to acquaint themselves with the applicable ethical standards, or refuse to abide by them.[58] The IPSA has had to go as far as 'naming and shaming' some twenty-six MPs who, in spite of repeated warnings, failed to repay money wrongly claimed on expenses, with the result that

[52] Shapiro (n 47) 349 and 351.
[53] See the discussion in ch 4.7. On eighteenth-century practices see ch 4.3.
[54] Nicholas Allen and Sarah Birch (2015), at 84, discussed in ch 4.8.
[55] Leif Helland and Rune Sørensen (2012).
[56] See generally Robert Winnett and Gordon Rayner (2009).
[57] Helland Sørensen (n 55) 205.
[58] http://www.telegraph.co.uk/news/politics/12194972/MPs-break-the-rules-because-they-do-not-agree-with-them-says-standards-watchdog-Kathryn-Hudson.html.

the losses were written off.[59] The individual sums involved might be small, but a repeated failure to acknowledge the authority of the IPSA on the part of an MP ought to lead to at least the threat of prosecution for the offence of misconduct in public office. If that seems unduly censorious, it should be borne in mind that a benefit claimant who failed repeatedly to pay back money wrongly claimed would certainly expect to face the threat of criminal prosecution or civil penalty, even if the sum involved was small.[60]

In regulatory contexts, it is an important function of the criminal law to be available to punish not only serious but also repeated breaches of the relevant standards that reveal a contemptuous attitude towards the regulating authority. More broadly, as the Law Commission has put it:

> A further advantage [of having criminal prosecution available] may be gained if compliance authorities know that the courts will, if ultimately called upon to do so, take a firm line on the demands of retribution in particular (as well as deterrence). Such knowledge arguably makes it more likely that regulators or other appropriate authorities will, at first, pursue non-criminal options aimed at securing compliance by consent. They will do this because they have confidence that the courts will accept that the criminal process stands at the apex of a response pyramid, where breach of standards is concerned.[61]

I consider the regulatory systems in place to prevent corruption in politics in Chapter 5.

Constitutionally, there seems much to commend in a system in which it is the task of an independent prosecution service, supported by the judiciary, to underpin such regulatory systems with the threat of criminal prosecution. In the UK political system, the temptations for MPs to misuse office for personal gain have proved far easier to give in to than any similar temptations facing the prosecution service and judiciary. Consequently, public trust in the judiciary and in law enforcement agencies to avoid personal corruption is in general far higher than it is in politicians.[62] So, there should no objection to the CPS and the judiciary taking a more consistently assertive role in the pursuit of an anti-corruption agenda in the political domain. The need for such an assertive role seems particularly important in cases of personal corruption, and is further considered in Chapter 4. There has long been mistrust or scepticism, on both the political left and right, about granting the judiciary any significant constitutional role in what is jealously regarded as Parliament's domain.[63] I will not enter into that debate here, except to make one observation. When it comes to holding officials to account for personal corruption, it is judges, not politicians, who are required to adhere most closely in public and private to the ideals of a republican state, and who are thus required to do most to deserve our trust. As Mr Justice Thomas, a judge in the Supreme Court of Queensland, has put it:

[59] http://www.theguardian.com/politics/2015/sep/10/mp-expenses-ipsa-names-shames-26-mps-who-did-not-respond-to-queries. See also http://www.independent.co.uk/news/uk/politics/mps-pursued-for-thousands-in-overpaid-expenses-9973765.html.

[60] See further Jeremy Horder (2015).

[61] Law Commission (n 3) para 3.64.

[62] See Transparency International (2010), at para 3.4.

[63] The classic work is J A G Griffith (2010).

We form a particular group in the community. We comprise a select part of an honourable profession. We are entrusted, day after day, with the exercise of considerable power. Its exercise has dramatic effects upon the lives and fortunes of those who come before us. Citizens cannot be sure that they or their fortunes will not some day depend upon our judgment. They will not wish such power to be reposed in anyone whose honesty, ability or personal standards are questionable. It is necessary for the continuity of the system of law as we know it, that there be standards of conduct, both in and out of court, which are designed to maintain confidence in those expectations.[64]

For example, under the Judicial Code of Conduct for England and Wales, respecting the obligation of propriety it is set down that:

A judge and members of the judge's family, shall neither ask for, nor accept, any gift, bequest, loan or favour in relation to anything done or to be done or omitted to be done by the judge in connection with the performance of judicial duties.[65]

By contrast, a study of MPs in 2005 (updated to 2015) showed that only 35 per cent of MPs considered that it would be corrupt to accept a gift of a crate of wine at Christmas from an 'influential constituent', as compared with 52 per cent of members of the public who regarded such conduct as corrupt.[66] It is demonstrably judges, not politicians, who occupy the moral high ground when one comes to consider who is best placed to pass judgment on the integrity and propriety of MPs' conduct.

What about the accountability of politicians to the public? As Larcinese and Sircar remark:

unlike in other dimensions of a politician's activity, it is very difficult for citizens to directly observe corruption, [and so] it is therefore only if and when abuses are reported by the media that they may become known to citizens.[67]

Following the so-called expenses scandal in 2009, generated by media exposure, the opportunity soon arose in the general election of 2010 for voters to punish MPs who had been exposed as abusers of their expenses. However, Larcinese and Sircar's study of the electoral fallout from the scandal reveals a complex picture of the reaction to the scandal. MPs exposed to a high degree of negative media coverage—disproportionately, women—were more likely to stand down and not seek re-election or, if they did seek re-election, would suffer a reduced vote share. Even so, overall, MPs' chances of re-election were not significantly affected by the scandal.[68] This is related to the crucial fact that political 'partisanship' plays a significant role in perceptions of MPs' responsibility for wrongdoing. Crudely, 'perceived involvement of an MP is reduced, *ceteris paribus*, when the MP belongs to the political party the respondent feels closer to'.[69] Broadened onto the international stage, the same point can be made, in that it is equally clear that an MP can expect to

[64] Mr Justice Thomas (1997), at 9.
[65] Judiciary of England and Wales (2013), at para 5.1.14.
[66] Allen and Birch (n 54) 84.
[67] Valentino Larcinese and Indraneel Sircar (2012), at 3.
[68] ibid 4.
[69] ibid 5.

survive corruption scandals more easily so long as he or she is supported by members of his or her own party.[70] As Larcinese and Sircar observe, 'biased perception and sticky beliefs can represent a formidable obstacle to accountability and points at the complexity of the role played by partisanship in voters' mind'.[71] It is this 'accountability gap' that prosecutors and the courts, unelected though they may be, can seek to fill through the use—in serious cases—of the deterrent power of the criminal law, in the interests of promoting clean government.

[70] http://qz.com/656324/south-africas-jacob-zuma-has-a-history-of-surviving-scandals-impeachment-is-just-the-latest/.

[71] Larcinese and Sircar (n 67) 27.

2

The Limits of Criminal Misconduct

> [A]s to political liberty, it is another branch of security — security against the injustice of the members of the Government.[1]

2.1 A Focus on the Abuse of Power

In this chapter, I will defend the view that the offence of misconduct in public office ought to be focused on an abuse of public powers, and then I will explore the theoretical justification for the offence, thus understood. The first task will, in part, bring my view into conflict with the Law Commission's proposals for reform of the offence.[2] On my account, there should be two offences of misconduct:

(a) Wilful neglect or misconduct (whether through act or omission[3]),[4] amounting to an abuse of a public position, power, or duty.[5] In appropriate cases, it should be possible to deal with this offence through the imposition of an administrative penalty.

(b) Misconduct (whether through act or omission), amounting to an abuse of a public position, power, or duty, caused by gross negligence on the part of a public organization, in which negligence on the part of senior managers played a substantial role.[6]

[1] Jeremy Bentham (John Bowring, ed: 1838–43), at 302.

[2] Law Commission, *Reforming Misconduct in Public Office* (2016b).

[3] There is, of course, a certain awkwardness in calling an omission an 'abuse' of a power or duty, but that awkwardness is not in itself enough to justify taking a different approach to omissions in breach of duty.

[4] In (a), it should be necessary to show that D was aware that he or she was exercising a public power or performing a public duty at the relevant time.

[5] For the Law Commission's definition of public power see Law Commission, *Reforming Misconduct in Public Office* (n 2) 4.56–4.62.

[6] In other words, as under the Corporate Manslaughter and Corporate Homicide Act 2007 ('the 2007 Act'), in deciding whether there was gross negligence, it should be possible to aggregate the negligence of different parties within the organization, so long as negligence on the part of senior managers is involved.

Without prejudice to their generality, the scope of these offences could be made clearer in at least three different ways.

First, further provisions could specify which public powers and duties would unquestionably be subject to these offences. So, for example, the Law Commission rightly suggests that officials who have powers of coercion, or duties respecting vulnerable people, should face the prospect of criminal liability for intentional or reckless (wilful) abuse of such powers.[7] Secondly, all departments of government could be given the task of drawing up a non-exhaustive list of the powers and duties falling under their aegis, including the powers and duties of non-departmental bodies exercising statutory powers delegated to them, the misuse of which would in the department's view amount to an abuse of power or duty in the context in question. This would give both officials, and the courts when called upon to interpret the scope of offences (a) and (b), some indication of conduct that ought to amount to misconduct in public office. As we will see in at 2.7 below, there are many examples to be found in which public bodies provide codes of conduct that could form the basis for such lists. The final responsibility for what appears on the list—which could enter into law as a revisable schedule to legislation—could be taken by the Ministry of Justice.[8] The advantage of this approach is that it embeds the offence in the evolving practice of the executive.[9] Thirdly, and finally, offences (a) and (b) could be supplemented with specific offences, although in theory the conduct in question falls within the scope of the existing misconduct offence (and of offence (a)). Two suggestions relevant to the conduct of MPs, discussed in Chapters 4 and 5, are a dishonest breach of the Ministerial Code or of the MPs' code of conduct, and the dishonest making of a false or misleading statement in relation to an obligation under one of those codes. As overall reform of the offence of misconduct is not central to the argument of this book, I will not defend all of these suggestions in great detail. However, some analysis is appropriate, so as to provide a contrast with the Law Commission's proposals.

The Law Commission proposes to divide the current offence into two. First, there would be an offence—the 'harm offence'—of breach of duty by a public office holder leading to or risking serious harm:

> We think that a distinct mischief arises when, by virtue of D's position of public office, D is under a particular duty to act, which if not fulfilled could give rise to a risk of serious consequences occurring and D is aware of this duty but nevertheless fails to fulfil that duty.[10]

Greater certainty would be provided by specifying particular groups of office-holders to whom this offence would apply, such as those entitled to use coercion and those with responsibility for vulnerable individuals.[11] Secondly, there would an

[7] Law Commission, *Reforming Misconduct in Public Office* (n 2) ch 5.

[8] It ought to be possible to use the schedule to modify case law development concerning the meaning of 'public power or duty'.

[9] The issue is discussed by the Law Commission, *Reforming Misconduct in Public Office* (n 2) ch 4.

[10] Law Commission, *Reforming Misconduct in Public Office* (n 2) para 5.4. The serious consequences in question would be death or physical injury, false imprisonment, serious harm to public order, and serious harm to the administration of justice.

[11] Law Commission, *Reforming Misconduct in Public Office* (n 2) para 1.30.

offence—the 'corruption offence'—that would be committed when a public office-holder abused his or her position in order to achieve an advantage of some kind for the office-holder or another, or to cause detriment to another, where to do so is seriously improper.[12] By contrast, my offence (a) above does not require the abuse of power or duty to involve 'serious' harm, or a risk thereof, or 'serious' impropriety. There is a very simple reason not to take the Law Commission's approach, in using seriousness as a threshold criterion, even though it would be right to say that the Commission's approach reflects the balance of existing authority in the common law world. Ordinary citizens are governed by a criminal justice system that knows no *de minimis* principle. There is, for example, no seriousness threshold that must be crossed before someone—including a public official—can be charged with bribery. Still less is there any such threshold when the issue is, say, whether a benefit claimant may be found guilty for drawing too much benefit.[13] In the case of bribery, the absence of any such threshold is explicitly intended to ensure that a culture of small bribe-taking does not become established in the course of business and government affairs.[14] I suggest that it is important that small-scale corruption is similarly deterred by the criminal law, especially where public officials are concerned. What should matter is solely whether there has been a wilful 'abuse' of power or duty, contrasted with something lesser, such as a mere error of judgment. The distinction is a matter ultimately for the jury.

Consider Example 1: A coroner's officer collaborates with a mortuary attendant to set up a system for regularly taking a lock of hair from deceased persons. The officer sells the locks of hair to anyone who offers a small sum for them.

Irrespective of whether there may have been a theft of the hair in this instance, other things being equal, such conduct should be capable of being regarded as criminal misconduct, in the form of an abuse of (an *ex hypothesi*) public position. In that regard, it should not be necessary for the prosecution additionally to show that what the coroner's officer did was 'serious', although in many cases the seriousness of wrongdoing will naturally contribute to a judgment that there was an abuse of position, power, or duty. The law should speak clearly and unequivocally in condemning all abuses of public position, power, or duty.

It is, of course, understandable that the Law Commission should wish to provide the definition of misconduct with a greater degree of certainty, by seeking to build into that definition some clear indications of what public officials must avoid: causing or risking various harms, or seeking to gain private advantages from office. I have already said that the aim of achieving greater certainty can be substantially achieved through indicative statutory guidelines. However, it is unclear that the Law Commission's proposed definitions are wide enough to capture all the conduct that ought to be included within the scope of the offence. The proposed definitions exclude, for example, spontaneous or demonstrative conduct, however offensive or objectionable it may be, because such conduct neither poses a risk of

[12] ibid para 1.36. This offence is analysed at length in ch 4.
[13] For general discussion see Jeremy Horder (2015).
[14] See TRACE International (2015).

serious harm nor involves corruption. An example involving the use of abusive language by a public official is given in section 2.5, but there are other examples. Suppose that a chief constable insists on the use of racist language when officers are speaking to him or her about black or minority ethnic suspects and offenders. That ought to be regarded as misconduct capable of amounting to a criminal offence. One advantage of the current definition is that it captures such cases.

2.2 Enforcing Virtue? Officials' Conduct, Lifestyles, and the Scope of the Offence

> [A]nother curiosity of current moral discourse about public life ... [is] the emphasis placed on those personal restrictions that compliment the lack of official restraint – the other side of the coin of public responsibility and irresponsibility. Public figures are not supposed to use their power openly to enrich themselves and their families, or to obtain sexual favors ... stress is laid on the personal probity and disinterest of public figures. This kind of personal detachment in the exercise of official functions is thought to guarantee their good moral stand ing ... When ... [personal transgressions] are inescapably exposed the penalty can be severe, for a delicate boundary of moral restraint that sets off the great body of public power and freedom has been breached.[15]

At the start of Chapter 1, I pointed out the importance of consistently ethical conduct, on the part of officials, to a flourishing constitution. In that regard, in England and Wales, most types of official—from MPs and judges downwards—are governed by codes of conduct. Such codes of ethical conduct, drafted to apply to public officials and backed by disciplinary sanctions—and in some instances, the threat of criminal prosecution—for breach, are one of the most important parts of the written element to the UK's constitution. A key issue constitutional lawyers and legal theorists have not devoted as much attention to as they might have done is the legitimate scope of such codes of conduct.

For example, under the House of Commons Code of Conduct, MPs are bound as follows:

> Members should act on all occasions in accordance with the public trust placed in them. They should always behave with probity and integrity, including in their use of public resources.[16]

The requirement seems entirely appropriate and fitting; but a key question is, how far does it extend into different dimensions of MPs' lives? For example, suppose that an MP with responsibility for government policy on families is found to be a serial adulterer. Is that a breach of the requirement that he or she 'should always behave with probity and integrity', and thus grounds to call into question his or her fitness to be an MP or minister? In the case of MPs very generally, answering the question is complicated by the fact that an MP has a representative function, in relation to his or

[15] Thomas Nagel (1979), at 76–77.

[16] House of Commons (2015), at para III, r 7.

her constituency. He or she could be deselected by his or her constituency party on such 'lifestyle' grounds. Putting that possibility on one side, our concern is whether it should be possible to take public, official action in law against an MP—or any other public official—in such circumstances.

To many, it will seem obvious that MPs, police officers, judges, NHS managers, and other public officials are entitled to a private life. Hence, so the argument runs, officials should not suffer adverse consequences respecting their public role in virtue of moral wrongdoing committed, or lifestyle choices adopted, in their private lives. We can call this the 'libertarian' view. However, the libertarian viewpoint is not that adopted in the UK, where the position is complex, differing according to a number of factors, including the nature of the public office held. For example, in the Judicial Code of Conduct for England and Wales, in relation to the judicial obligation to maintain integrity, it is clearly stated that judges 'must ... avoid situations which might expose them to charges of hypocrisy by reason of things done in their private life'.[17] By contrast, no such obligation necessarily binds politicians. Their dependence on the support of their constituencies (referred to above) means that, although they may lose such support following the disclosure of something discreditable about their private lives, if they are popular enough they may equally survive in office even following (say) a criminal conviction.[18] Clearly, however, the popularity of judges, even if it could be measured, does not look like a sound guide to whether or not we should overlook failures on their part to behave with integrity in their private lives.

It is possible to find other examples of private lifestyle restrictions binding on (would-be) public officials. The Code of Conduct governing the appointment of police officers includes the following advice about tattoos and facial piercing:

> The number and size of tattoos will also be factors to consider in terms of the impression they may give to members of the public or colleagues. Similarly, there will be a need to consider whether the prominence and location of facial piercing would undermine the dignity and authority of the office of constable and whether there may be implications for an officer's safety.[19]

I will come back shortly to consideration of the wording used in this advice. Clearly, even in a liberal democracy such as the UK, it is considered appropriate to make someone's fitness to hold (certain kinds of) public office—or to discharge certain duties associated with it—in part dependent on the lifestyle choices they make, at least where the choices are liable to come to the notice of, and perhaps affect the behaviour of, the public. This is so, even if there is nothing discreditable about those choices. Consideration of such examples leads to a broader issue that goes to the heart of the matters discussed here. Can the offence of misconduct in office be used to condemn and punish private failings on the part of public officials? The broader

[17] Judiciary of England and Wales, *Code of Conduct* (2013) para 4.1.

[18] What is more, it may be important that they can survive in office, in such circumstances. An example might be when the criminal conviction stems from conduct closely linked to an MP's politics, such as a public order offence committed at a demonstration.

[19] See Home Office (2003), guidance point 2.

issue will also have a resonance in the discussion of MPs and private corruption in Chapter 4. If, say, an MP's private family firm stands to benefit from decisions taken by the Government of which the MP is a member, would it be right to threaten the MP with (criminal) sanctions if he or she fails to declare that interest?

On the libertarian view, the threat of criminal sanctions for misconduct is appropriate only when an official behaves in a way that betrays his or her official functions as a holder of public powers and duties.[20] Other kinds of failing when in office (unrelated to the exercise of such functions), even conduct involving the commission of a crime, should not fall within the purview of the misconduct offence. If, for example, a Crown Court judge is caught shoplifting, that wrongdoing has nothing to do with the performance of his or her official judicial functions. So, the argument runs, there is no particular reason to regard such an act as misconduct in office, even if it amounts to the offence of theft. Nonetheless, on the libertarian account, there may be some—exceptional—occasions when a private lifestyle choice is or may be incompatible with the effective performance of a public function. There is such a suggestion at the end of the Home Office guidance on facial piercing, cited above, when it indicates that some kinds of facial piercing may put the officer's safety in jeopardy. The suggestion implies that some kinds of facial piercing may tend to provoke a hostile reaction in members of the public, a reaction that will impair the officer's capacity to carry out his or her duties and hence perform his or her function properly. Quite conceivably, then, on the libertarian account, it might in some instances be appropriate to charge an officer with misconduct in public office respecting a private lifestyle choice. One example might be where the officer was shown to have had a highly prominent racist slogan tattooed on his or her face, the day before going on duty at a protest involving ethnic minority participants.

At the other end of the spectrum is what I call the 'austere republican' account of the scope of misconduct. The difference between the libertarian and the austere republican accounts is well summarized by Quentin Skinner, in the distinction that he draws between two contrasting understandings of the conditions in which government flourishes, which we can call institutional–functional and individual–virtuous:

> One [institutional-functional understanding] stresses that government is effective whenever its institutions are strong, and corrupt whenever its machinery fails to function adequately ... The other approach [individual-virtuous understanding] suggests by contrast that if the men who control the institutions of government are corrupt, the best possible institutions cannot be expected to shape or constrain them, whereas if the men are virtuous, the health of the institutions will be a matter of secondary importance. This is the tradition ... which stresses that it is not so much the machinery of government as the proper *spirit* of the rulers, the people and the laws which needs above all to be sustained.[21]

Under an austere republican account of misconduct in public office, *all* failings in point of virtue should be regarded as potentially threatening to the fitness of the individual in question to hold public office. Living a virtuous life does not necessarily

[20] See Law Commission, *Reforming Misconduct in Public Office* (n 2) para 6.50.
[21] Quentin Skinner (1978), at 44–45, cited by Thomas W Simpson (2017), at 51.

fit someone to hold public office (other qualities are typically needed for such fitness). However, it is part of the role of all public officials to inspire the trust, confidence, and respect of the public in the performance of their functions. This, the austere republican theory holds, they will not do unless, in the relevant respects, they live virtuous lives (especially in the case of high-ranking officials), a suggestion implicit in the passage cited from Nagel's work at the beginning of section 2.2. In other words, it is not enough that the official can make or is making a good job of the official function he or she is assigned to perform (the narrow, libertarian approach). Consider a case in which a minister leading a Home Office initiative against the drug trade is found to have been selling drugs him or herself to friends. In such a case, however well the initiative is going under the minister's leadership, the minister is liable to suffer a fatal loss of credibility when his or her personal wrongdoing is exposed. According to the austere republican theory, that would be enough in itself to justify the intervention of the criminal law, in the form of the misconduct offence, because the minister has knowingly undermined the *moral* basis on which he or she can credibly remain in office. The austere republican will, for example, ask rhetorically: 'How can we have confidence in a family law judge who him or herself concealed assets when divorcing, or in a Crown Court judge who has been found guilty of theft? Their offence is that such judges, however well qualified legally or experienced judicially, have wilfully rendered themselves unfit for an office the dignity and authority of which they undertook to uphold'.

Looking back once more at the Home Office guidance on facial piercing and tattooing cited above, we can detect the influence of elements of austere republican thinking, albeit not directed at the scope of the misconduct offence. The guidance places emphasis not only on whether some kinds of visible and prominent piercing or tattoo might impair an officer's ability to perform his or her function, but also on whether such piercings or tattoos might 'undermine the dignity and authority of the office'. Some, albeit not all, public offices or functions are supported by the public good constituted by the 'dignity and authority' associated with holding the office.[22] This public good can be undermined by acts and omissions on the part of officials going beyond failures to fulfil their function. If, for example, an off-duty police officer or a judge involved in a car accident engages in a widely shared foul-mouthed rant in front of witnesses, such conduct is just as capable of undermining the dignity and authority that ought to accompany his or her office-holding as a betrayal of his or her public functions when on duty. So, for austere republicans, it is arguable that such conduct should fall within the scope of misconduct in office. Whether or not it does so in English law is an important question.[23] So far as the broader descriptive adequacy of the theory is concerned, austere republicans can point to the clear possibility of dismissal, or of other disciplinary sanctions, that would undoubtedly be available in such cases against public officials. The fact that we contemplate disciplining officials, and perhaps even dismissing them from their jobs, for what would

[22] On the meaning of public goods in this context see ch 2.5.

[23] On which see the useful discussion by the Law Commission, *Reforming Misconduct in Public Office* (n 2) paras 2.83–2.84, and paras 5.21 ff.

outside the realm of public office be regarded as private wrongdoing, seems to show that austere republicanism has a strong foundation in English constitutional ethics and law.

True enough. Libertarians could, however, answer this by questioning the theoretical security of the austere republican argument. That argument appears to move from the proposition that the dignity and authority of a public office is in fact undermined in the eyes of others by private wrongdoing, to the proposition that we should use this as a basis for taking legal action (be in civil or criminal) against officials. But how does this necessarily follow? On the contrary, one could argue that the public should instead be educated to judge officials solely by reference to the dedication, competence, and skill with which they discharge their functions. The temptation to let one's judgment be affected by broader ethical failings of officials should be resisted. Suppose that the public tolerates a hard-drinking culture amongst male police officers (publicity about it does not affect the dignity and authority of office-holding by male officers, at least in the eyes of the public), but if such conduct is engaged in by female officers, they lose dignity and authority in the eyes of the public. Surely, the libertarian might ask rhetorically, would we really follow through this finding by tolerating disciplinary action being taken against female officers, but not against male officers, when evidence of hard-drinking emerges? If we would not tolerate it, this shows that the 'dignity and authority' of office is a contested matter about which the public may need to be educated, so as to avoid unrealistic or unacceptable expectations. It follows that the public—and a fortiori enforcement authorities—could, and on the libertarian argument should, be educated to separate betrayals of specific public functions from other (*ex hypothesi* private) forms of wrongdoing, and to tolerate the latter but not the former. It is important to note that one can, of course, seek to be a libertarian about the scope of the criminal law of misconduct, without necessarily advocating that approach in the sphere of private law, although to adopt such a stance somewhat weakens the force of libertarian thinking. The libertarian may argue that taking a more austere republican, individual–virtuous approach to the law governing employment discipline should be enough to support the public goods of dignity and authority attaching to public office-holding. On that argument, there is no additional need to invoke the criminal law in order to do this. The criminal law should be confined more narrowly to institutional–functional betrayals of office.

Putting aside the proper scope of private law, preferable is a view of the limits of the misconduct offence that rejects the austere republican viewpoint, but supplements the libertarian approach. According to this middle-ground view, the public goods associated with the discharge of public office, such as the dignity and authority of an office, can sometimes legitimately be protected and promoted by the criminal law, as well as by the civil law. It should not only be where an official has betrayed his or her function that the misconduct offence applies. It should also apply when an official has misused a special bureaucratic or role-specific feature of office: what one might call one of the 'trappings' of office. For example, suppose a police officer hires out his uniform, an MP gives a parliamentary pass to an influential constituent, a firearms officer allows a friend to handle a submachine gun, or a judge permits a relative to do business from her office in the Royal Courts. Such instances of misconduct are not merely a private failing unconnected to holding office, but it is also not altogether clear that they all involve a betrayal of official functions. Instead, it is more accurate to say that each person knowingly misuses one of the (role-specific) trappings of office.

One common way of seeking to express this middling approach is through some kind of proximity test. In the Hong Kong case of *Sin Ksam-Wah v HKSAR*,[24] the kinds of misconduct properly caught by the offence were described as those in which the wrongdoing is 'so closely connected to the public office', that it 'bring[s] the public office into disrepute'. The difficulty with this kind of test is that it has no qualitative element. The test fails to identify what kind of connection the wrongdoing must have to public office, if it is to bring the office into disrepute. To go back to an earlier example, if a minister charged with revitalizing 'family values' admits to an adulterous liaison, does the nature of his or her ministerial role establish the 'close connection' required? To return to another earlier example, of the Home Office minister who has been dealing in drugs whilst in charge of an initiative to counter the drugs trade, does the fact that the wrongdoing he or she committed is identical to that which, in an official capacity, he is charged with countering, establish the kind of 'close connection' required in *Sin Ksam-Wah*? If it could do, then it is hard to see how the proximity approach differs much from full-blooded austere republicanism. In other words, the *Sin Ksam-Wah* test is too broad, because it is capable of being satisfied simply by the way that D's behaviour in private reflects on his or her office, and is not limited to abuse of functions or (crucially, also) special features of that office.

The middle-ground view I support is, by contrast 'institutional', but it is not (purely) 'functional' in its approach to the limits of the misconduct offence. Institutions can have dignity and authority in virtue of the way that the trappings of office are used, and not solely through the way that the office's functions are performed. To be sure, the examples I have given in which the defendant (D) abuses one of the trappings of office (such as a parliamentary pass) that give it dignity and authority may tend to fall at the lower end of the scale in terms of seriousness but, as pointed out in section 2.1, English law has no *de minimis* principle in general.[25] It is hard to see why this principle should operate in an offence applicable to public officials when it does not apply to any other kind of offence or offender. It is for this reason that, under the proposed offence (a) above, it is possible to impose a civil penalty for wrongdoing. In the seventeenth century, in more minor cases, the Star Chamber was not above ordering corrupt officials to ride backwards on an ass, in part to secure more publicity for the punishment.[26] Eschewing any undignified

[24] [2005] 2 HKLRD 375.

[25] A *de minimis* principle is a principle that requires non-prosecution in cases where an instance of a criminal offence is very trivial, or even regards such conduct as falling outside the scope of the offence altogether. See eg the relevant provision of the Model Penal Code: Model Penal Code s 2.12: 'De Minimis Infractions: The Court shall dismiss a prosecution if, having regard to the nature of the conduct charged to constitute an offense and the nature of the attendant circumstances, it finds that the defendant's conduct . . . (2) did not actually cause or threaten the harm or evil sought to be prevented by the law defining the offense or did so only to an extent too trivial to warrant the condemnation of conviction'.

[26] Steve Hindle (2000), at 88.

treatment of animals, the introduction of civil penalties would be a new development in this field. Such penalties are more typically applied *by* public office-holders *to* businesses and ordinary member of the public. But what is the principled objection to the use of such penalties against public office-holders? It is hard to know what it might be.

The Law Commission's definition of misconduct links abuse of (public) position with conduct involving D '*exercis[ing]* that position, power or authority'.[27] This is the libertarian, institutional-functionalist approach to the limits of the offence.[28] On this view, whatever the right approach in civil law may be, the misconduct offence should be confined to circumstances in which it is D's legal position or power, *qua* official, that has been abused (including cases in which D culpably fails to exercise a power or perform a duty when he or she should do so). A simple example would be where D, a planning officer, agrees to recommend the grant of planning permission because the applicant is a friend. As we have seen, on this libertarian approach, it is not enough that D has brought him or herself into disrepute or disgrace by some illegal or immoral conduct that did not involve an exercise of his or her official position or power: one can be both an outstanding public servant and a wholly irresponsible private citizen. At the other end of the scale, the austere republican theory was expounded by the Victorian Supreme Court in *R v Quach*:[29]

> [T]he relevant misconduct need not occur while the officer is in the course of performing a duty or function of the office. Certain responsibilities of the office will attach to the officer whether or not the officer is acting in the course of that office. Where the misconduct does not occur during the performance of a function or duty of the office, the offence may be made out where the misconduct is inconsistent with those responsibilities. It may be connected to a duty already performed or to one yet to be performed or it may relate to the responsibilities of the office in some other way. The misconduct must be incompatible with the proper discharge of the responsibilities of the office so as to amount to a breach of the confidence which the public has placed in the office, thus giving it its public and criminal character.[30]

In a criminal law context, a major objection to austere republicanism is that by its nature it gives very little guidance on what kinds of conduct will be regarded as (to use the court's words in *Quach*) 'incompatible with the proper discharge of the responsibilities of the office'. When what is at stake is criminal conviction, this is a serious concern. In confining the offence through use of the institutional-functionalist approach, the Law Commission rightly places the value of greater certainty above the demands of the austere republicanism advocated in *Quach*. Perhaps more importantly, an austerely republican interpretation of the scope of the misconduct offence involves a risk of an unduly punitive legal moralism creeping in to the assessment of official failures. A misconduct offence defined on austerely republican lines wrongly risks elevating the 'sin' of rank hypocrisy on the part of officials into a serious criminal offence (as in the example of the drug-taking Home Office minister,

[27] Law Commission, *Reforming Misconduct in Public Office* (n 2) 6.50 (Provisional Proposal 28) (my emphasis).

[28] ibid paras 5.21–5.30 (Provisional Proposal 6).

[29] [2010] VSCA 106.

[30] ibid para 40.

given earlier). It is not, of course, that we should be indifferent to whether officials are people of moral integrity; far from it. It is just that employment sanctions such as dismissal should be quite enough to deal with the kinds of examples just discussed, where the problem is really that wrongdoing of some kind has undermined D's credibility as a public official. It involves no moral inconsistency to defend austere republicanism in the sphere of private law, whilst endorsing (modified) libertarianism as the right approach for the criminal law.

However, it must be recognized that the courts are likely to come under pressure to give a broad interpretation to the idea of misuse of the exercise of a public position or public power, an interpretation that is capable of reflecting the value of the dignity and authority of public office over and above the way that a function has been performed. Some simple examples where a broad interpretation would be needed were given above, including (i) a police officer is found to have been making money on the side by hiring out his or her uniform, (ii) an MP is caught making copies of parliamentary passes that he or she intends to provide to influential constituents. In these examples, there is a difference from the examples above involving the judge who stole and the judge who concealed assets when divorcing. In both the police officer and the MP examples, there is a special connection between the misconduct and D's role as an official, in virtue of the fact that the misconduct relates to a formal or bureaucratic feature peculiar to that role (the 'trappings' of office). In these examples, was D (to use the Law Commission's language) 'exercising [his or her] position, power or authority', as a police officer or MP, in committing the wrongdoing? If so, then the examples are covered by the Law Commission's institutional-functionalist approach. However, I think it is more accurate to say that the wrongdoing in the examples arises from exploitation of a special official feature or mark of the position that D holds—respectively, the possession of the uniform and the pass—and does not involve the misuse of a power or duty inherent in that position as such. If that is right, what it suggests is that if we wish the misconduct offence to cover such examples—and I believe that we should—we should endorse the middle-way 'institutional' test for misconduct offence, explained above. Such a theory goes further than the institutional-functionalist account, beyond the misuse of powers or duties constitutive of a public position, to cover some forms of misconduct inconsistent with the moral integrity required of those holding public office. However, the middle-way test is restricted to instances of such misconduct that involve the wrongful exploitation of special formal or bureaucratic features of the office held, features associated with the dignity and authority of the office.[31] In that way, the moderate theory seeks to avoid the punitive legal moralism of the austerely broad republican theory.

[31] It is important to stress that it is insufficient, on this theory, that D's wrongdoing is merely connected causally to his or her position. The wrongdoing must stem from some official feature of the position that D holds. It could be that D's position as an MP makes it easier for him to enter into adulterous liaisons. However, although such misconduct is hence causally connected to D's official position, it does not stem from some official feature of that position, unlike the example in which the MP makes copies of the parliamentary pass. Accordingly, the adulterous MP should not be regarded as guilty of misconduct in office, on the moderate republican theory.

To illustrate the latter point, consider a case in which a senior official in the Serious Fraud Office is caught using an official credit card to make private purchases.[32] Under the austere republican theory, such behaviour should fall within the scope of the misconduct offence. That is because, having regard to the importance attached by this theory to the moral integrity of public office-holders, such behaviour is incontrovertibly inconsistent with the public office that he or she holds: the official has wilfully rendered him or herself morally unfit to hold office. By contrast, according to the libertarian, institutional-functionalist theory, the official's conduct will fall clearly outside the scope of the misconduct offence, because it does not involve the exercise of one of his or her official functions *qua* member of the Serious Fraud Office.[33] In this example, the middling, institutional theory sides with the libertarian, institutional-functionalist theory, but the reasoning is different. For the institutional theory, what matters is that the issuing of an office credit card is not a unique or special feature of the public office that the official holds (many employees in the private sector are also trusted to use company credit cards), and possession of the card is not connected to the dignity and authority of that office. That being so, whilst the officer might be guilty of fraud, he or she is not properly found guilty of misconduct in public office. The example is not to be equated with misconduct associated with the possession of a police uniform by a police officer, or (say) the access to weapons enjoyed by a firearms officer, both special features of the office held connected to the authority of their office.[34]

2.3 Liability for Misconduct: The Organizational Dimension

We should now consider a different dimension to the reach of the offence. An advantage of the current offence is that, in principle, it is not confined to the actions of the actual perpetrator of misconduct. It could also extend to the public officials who were responsible for supervising the actions of the perpetrator, but culpably failed to prevent him or her from acting. This feature of the offence would to some extent be lost under the Law Commission's proposals. For example, in relation to its corruption offence,[35] there is a need for the perpetrator to act with the purpose of gaining an advantage or causing a detriment. It follows that, short of a finding of complicity, there is little scope to prosecute a higher level official who connived at such conduct on the part of a lower-level official without engaging in it him or herself. This could, of course, be remedied by the inclusion of a clause making senior managers liable for the offence if it occurs through consent or connivance.[36] However, the focus in

[32] For a case of this nature see *R v W* [2010] EWCA 372.

[33] See Law Commission, *Reforming Misconduct in Public Office* (n 2) para 6.24.

[34] I am very grateful to have had the opportunity to discuss the limits of the 'middle way' theory with Andrew Simester and with participants in the Criminal Law Conversations seminars at King's College London. My views have been much influenced by the discussion, although only I am responsible for the development of the argument.

[35] See section 2.1; also discussed in more detail in ch 4.

[36] Such clauses are common place in ordinary criminal offences. See the discussion in Law Commission (2010), at ch 7.

offence (a) on abuse of public power would make this an unnecessary complication. All instances of consent and connivance may fall within the scope of 'abuse' of power or duty.

I now turn to offence (b). It illustrates the desirability of extending the offence beyond 'wilful' misconduct, to encompass gross negligence as a fault element. This is particularly important in cases involving public organizations, which currently seem to be excluded from the scope of the Law Commission's two proposed offences. In the case of Jean Charles de Menezes, mistakenly shot by armed officers from the Metropolitan Police in 2005, the Metropolitan Police organization was subsequently convicted and fined £175,000 for breach of section 3 of the Health and Safety at Work Act 1974 ('the 1974 Act').[37] The Metropolitan Police might have incurred liability under the Law Commission's proposal (outlined earlier) for an offence of breach of duty leading to serious harm done. However, rather like this proposed offence, the 1974 Act is restricted in scope. Its applicability to organizations depends on the existence of risks to physical or mental health and safety in what that organization does. So, the 1974 Act offences are not apt to cover cases where an organization's activities pose other kinds of risk. For example, it is possible to imagine obvious weaknesses in the Department of Health IT systems, persistently overlooked for years by management, leading to the release into the public domain of thousands of private medical records.[38] Alternatively, imagine a decision by senior managers at HMRC, influenced by racist assumptions, to conduct raids on the business premises of hundreds of Asian people.[39] It ought to be possible to charge misconduct in public office against an organization in these kinds of circumstances, where there has been extreme negligence or indifference at a high level. Even in a case such as de Menezes, which recalls the glaring management failures that led to the killing of IRA suspects on Gibraltar,[40] the wide exemptions from liability enjoyed by public organizations such as the police under the Corporate Manslaughter and Corporate Homicide Act 2007 mean that adequate labelling of an organization's offences may only be achieved through use of the misconduct offence against that organization.

For a variety of reasons, organizations are also liable to cover up wrongdoing by individual members, and the worst examples of such cover-ups could be charged as instances of offence (b). The concealment by officials of sexual offences committed by organization members is a possible example. In a 1995 BBC documentary, 'Westminster's Secret Service', former Conservative Party Whip Tim Fortescue said the following about what the whips would do for MPs who were in danger of being mired in scandal:

[37] https://www.theguardian.com/uk/2007/nov/01/menezes.jamessturcke2.

[38] On data protection in this context see Law Commission, *Reforming Misconduct in Public Office* (n 2) paras 3.297–3.303. According to one organization, between 2008 and 2011, there were at least 806 incidents in which NHS employees breached data protection policies and compromised the private medical information of patients: Big Brother Watch (2011), at 2.

[39] In 2015–2016, HMRC raided 761 properties (usually early in the morning), a 53% increase on the figures for 2010–2011 https://www.accountancyage.com/2016/09/26/hmrc-ramps-up-number-premises-raids/.

[40] *McCann and Others v United Kingdom* (1995) 21 ECHR 97 (GC).

> For anyone with any sense, who was in trouble, would come to the whips and tell them the truth, and say now, 'I'm in a jam, can you help?' It might be debt, it might be … a scandal involving small boys, or any kind of scandal in which, erm er, a member seemed likely to be mixed up in, they'd come and ask if we could help and if we could, we did. And we would do everything we can because we would store up brownie points … and if I mean, that sounds a pretty, pretty nasty reason, but it's one of the reasons because if we could get a chap out of trouble then, he will do as we ask forever more.[41]

Such action on the part of an individual whip amounts to criminal bribery; but in so far as such action also reflects a whip's office—and hence, a party—policy, it ought to be possible to charge the party with offence (b). Even under the existing law, the toleration of criminal activity should be regarded as in itself misconduct in office.

2.4 The Vagueness of the Offence and the Demands of the Rule of Law

The central definitional place given to the concept of an abuse of a public position, power, or duty in offences (a) and (b), in section 2.1, is meant to reflect the special obligations of propriety carried by those in such positions or with such powers and duties (well explained by Nagel, in the passage cited at the beginning of section 2.2). Anyone, including a public official, can fail to live up to expectations respecting the obligations that they have undertaken to discharge. In itself, that does not call for the application of the criminal law. However, as we will see in Chapter 3, a long tradition in English law distinguished such cases—mere failures in point of duty, appropriate only for civil law remedies—from *abuses* of public position, power, or duty. The latter are a betrayal of one or more of those obligations, and hence a fit subject of criminal prosecution and punishment. There is a sense in which the Law Commission's revised offences treat the occupation of public office as little more than a 'gateway' condition for extended criminal liability. On the Law Commission view, if one is a public official, then it becomes appropriate to extend the reach of the criminal law somewhat further—for example, to cover the creation of risks of harm—than would be appropriate in the case of an ordinary citizen. Whilst such an approach is not wrong, it does—quite intentionally—deprive the law of one important republican virtue, the sharp focus on misuse of public authority as the wrong itself.

One reason the Law Commission takes its chosen path is to give the offence of misconduct a greater degree of certainty, so far as the identification of wrongdoing in advance is concerned. Laudable though that aim is, it is arguably a less significant goal, in this context, than would ordinarily be the case with reform of an offence attracting moral stigma upon conviction. The misconduct offence reflects the

[41] http://www.telegraph.co.uk/news/politics/10952138/Member-of-Edward-Heaths-government-boasted-he-could-cover-up-a-scandal-involving-small-boys.html.

'authoritarian' principle in criminal law.[42] Under this principle, judges have a role to play in the development of the criminal law:

> [T]here is in [the King's Bench] a residual power, where no statute has yet intervened to supersede the common law, to superintend those offences which are prejudicial to the public welfare . . . [to fill] . . . gaps [that] remain and will always remain since no one can foresee every way in which the wickedness of man may disrupt the order of society.[43]

In this respect, the misconduct offence is an open-ended offence, in definitional terms.[44] Accordingly, guided by the authoritarian principle, the offence gives the courts considerable 'superintendence' power to include new forms of conduct within its scope. That will be true even if the use of the power of superintendence, and hence the expansion of the criminal law, is subject to the restriction that the courts' use of the power must have been reasonably foreseeable (with legal advice, where appropriate) in relation to the conduct in question.[45] When such crimes are applicable to ordinary citizens—as in the case, say, of cheating the public revenue—there are strong arguments based on the rule of law to object to their open-ended nature. In such cases, there are equally strong reasons to reject—as morally and constitutionally inappropriate—the invocation of the authoritarian principle, as a basis for superintending wrongdoing with a view to criminalization.[46] Even so, these arguments are not decisive across the board. They are weaker when:

(i) the offence targets a predetermined and voluntarily formed group of people (rather than the public at large);
(ii) members of that group of people know and agree that they are bound to uphold a common set of standards of integrity amounting to a public good, and have access to advice on the legal status of those standards;
(iii) allowing misconduct to go unpunished might undermine *ésprit de corps* amongst the group, as that bears on its members' identification with need to uphold the common standards; and
(iv) allowing misconduct to go unpunished might undermine people's confidence in the integrity of the group as a whole, in circumstances where the role of the group in society is too important for such an undermining to be tolerated.[47]

There are two dimensions to this 'group-based' theory. First (points (i)–(ii) above), it explains why a misconduct offence defined vaguely by reference to 'abuse' of position, power, or duty is not contrary to the rule of law. It will not be contrary to the rule of law if, in virtue of being a member of the group, someone will become

[42] For discussion see Jeremy Horder (2016), at ch 4.5.
[43] *DPP v Shaw* [1962] AC 220, at 225 (Viscount Simonds).
[44] See generally Law Commission (2016a).
[45] For this kind of analysis, in relation to open-ended common law crimes see *R v Rimmington; R v Goldstein* [2005] UKHL 63.
[46] See, in relation to cheating the public revenue, David Ormerod (1998).
[47] It might very well be that the satisfaction of conditions (i), (ii), and (iv) would be enough, even without the satisfaction of (iii), to justify the adoption of a supervisory approach.

informed or aware of their responsibilities, *qua* public official, with a sufficient degree of certainty to guide them, and hence avoid wrongdoing. It is not, nor ever has been, and could not ever be an essential task of the criminal law to provide a complete statement in every case of when someone will incur liability. As we will see in ensuing sections, public officials are commonly well informed about their responsibilities, and about what failure in that respect involves, with the ensuing risk that the criminal law may intervene. The second dimension to the group-based theory concerns the role of prosecutors and the courts (points (iii) and (iv)). Without willingness on the part of prosecutors and courts to work together to extend the misconduct offence to new forms of abuse—the adoption of a 'superintendence' approach—our constitutional arrangements bearing on the misconduct of public officials, especially the highest ranked officials, will lack adequate balance: the issue of 'Who will guard the guards?', addressed in Chapter 1. In Chapter 4, it is argued that the misconduct offence should be reinvigorated as a powerful anti-corruption weapon designed to punish abuses and to create better incentives, amongst MPs in particular, to behave with integrity as a group. In that regard, a test of prosecutors' and courts' willingness to use the offence to superintend deterrence of corruption amongst MPs, would be whether they were willing to apply it to the conduct I mentioned earlier as worthy of criminalization: dishonest breaches of the Ministerial Code or the MPs' code of conduct, and the dishonest making of false or misleading statements in relation to obligations under those codes.

2.5 The Public Law Role of the Offence of Misconduct in a Public Office

In this chapter, I will mainly be concerned with the theoretical underpinning of the misconduct offence, particularly as it bears on my focus on abuse of position, power, or duty as the essence of the offence. The misconduct offence holds officials to account, along with those exercising public powers and performing public duties more broadly, by reference to standards of behaviour they are required to observe. Those standards are not, however, always directly concerned with a risk of harm stemming from a departure from them (although that may sometimes form part of the picture, where criminalization is concerned). Instead, they are standards of behaviour essential to the conduct of public life under a flourishing constitution, standards such as honesty, openness, integrity, accountability, self-restraint, and impartiality. A collective commitment amongst officials to uphold such standards across the board is a 'public good' (a concept explained shortly). The criminal law plays a constitutional role in seeking to reinforce that commitment, through deterring and punishing departures from it so serious that they amount to abuses of authority, going beyond mere shortcomings.[48] To use some language familiar to legal theorists, this constitutional role may appear to be an example of the criminal law being employed to enforce or uphold moral standards for their own sake; and so

[48] For the historical foundations of this approach see ch 3.

it is. In the discussion that follows, I provide some reasons for thinking that, where public morality is concerned—the standards required to be upheld if constitutional government is to flourish—there is nothing wrong in this.

The modern understanding of the crime of misconduct in a public office is set out in the decision of the Court of Appeal in *Attorney-General's Reference (No 3 of 2003)*.[49] In this case, a man died in police custody following an incident in which he had been handcuffed unconscious in a face-down position at the station. He developed breathing difficulties and died. The defendants were police officers who had arrested the man at a hospital where he was due to be treated for head injuries. A doctor certified that the man was fit to be detailed, so the man was taken to the police station. Although he was unresponsive, he was placed on the floor of the custody suite, under restraint, in the semi-face down position rather than in the recovery position. When he developed breathing difficulties, the handcuffs were removed from him but he died minutes later. On the particular facts, prosecutions for both gross negligence manslaughter failed and (in the alternative) for misconduct in a public office.[50] In answer to a question referred to it by the Attorney-General, namely 'What are the ingredients of the common law offence of misconduct in a public office?', the Court of Appeal said:

> The elements of the offence in a public office are: (1) a public officer acting as such . . .; (2) wilfully neglects to perform his duty and/or wilfully misconducts himself . . .;[51] (3) to such a degree as to amount to an abuse of the public's trust in the office holder . . .; (4) without reasonable excuse or justification.[52]

The crime has been extensively criticized by those who object to its alleged uncertainty, in point of definition, and also to its use in cases where clearer, statute-based offences would better reflect the nature of the wrongdoing.[53] The *Attorney-General's Reference* case has, however, in all probability done enough to render the offence's definition sufficiently clear to withstand an Article 7 challenge on the basis of uncertainty.[54] The Court of

[49] [2004] EWCA Crim 868.

[50] That constables may be indicted for neglecting their duties is a long-established principle: see eg *Crouther's Case* (1599) 2 Hawk PC 116, and *R v Wyat* (1705) 1 Salk 380.

[51] Some writers argue that there have always been two separate offences of misconduct in a public office, one concerned with neglect of duty, and the other with breach of trust: see Terence F Williams (2010), and the Canadian case of *Boulanger* (2006) SCC 32. In what follows, I will adopt the line taken in the *Attorney-General's Reference* case that the law should be considered to be comprised of a single offence, that may be committed by omission as well as by a positive act.

[52] *Attorney-General's Reference (No 3 of 2003)* (n 49) para 61. Each ingredient is helpfully discussed in Simon Parsons (2012), at 181–83.

[53] See eg John Spencer (2010); Simon Parsons (n 52); Terence F Williams (2010).

[54] The offence now requires proof, inter alia, of knowledge or recklessness ('wilfulness') with regard to whether there was a duty, the breach of which is the focus of the charge: *Attorney-General's Reference (No 3 of 2003)* (n 49) para 30. That ought to be enough to ensure that the offence satisfies any art 7 requirement for fair warning, even if there is also a purely evaluative element to the test for liability, namely whether D misconducted him or herself—or neglected his or her duties—'to such a degree as to amount to an abuse of the public's trust in the office holder'. The mere fact that an offence definition hinges on an evaluative question will not entail that the offence will fail an art 7 challenge: see eg *R v Misra and Srivastava* [2005] 1 Cr App R 328. In Hong Kong, the offence has not been found to be so imprecise as to be unconstitutional under the basic law: *Kwok Sher v HKSAR* [2002] 5 HKCSAR 381.

Appeal[55] has also indicated that offences of this kind should not be charged if the relevant aggravating feature—here, that D abused his or her position as a holder of public office—can be adequately reflected in the sentence handed down upon conviction for a clearer, statute-based offence.[56] As Wasik has pointed out, however, in relation to the use of the offence in the context of computer misuse and data protection violations, not only may the relevant statutes be unclear, but (thanks to the positivity of statute law) it may be obvious that they contain inexplicable or unwarranted gaps that only the misconduct offence can fill.[57] An example is given shortly.

The offence of misconduct in a public office has a distinctive place in the armoury of weapons designed to address wrongdoing by those to whom the state has entrusted the provision of public services. Broadly understood, 'public sector wrongdoing' (as we may speak of it) may take forms very familiar to public lawyers as giving rise to well-known causes of action. Textbook examples of wrongdoing (in the broad sense) include an irrational or biased decision, the adoption of a flawed decision-making process, a breach of statutory duty, a nuisance, or, of course, misfeasance in a public office in its guise as a tort.[58] In such cases, the accountability of the authority or person in question depends, amongst other things, on whether the conduct at issue either has the kind of normative character that makes it judicially reviewable, or has been the cause of loss or harm for which someone may claim a remedy in civil law. Public sector wrongdoing may, however, manifest itself through conduct that does not have the normative characteristics that will make it judicially reviewable, or through conduct that has not caused actionable loss or other harm. It is here that the criminal law—and the offence of misconduct in a public office in particular—can play a legitimate role, by punishing and deterring public sector wrongdoing.

Consider an example in which a police officer on duty behaves or speaks in a highly abusive way towards a group of people taking part in a demonstration. Such conduct neither has the kind of normative character that makes it susceptible to judicial review, nor provides a basis on which it is likely that a claim for

[55] *R v Sookoo* [2002] TLR 10/04/02. See also the Crown Prosecution Service guidance on prosecuting the misconduct offence: www.cps.gov.uk/legal/l_to_o/misconduct_in_public_office/#a015: 'Where there is clear evidence of one or more statutory offences, they should usually form the basis of the case, provided the offences give the court adequate sentencing powers'. See also *Attorney-General's Reference (No 3 of 2003)* (n 49) para 64.

[56] Merely because a clearer, statutory offence applies to the facts of particular cases will not necessarily make that offence more suitable than a prosecution for the misconduct offence. The sentencing powers for the statutory offence may simply be inadequate, or a co-defendant may have charged with an indictable offence and the relevant statutory offence applicable to the holder of public office is summary only, posing difficulties for adequate presentation of the case.

[57] See Martin Wasik (2008).

[58] See *Three Rivers DC v Bank of England (No 3)* [2003] 2 AC 1. The ingredients of the tort of misfeasance in a public office differ from the ingredients of the crime, and for reasons that will become clear, discussion of the tort is not relevant here.

damages can be made by any individual member of the group (although this may depend on precisely what the officer said or did). Moreover, even if compensation were available to members of the group, there are many instances in which the law regards wrongdoing as appropriately criminalized because (amongst other things) leaving the generation of deterrent effect to the use of civil law remedies will not be enough to do the necessary deterring.[59] Consequently, other things being equal, this kind of public sector wrongdoing can permissibly be dealt with through the criminal law.[60] In the example given, the officer's conduct might be prosecuted under section 5 of the Public Order Act 1986, as an assault,[61] or at common law (assuming it is sufficiently egregious) as misconduct in a public office. The latter offence may well be the only appropriate prosecutorial option, in terms of 'fair labelling' of the offender,[62] if the abusive conduct does not meet the precise requirements of section 5, or of assault.[63] If the officer's conduct does not amount to a public order offence and does not constitute an assault, then why might it be important that his or her abusive conduct falls within the scope of the misconduct offence, even if the punishment should be no more than an administrative penalty?

The justification for the misconduct offence must be seen in the light of what I will call the 'role' theory of criminalization, explained in greater detail below. The occupation of a role provides a well-known exception to the dictum that an 'ought' cannot be derived from an 'is'.[64] If, say, I am a police officer, then I ought to do what police officers are meant to do.[65] Should I fail in that respect, I lay myself open to criticism simply in virtue of having failed in my normative role. What, then, is the general normative role in question here? In many contexts, part of what it means to be a public servant—to take on a role as a public service provider—is to uphold and promote one or more 'public goods' in one's work. A failure to live up to one's role, in that regard, may not merely be to fail to do as one's contract of employment demands, but to compromise

[59] The criminalization of unacceptable trade practices by companies providing goods or services to consumers is a source of examples.

[60] The mere fact that a certain kind of misconduct could be dealt with through a disciplinary code should clearly not be sufficient to justify withholding the possibility of criminal prosecution in such a case.

[61] See *R v Dunn* [2003] Cr App R (S).

[62] That is, in terms of finding a good moral, as well as legal, 'match' between the offence charged and the nature of the defendant's wrongdoing: for the seminal discussion see Andrew Ashworth (1981). See also Victor Tadros (2012).

[63] Suppose, for example, that there is only a risk that the officer's conduct will cause harassment, alarm, or distress to someone within sight or hearing of the behaviour, rather than this consequence being, as section 5 requires, 'likely' to occur. The Court of Appeal has indicated that where a specific statutory offence is inadequate—in terms of labelling and sentencing powers—to capture the wrongdoing in question, then a general common law offence such as misconduct in a public office may be charged in such circumstances. However, a misconduct charge should not merely be added as a 'long-stop' option: *R v Sookoo* (n 55).

[64] See for general discussion Alasdair MacIntrye (1981), at 148–50. See also John Searle (1964).

[65] For an outstanding discussion of this point see John Gardner, *The Constitution of the Criminal Law* (2013a).

or imperil those goods.[66] A helpful definition of a public good is given by Joseph Raz. It is a good that:

> refers not to the sum of the good of individuals but to those goods which, in a certain community, serve the interests of people generally in a conflict-free, non-exclusive, and non-excludable way.[67]

Public goods will be considered in more detail later, but their immediate relevance is that the public practice of manifesting self-restraint and civility in dealing with others has some of the key features of a public good. A society in which the citizens behave in a self-restrained and civilized manner is capable of benefiting all those in that society in broadly the way that Raz describes. As a good, the manifestation of self-restraint and civility will be enjoyed in a conflict-free way if it is not a scarce resource for which one has to fight others for a share. It is also non-exclusive, if the benefits are not confined to limited sectors of the public. However, it is not a pure public good, since it is excludable. It is obviously perfectly possible that a society could in practice deny it to, say, those deemed to be foreigners.

A society will have a deserved reputation for self-restraint and civility—the public goods in question will exist—if the vast majority of its citizens manifest these qualities most of the time, in a conflict-free and non-exclusive way. It will rightly enjoy such a reputation whether or not citizens manifest the qualities as a matter of obligation or quite spontaneously, and even if there are some citizens who do not join in. However, so far as public officials—such as police officers—are concerned, the position is qualitatively different. The mere fact that it comes naturally to most police officers to behave in a restrained and civilized way is not enough, although that is welcome. It is part of the role of a police officer—a matter of high obligation—to behave in a restrained and civilized manner. Further, it is a stain on the police service if there are some officers—even a tiny number—who lack the qualities of self-restraint and civility in dealing with members of the public. A collective commitment amongst officers to behave in a restrained and civilized way, non-exclusively and whatever the provocation, is the hallmark of a properly functional and flourishing police service (even in a society otherwise noted for its boorish behaviour in public). Consequently, when an officer fails to exercise self-restraint or behaves in an uncivilized way, as John Gardner rightly observes (although he is speaking of different kinds of wrongs an officer might commit): 'the officer has a ceteris paribus harder job of defending his or her actions than he or she would have if he or she were an ordinary member of the public who did the same thing'.[68] It is the sense that an officer has not merely done something wrong by, say, verbally (or a fortiori physically) abusing a member of the public, but has betrayed his or her role as a public servant, which can provide a basis for justifying criminalization of that behaviour. The misconduct offence is the most potent and apt offence, in labelling terms, to characterize these kinds of betrayals,

[66] This point is particularly well explained by Gardner, *The Constitution of the Criminal Law* (n 65).
[67] Joseph Raz (1994), at 52. See also Inge Kaul, Isabelle Grunberg, and Mark A Stern (1999), at 40.
[68] See Gardner, *The Constitution of the Criminal Law* (n 65) 102.

and the definition of it in terms of an 'abuse' of public position, power, or duty is meant to reflect that.

2.6 The Harm Principle and the Role Theory

In making my case for reform of the misconduct offence, I am moving somewhat beyond the range of orthodox thinking about the legitimate foundations of criminal liability. In particular, I shall suggest that the misconduct offence is not best explained and justified by some version of the 'harm principle', attributed to J S Mill.[69] This is so, even though in Joel Feinberg's famous gloss on the principle, the notion of harm is imaginatively extended to include 'harm to important public institutions and practices'.[70] The misconduct offence is best explained by the 'role' theory of criminalization.

To begin with, the role theory has a part to play in making the harm principle itself fit for its justificatory purpose, in cases where some ostensibly harmless piece of conduct may cause or risk remote harm. Suppose that I sell you some meat from my fridge that, unbeknownst to me, is diseased. Fortunately, you discover the facts before serving the meat to some friends. The mere fact that my conduct in selling the meat poses a risk of harm is not enough to justify making it a criminal offence. However, the position would be different if, when I sold it to you, I did so in my capacity as a butcher.[71] Why? It is integral to a butcher's role that he or she sells meat that is fit to eat. As Simester and von Hirsch rightly observe, the range of someone's responsibilities in criminal law can depend on the nature of the role they occupy:

> The extent of responsibility of a vendor, for example, depends on his social role – which provides clues about what he is implicitly representing to customers concerning his product. The responsibilities of a manufacturer or civil servant likewise will depend on their respective roles.[72]

In the case of meat that is unfit to eat, a seller's responsibility clearly relates to the risk that harm may be done. What Simester and von Hirsch do not explore is the possibility that the role theory may also justify criminalization in circumstances where the possibility of more or less remote harm is not, as such, the primary concern. I will be exploring such circumstances.

I will focus on cases in which someone has voluntarily[73] taken on a role the value of which comes from the part the holder of the role will play in honouring and sustaining important public goods, such as honesty, integrity, openness,

[69] John Stuart Mill (1859), at ch 1, para 9: 'the only purpose for which power can be rightfully exercised over any member of a civilized community against his will, is to prevent harm to others. His own good, either physical or moral, is not sufficient warrant'.

[70] Joel Feinberg (1984), at 11.

[71] See the well-known case of *Hobbs v Winchester Corporation* [1910] 2 KB 471.

[72] A P Simester and Andreas von Hirsch (2011), at 64.

[73] This term is to be understood in a broad sense consistent with the way in which public office may be assumed. So, alongside a decision to enter a regulated trade or industry, or to sign a contract to become a public servant, 'voluntarily' assuming a role includes instances in which, for example, a deputy leader of a Council becomes its leader following the sudden death of the incumbent.

accountability, self-restraint, and the maintenance of discretion in relation to confidential information.[74] In such cases, the role theory can justify the criminalization of conduct dishonouring those goods, irrespective of whether the conduct is of a type that risks remote harm. This is because the honouring and sustaining of such goods plays an essential role in maintaining and enhancing the intrinsic value of ethically well-ordered public institutions. It follows that the role theory is, in part, a consequentialist theory of criminalization, aimed at underpinning the commitment of public officials to the promotion of key public goods. However, unlike cruder forms of consequentialism, it is not a theory that is by its nature hostile to (or in tension with) individual autonomy.[75] On the contrary, not only does D's voluntary participation in a relevant role play a crucial part in the justification for criminalization, but a society that seeks to promote ethically well-ordered public institutions, if need be through criminalization, is perfectly capable of being (and in all probability will be) an autonomy-enhancing society.[76] The role theory is thus indirectly supported by a concern for autonomy, but this is a concern about the conditions in which autonomy flourishes rather than a concern about (harmful) set-backs to autonomy.

This abstract claim must be substantiated before we return to consider the proper nature and scope of the crime of misconduct in a public office. I will start by asking whether the misconduct offence is securely captured by a relatively straightforward application of the harm principle. The answer will be 'not very securely'. I will then make my case for the role theory as the theory of criminalization best suited to explain and justify the offence. In so doing, I will compare and contrast the role theory with a more sophisticated extension of the harm principle that I will call the 'common pool resources' theory.

2.7 The Limits of an Orthodox Application of the Harm Principle

Here are some examples of misconduct in a public office that, in themselves, involve harmless wrongdoing:

Example 2: A planning application is being heard by a local planning committee. X, a member of the committee, knowingly fails to reveal that the applicant is his or her daughter, even though X makes no contribution to the discussion of the application.[77]

[74] See eg the core values of the Civil Service, as expressed in cl 3 of its Code of Conduct: Civil Service (2014), at para 3: 'integrity, honesty, objectivity and impartiality'.

[75] As outlined by J S Mill (n 69), the main purpose of the harm principle was to provide a bulwark protecting personal autonomy against unrestrained utilitarianism. The principle is not engaged in the same way when autonomy-enhancing consequentialist theories are in issue.

[76] See Joseph Raz (1986), at chs 8 and 10, on the relationship between collective goods and personal autonomy.

[77] See *Speechley* [1982] QB 1053, in which D influenced the re-routing of a road near his property, without disclosing this personal interest, but claimed not to have been motivated by any consideration of personal benefit, discussed in Terence F Williams (2010), at 344. For an analogous Canadian case see *Arnold* (1892) 23 OR 201.

Example 3: A public sector accountant, Y, 'cooks the books' to make it appear that a local council has spent far less on entertaining visiting dignitaries than it actually has, by concealing some of the expenditure under a different heading.[78]

Example 4: Out of curiosity, Z, a judge's clerk in the Royal Courts of Justice, makes use of the fact that an office is temporarily unoccupied to view confidential information about the administration of justice on the screen of a shared computer. Z was just curious, and never had any intention to pass on the information.[79]

In his famous examination and development of the harm principle, Feinberg defines harm as a 'thwarting, setting back, or defeating of an interest',[80] where central to the notion of an 'interest' is the interest of an individual.[81] In none of the examples just given does any individual suffer a set-back to their interests, thus defined, as a result of the wrongdoing in each case. Even so, some might think that there is a straightforward way in which to invoke the orthodox harm principle to justify criminalization in these examples. The harm principle has always been interpreted so as to allow criminal prohibition of harmless wrongdoing, if and when such wrongdoing as a *type* of conduct tends to lead to the thwarting, setting back or defeating of individual interests (harm).[82] In example 2, we could take the view that failures to disclose personal connections to the case are a type of conduct liable wrongfully to set back people's interests, even if such a failure may not have this effect in an individual example.

In approaching this issue, we need to distinguish two ways in which criminal prohibitions can permissibly be applied to harmless wrongdoing.[83] First, there are cases in which problems of vagueness will be encountered in distinguishing harmless from harmful wrongdoing, necessitating the extension of a criminal prohibition on the latter to the former.[84] Although his work long predated Mill's exposition of the harm principle, Sir William Blackstone himself highlighted this feature of legitimate criminalization, in the case of battery. He justified the criminal prohibition of the slightest (harmless) touching of another, by pointing out it may be difficult to distinguish between a touch and a harmful slap or push, and between a slap or a push and an even more harmful blow. So, his argument runs, if the law tolerated (harmless) minor interferences with others, as a type of conduct, people would inevitably mistake the limits of the law's tolerance and wrongfully cause unjustified

[78] Y's conduct would not amount to false accounting contrary to s 17 of the Theft Act 1968, because Y does not intend to benefit himself or another, or to cause loss to another, in the sense of financial or proprietary gain and loss.

[79] See *R v Pike-Williams* [2004] EWCA Crim 2400 for a closely analogous case, in which it was held that D's sentence for misconduct in a public office should be a community penalty (D's original sentence of two months' imprisonment was quashed).

[80] See Feinberg, *Harm to Others* (n 70) 33.

[81] ibid 34: 'One's interests ... consist of all those things in which one has a stake ... the things these interests are *in*, are distinguishable components of a person's well-being . . . '. (Feinberg's emphasis). Feinberg's basic notion of an interest can be extended easily enough to include the interests of groups, such as racial or religious groups, who can suffer a set-back to their interests as a group; but that kind of extension is not in issue here.

[82] See now A P Simester and Andreas von Hirsch (n 72) 50–51.

[83] The two ways appear to me to be run together in Simester and von Hirsch (n 72) 51.

[84] See more generally S G Williams (2004).

harm in the form of slaps, shoves, and blows.[85] The same kind of argument can be applied to justify the criminalization not merely of (inherently risky) 'careless' driving, but also of merely (annoying but not necessarily inherently risky) 'inconsiderate' driving.[86] There may frequently be no discernible point at which the latter turns into the former, that fact being sufficient in itself to provide a justification for the prohibition of both.

Secondly, there are cases where, in broad terms, the justification for criminalization is that although wrongdoing is harmless, it is nonetheless of a type liable to pose an unacceptable risk of harm.[87] It is this second path to justified criminalization that is relevant here. In such cases, one might argue as follows. Suppose that the wrongdoing in the three examples above does not happen to thwart, set back, or defeat any individual's interests (or risk this consequence) in the particular circumstances. Even so, to tolerate wrongdoing of this type would in all probability lead to public sector workers sometimes engaging in it when it did—or was likely to—go on to have such harmful effects.[88] Since we cannot allow that to happen, does it not follow that it is permissible, for good old-fashioned harm principle reasons, to prohibit all such wrongdoing? In answering this question, it is important to distinguish grounds on which conduct is permissibly criminalized, from grounds on which such conduct should in fact be criminalized, even if these grounds overlap to some extent. Having permission to do something is, after all, in itself no reason to do it.[89] We may grant, then, that where, as a type, harmless wrongdoing might pose a risk of harm there is likely to be permission to criminalize that wrongdoing; but this hurdle is a low one to surmount. By contrast, providing a justification for a decision to criminalize harmless wrongdoing, because of the risk of harm that it poses as a type of conduct, should (in theory) involve surmounting a much higher hurdle. What is more, the justification for criminalization on such grounds is vulnerable, not only at the time the decision is taken but also throughout the time that the offence is on the statute book, to being undermined by proof that the potentially harmful effects of the wrongdoing are or have become too unlikely, or too trivial, to warrant (continued) criminalization.[90]

That being so, a harm principle argument is best viewed as providing only auxiliary or supporting justification for criminalization in relation to examples 2–4. We

[85] This is my interpretation of the passage in Sir William Blackstone (1765), at vol iv, 120, where he says: 'The law cannot draw the line between different degrees of violence, and therefore prohibits the first and lowest stage of it, every man's person being sacred, and no other having a right to meddle with it, in any the slightest manner'.

[86] See now s 3 of the Road Traffic Act 1988.

[87] A highly sophisticated exploration of this basis for criminalization, drawing a variety of significant distinctions, can be found in Simester and von Hirsch (n 72) 79–85.

[88] So, in example 3, it might be that the accountant's conduct sets back the interest of an auditor under a duty to certify that the accounts are a truthful and honest account of spending incurred.

[89] See John Gardner, 'Justification under Authority' (2010), at 78: 'Consent is not a reason for anyone to do anything. This follows from the fact that consent may be permission-granting or power-conferring, but is never directly duty-imposing. Unlike a duty, neither a permission nor a power is a reason (or entails or even suggests the existence of a reason) to act as one is permitted or empowered by it to do'.

[90] See the discussion in John Gardner (2011).

may also ask how helpful it really is, in seeking to make the justification, to extend the notion of harm (as Feinberg does) to include 'harm to public institutions and practices'?[91] It is only helpful if one is willing to add a phrase such as 'ethically well-ordered', to 'public institutions and practices'. Public institutions are normatively capable of forming their own—perhaps dysfunctional—understanding of what benefits them and what harms them. Without the addition of a value-directed descriptor, such as 'ethically well-ordered' to 'public institutions and practices', one might end up in the strange position of having to say about example 3 that Y's conduct is not potentially harmful to the institution, because the institution—the local authority—saw Y's conduct as helpfully enabling it to avoid any damaging embarrassment over spending decisions.[92] Suppose, then, that in order to locate the 'harm' done to a public institution by Y's wrongdoing, one has to add this element of value judgment (i.e. that public institutions and practices should be ethically well-ordered) to the factual element of something being a 'public institution [or] practice'. That suggests that the central focus in point of criminalization is not really the risk of harm to public institutions posed by the misconduct. The central focus is really the way in which Y's misconduct (like that of X and Z) dishonours or undermines the values constitutive of ethically sound public institutional practice.

In that regard, in X's case, in example 2, there is a failure in point of honesty and openness, as these affect complete impartiality, where impartiality—as it must always do in this context—includes being seen to be free of significant possible biases, as well as actually acting in an unbiased way. Codes of Conduct for public officials commonly contain obligations meant to ensure that such failures do not occur. Here is an example commonly used (with minor variations) by many local councils and police authorities:

> 9(1) ... [W]here you have a personal interest in any business of your authority and you attend a meeting of your authority at which the business is considered, you must disclose to that meeting the existence and nature of that interest at the commencement of that consideration, or when the interest becomes apparent.[93]

Few, if any, mentioned it at the time, but on this basis Lord Hoffmann might have been a legitimate candidate for a charge of misconduct in a public office, when he heard (and was party to the decision to allow) the Spanish prosecutor's appeal against a lower court's ruling that Augusto Pinochet, as the head of state in Chile at the relevant time, had immunity from prosecution for torture and hostage-taking. At the time of hearing the appeal, Lord Hoffmann had failed to disclose his position as director and chair of one of the parties to the case, Amnesty International.[94]

[91] See Feinberg, *Harm to Others* (n 70) 11.

[92] One of the few offences that I can think of that authentically reflects a harm-to-public-institutions rationale is the old offence of unlawfully and maliciously setting fire to a public building, contrary to s 5 of the Malicious Damage Act 1861. Clearly, that is not what Feinberg had in mind.

[93] https://democracy.swansea.gov.uk/documents/s29695/Code%20of%20Conduct.pdf para 11.1. See also www.southwalespoliceauthority.org.uk/en/content/cms/library/members_and_officers/code_of_conduct/code_of_conduct.aspx.

[94] For a critical account of Lord Hoffmann's role see Joshua Rosenberg (2009).

In Y's case, in example 3, there is similarly a failure in point of honesty and openness, but this time these failures dishonour or undermine the value of proper public accountability rather than suggesting bias.[95] In that regard, in relation to provision of financial information to the public about its income and expenditure, the National Association of Local Councils' practitioner guidance on accounting practices requires a local council to ensure that:

4.27 ... The financial information provided is reliable and,
- reflects the substance of the transactions and other events that have taken place;
- is free from deliberate or systematic bias;
- is free from material error;
- is complete within the bounds of materiality; and
- under conditions of uncertainty, is prudently prepared.[96]

In Z's case, in example 4, there is a failure in point of 'discretion'; the need for those with public responsibilities not only to keep confidential much information to which they are privy,[97] but also to remain studiously ignorant of confidential issues that are not their professional concern.[98] Once again, codes of conduct issued to public service workers typically contain strong guidance on the importance of maintaining confidentiality.[99] An example is provided by the Model Code of Conduct for members of local authorities, section 4 of which says:

You must not-

(a) Disclose any information given to you in confidence by anyone, or information acquired by you which you believe, or ought reasonably to be aware, is of a confidential nature ...[100]

These are not the only values it is a public sector worker's responsibility to honour and promote, as part of their duty to embrace a public service ethos.[101] Equally

[95] In Weber's analysis of bureaucracy, accountability was always 'internal'—to one's superior, in particular—rather than being 'external', to the public, an aspect respecting which Weberian analysis needs to be supplemented or updated: see Beetham (1996), at 33–35 and at 94–95.

[96] See the Joint Practitioners Advisory Group (2010).

[97] See *R v Fletcher and Parr* (unreported www.bbc.co.uk/1/hi/england/nottinghamshire/6088150.stm), cited by Wasik (n 57) 138, where the defendants were police officers who passed on confidential information to suspected criminals in a serious crime investigation. A similar case is *R v O'Leary* [2007] EWCA Crim 186.

[98] I put on one side here instances in which a duty to disclose confidential material (to become a 'whistle-blower') comes from the misuse of confidentiality within an institution. Whistle-blowers are protected from dismissal or adverse treatment under the Public Interest Disclosure Act 1998.

[99] See eg the guidance given to police officers by Cleveland Police: 'Information which comes into the possession of the police should be treated as confidential. It should not be used for personal benefit and nor should it be divulged to other parties except in the proper course of police duty': www.clevelandpf.org.uk/regulations/discipline.pdf.

[100] Local Authorities (Model Code of Conduct) Order 2007.

[101] In his seminal work on white-collar crime, Stuart P Green makes an important argument for criminalizing public sector wrongdoing by characterizing such wrongdoing as evincing 'disloyalty': see Stuart P Green (2006), at ch 8. That argument may go both too far, and not far enough. It goes too far, in that in some instances it will be clear that a public servant should be honest and open, rather than loyal to a superior or to an institution, when these values clash. The argument does not go far enough, in

important, for example, are 'integrity' (a commitment to be *consistently* ethical in one's conduct: not only behaving ethically when it is convenient or personally advantageous), and 'self-denial' (not taking up personal advantages that present themselves in virtue of one's public sector work).[102] So, for example, paragraph 1.5 of the Code of Conduct issued by Gateshead Council[103] instructs its members:

> You ... must not use or attempt to use your position as a member improperly to confer on or secure for yourself or any other person, and advantage or disadvantage.[104]

Understood broadly, the need to honour and sustain the demands of self-restraint can help to explain why, in the example given in section 2.5 above, the police officer misconducts him or herself by behaving abusively in public, whether or not the behaviour is likely to cause harassment, alarm, or distress (and thus fall foul of section 5 of the Public Order Act 1986). A lack of self-restraint can be displayed by a public official not only through greed or opportunism ('feathering one's own nest'), but also by an inappropriate emotional display. This is made plain, for example, in clause 3 of the guidance issued by the Cleveland Police Federation to its officers: 'Officers should treat members of the public and colleagues with courtesy and respect, avoiding abusive or deriding attitudes or behaviour'.[105] The forming of a relationship with a victim or witness by a criminal justice official may also exemplify a wrongful failure of self-restraint, if it has the capacity to affect the discharge of an official's powers or duties (the libertarian, institutional-functionalist test). Such conduct has hence rightly led to prosecution of officials for the misconduct offence.[106] The example of self-restraint as a public good is particularly helpful in that it illustrates how all of the values discussed are of importance in the way that they link together. They are not valued only separately, for bringing something distinct to the development of a public service ethos. So, for example, abuse or derisive behaviour is closely linked with the risk that impartiality and integrity may be abandoned,[107] and the maintenance of confidentiality is linked with resisting the temptation to exploit an opportunity to benefit oneself, where that includes the social benefit derived or pleasure from releasing confidential information as a juicy piece of gossip.[108]

that—as I am suggesting—there are many more values to be honoured than loyalty, as intrinsic elements in the delivery of public services.

[102] See eg College of Policing (2014), at 5 ('honesty and integrity').

[103] A code of conduct very similar to those adopted by many other councils.

[104] Gateshead Council (2017), at para 5.

[105] http://www.clevelandpf.org.uk/regulations/discipline.pdf para 3. See also https://www.nottinghamshire.police.uk/sites/default/files/documents/files/CODE%20OF%20CONDUCT.pdf. See further Gardner, *The Constitution of the Criminal Law* (n 65).

[106] *Witcher and Lang* (unreported, Guildford Crown Court 2005), and see the cases discussed by Wasik (n 57).

[107] See Gardner, *The Constitution of the Criminal Law* (n 65).

[108] See Sarah R Wert and Peter Salovey (2004).

2.8 The Role Theory of Criminalization: Public Goods and Common Pool Resources

It has frequently been argued that the harm principle does not stand in the way of alternative theories of criminalization, even though JS Mill himself expressed the view that the *only* justification for the use of coercion was that (other things being equal) it prevented 'harm to others'. In other words, most theorists argue that there can be exceptions to it. Some have said, for example, that coercion can be used in certain circumstances to deter and punish offensive (but harmless) behaviour,[109] and that coercion may sometimes be justified paternalistically, to punish and deter the causing of harm—or the risk of harm—to the self rather than to others.[110] Perhaps less well explored is the possibility that there might be an alternative theory of criminalization that is capable of meeting—rather than being an exception to—the two key tenets of the harm principle, and yet itself not be founded on that principle. These tenets are, very briefly and broadly, first, that state coercion should not be used merely to try to improve someone's moral or personal well-being (the autonomy sub-principle).[111] Secondly, assuming the first tenet is satisfied, the state must believe—on the basis of a combination of judgmental and evidential factors[112]—that in pursuit of the relevant goal the use of coercion is a balanced response (the balance sub-principle).[113] A decision to license the use of coercion through the criminal law must be a 'balanced' and proportionate response, but it need not be a strictly 'necessary' response, because the latter test would be too strict. The state is perfectly entitled, other things being equal, to experiment with criminalization. It is not bound to use the criminal law only as a last resort, or only in the absence of any other available measure. More importantly, neither of these tenets or sub-principles rules out the use of coercion to uphold and promote standards in public life: the issue at the heart of the role theory.

[109] See Joel Feinberg (1985). By contrast, Simester and von Hirsch are much more cautious, defending the view that offensive conduct may be criminalization only if there is some kind of connection with the harm principle: see Simester and von Hirsch (n 72) Pt III.

[110] See Joel Feinberg (1986). The authoritative modern discussion is Simester and von Hirsch (n 72) Pt IV.

[111] See Mill (n 69). This aspect of the harm principle represented, of course, Mill's introduction of a bastion shielding personal autonomy from the more unrestrained excesses of some utilitarian thought: see Alan Ryan (1972).

[112] The balance sub-principle of the harm principle demands an investigation and evidence-base for the making of balanced judgments that is characteristic of bureaucratic thinking, the kind of thinking that, as a lifelong civil servant in the East India Company, J S Mill (n 69) would have been all too familiar and comfortable with: see Ryan (n 112), and the discussion of *zweckrationell* (goal rationality) in Max Weber (1947), at 337. See also Feinberg, *Harm to Others* (1984) 226: 'In applying the harm principle, then, the legislator must acquire the best empirical information he can get about the readiness of persons generally (and also their opportunities and abilities) to act in the way whose prohibition he is considering'.

[113] For a more detailed account of what needs to be shown if coercion is to be regarded as a balanced response see Simester and von Hirsch (n 72) 45.

So far as the first tenet or sub-principle is concerned, to coerce someone into performing their public role, in upholding public goods, is not to trespass within a protected domain of freedom where individuals should be at liberty to accept or reject *personal* roles (husband; career woman; political activist; and so on) or private standards (the values of my parents' generation; religious values, and so forth). Subject to the application of the balance sub-principle, coercion through the criminal law may be used to secure conformity by those occupying public roles to the demands of public goods, because it is not the individual's—the public service provider's—*own* good that the coercion is being employed to promote. It is the good intrinsic to his or her public role. When someone occupies a public role, they may legitimately be required to do or abstain from doing certain things—a requirement backed by the threat of coercion in cases of transgression—that should never be coercively demanded of them in a personal role. We explored some aspects of that point in section 2.2, when contrasting the libertarian and austere republican accounts of the scope of the misconduct offence.

The role theory of criminalization is engaged when a role has two key features, mentioned earlier. First, the role must have been freely chosen[114] and, secondly, the role must gain its intrinsic value from the public goods to be honoured and sustained in discharging it. The obvious candidate roles are the ones under discussion to date, namely public service roles. We saw in the last section how these roles are given value through the honouring and sustaining of goods such as integrity, openness, accountability, and so on: goods that form an essential part of the intrinsic value of ethically well-ordered public institutions. More needs to be said, however, about the theoretical basis of the role theory, beyond its crucial role—considered earlier—in bolstering the harm principle. Superficially, the role theory seems puzzling. The mere fact that I consent to a code of conduct of some kind, breach of which is made a criminal offence, seems wholly inadequate by itself to justify exposing me to such liability. Yet, mutatis mutandis, in liberal societies the criminal law cannot ordinarily be used simply to protect or promote the integrity and importance of a code of values for their own sake. So, how can these two factors, both insufficient in themselves to justify criminalization, together provide an adequate justification?

Care must clearly be taken, in deciding that people occupy roles involving certain kinds of responsibilities, if that decision is related to the imposition of criminal liability on role-related misconduct. Nonetheless, the element or choice (or of voluntary assumption of responsibility) in accepting a particular role can make one permissibly subject to a range of prohibitions and sanctions bearing on one's role that the state would or might otherwise not be permitted to deploy against one. By one's choice, one may change one's normative position, by expressly or impliedly subjecting oneself to the duty-imposing powers of those whose task it is to safeguard the values constitutive of the role one now occupies.[115] Having said that, the

[114] Or, at least, in the case where one official automatically comes to occupy another's role, because that other has died or unexpectedly resigned, the role must not have been disclaimed by the official in question (and hence impliedly assumed voluntarily).

[115] On this feature of permissions see Gardner, 'Justification under Authority' (2010).

mere fact that one has chosen to occupy a public role of some kind cannot justify criminalization of *any* failure to live up to the role's expectations. To make oneself permissibly subject to the duty-imposing power of the state respecting the values constituting a given role does not mean that 'anything goes', when it comes to the creation of criminal prohibitions underpinning and shaping that role. It is a further and partially independent question whether there were or are sufficiently persuasive and compelling reasons for the state to seek to shape the role in issue by creating such prohibitions.

Consider, by way of example, the offence created by section 16 of the Armed Forces Act 2006:

16 Malingering

(1) A person subject to service law commits an offence if, to avoid service—
   (a) he pretends to have an injury;
   (b) by any act he causes himself an injury;
   (c) by any act or omission he aggravates or prolongs any injury of his; or
   (d) he causes another person to injure him.

In the special context of voluntary participation in service life, such offences may permissibly be applied to service personnel, for the purpose of maintaining an (ethically sound) *esprit de corps* essential to the conditions in which the armed services will flourish. One does not have to be of a warlike disposition to see that ethically sound service culture—'courage, dedication and professionalism in [soldiers'] service of their country'[116]—is capable of making a vital contribution to the public good of national security. That kind of justification would not, however, be available to justify a similar offence in (non-voluntary) civilian life, because the harm principle rules out justifications for criminalization rooted solely in the desire to make people—either individually or collectively—better people, whether they want to be or not.

In that respect, the role theory (as I have presented it) should be contrasted with the treatment of more controversial examples of what might be called 'inherent' roles, roles that I must fulfil (say) in virtue of being human, or in virtue of being a citizen. Attempts to coerce people into fulfilling such roles, for their own sake, are liable to fall foul of the autonomy sub-principle of the harm principle. That I will be a better human being if I pay more attention to my friends, or a better citizen if I tone down my protests about my country's involvement in an (*ex hypothesi* just) self-defensive war, is no basis for coercing me through the criminal law into doing either. However, in connection with the harm principle, some thinkers have sought to make something of such roles as a source of responsibilities, failure in which may legitimately be criminalized if the failures threaten or cause harm. For example, when discussing role-responsibility, Simester and von Hirsch suggest that, beyond roles that are chosen (such as one's role as a

[116] The words of Robert Ainsworth, in Ministry of Defence (2008) preface. Ainsworth was an MP and Minister of State for the Armed Forces.

company director) 'every person has certain responsibilities as a citizen – for example, the obligation to contribute one's share of taxes'.[117] I will come back to the relationship between a failure to pay tax and the harm principle shortly; but how securely founded on someone's inherent role as a citizen is the obligation to pay taxes? I suggest that the obligation is not securely founded on that basis, an illustration of the contentious nature of inherent roles in general and citizenship obligations in particular.

Both UK companies, and individuals working temporarily in the UK, must pay tax in the UK, even though they are not 'citizens'. Overseas companies must pay tax on high value residential property in the UK, even though they may have no legal existence in the UK.[118] Similarly, even as an individual, if I buy and sell a property in France, I will have to pay the equivalent of capital gains tax in France, even if I have never set foot in France and have no other connection there. Perhaps, the obligation to pay tax can be linked to some kind of domestically or internationally applicable benefit-and-burden theory. Even so, such a theory would not be co-extensive with citizenship status. To be sure, all citizens face obligations arising out of benefit-and-burden; but these obligations might legitimately in some cases remain on someone who continued to reside in a given jurisdiction, even if that person was stripped of citizenship status. The duty to pay tax does, however, raise a key question in relation to the theory being developed here. It raises the question whether there is an as-yet-unexplored basis on which the harm principle can account for the criminalization of the dishonouring of public goods. This basis can be called the 'common pool resources' theory of harmdoing.

In *Harm to Others*, Feinberg identifies a kind of harm that he called 'accumulative harm', the threat of which may justify the use of criminal sanctions.[119] If the vast majority of people could be relied on to pay enough tax voluntarily, there would be no need to make tax 'evasion' a criminal offence. However, the greater the numbers of people who—perhaps in hard economic times—might make use of such a legal freedom not to pay tax, the more 'social harm'[120] would in consequence result from the inability of government to pay for vital services. In order to minimize the risk of such an 'accumulative' harm occurring, thus, the threat of criminal sanctions to coerce the unwilling into paying tax can be justified. Simester and von Hirsch develop a similar thesis, calling such harm 'conjunctive harm'.[121] Of this type of harm, they say:

> In these cases, the conduct to be prohibited does the feared injury only when combined with similar acts of others ... There are, we accept, certain basic duties of co-operation which are owed by each person in his capacity as a citizen, concerning such matters as the payment of taxes, the administration of justice, and so forth. These basic duties of citizenship support generally application prohibitions.[122]

117 Simester and von Hirsch (n 72) 64.
118 See Her Majesty's Revenue and Customs (2014).
119 See Feinberg, *Harm to Others* (n 79) 225–27.
120 ibid 226.
121 See Simester and von Hirsch (n 72) 85–88.
122 ibid 85, 87.

I have already dealt with the issue of whether it is the status of 'citizenship' that grounds the basic duties of cooperation.[123] More significant is the question of how the non-payment of taxes, to use that example, comes to be regarded as harmful.

The resources generated by taxation, like (say) the freshness and purity of the water in a lake, are 'common pool resources', rather than what I have been referring to as public goods. The distinction is well explained by Karen Yeung:

> Common pool resources are not... "pure public goods" because consumption of the pooled resources is rivalrous. Because a common pool resource system generates a finite supply of resource units, one person's appropriation from the pool diminishes the quantity of resource units available to others, slightly degrading the overall health and quality of the resources system and thus exposing it to problems of overcrowding or overuse ... [T]he ocean is a common pool resource: by extracting fish from the ocean, I diminish the number of fish available to others.[124]

In the case of taxation, a failure to contribute one's due[125] to the common pool obviously diminishes the quantity of resource units available to others just as much as an unauthorized appropriation from the available resource units; and a failure, in breach of a duty to act, to improve others' prospects can be to harm them.[126] From here, it is but a short step to the perfectly sound proposition that such a failure to contribute causes or threatens harm, in the form of a diminution of the resources available to satisfy calls on tax revenue. It follows that Simester and von Hirsch are right to identify the failure to pay one's due to the common pool, in the form of tax, as conduct that causes or risks harm.

However, as Yeung indicates, common pool resources must be distinguished from public goods, even though both are protected by the offence of misconduct (amongst other offences). By way of contrast with common pool resources, the nature of public goods means that their diminution is not best analysed in terms of harm done or risked. According to Kaul, Grunberg, and Stern:

> The ideal public good has two main qualities: its benefits are non-rivalrous in consumption and non-excludable... Peace is an ... example of a pure public good. When it exists all citizens of a country can enjoy it; and its enjoyment by, say, rural populations does not distract from its benefits for urban populations. A similar case can be made for law and order or good macroeconomic management.[127]

As Kaul, Grunberg, and Stern go on to point out, whilst a true public good has these two qualities (it will be non-competitive in consumption and non-excludable), many

[123] In relation to the example of an obligation to respect the due administration of justice, given in this passage, it is equally questionable whether that obligation rests on a citizenship obligation in the relevant jurisdiction. If two residents of France, who have never set foot in England, conspire in Paris to pervert the course of justice in England, that is just as much an offence indictable in England as if it had been committed by two life-long English citizens in London: *Somchai Liangsiriprasert v United States* [1991] 1 AC 225 (PC).

[124] Karen Yeung (2011), at 19.

[125] Assessed according to whatever theory best accounts for fair taxation: benefit-and-burden, citizenship, or whatever.

[126] See the discussion in Joseph Raz (1987).

[127] Kaul, Grunberg, and Stern (n 67) 3, 4.

public goods are in reality what they call 'impure' public goods, because they lack one or other of these qualities to some extent.[128] Further, the 'impurity' may come about through human (in)action. As we saw earlier, for example, the public good of self-restraint exercised in public may not be extended to some members of a community (foreigners; demonstrators, and so on). Where public officials are concerned, however, ethically well-ordered public institutions seek to guard against the very possibility that such exclusions may take place. Recall the wording of the Cleveland Police Federation to its officers: 'Officers should treat members of the public and colleagues with courtesy and respect, avoiding abusive or deriding attitudes or behaviour'.[129] Implicit here is an endorsement of the view that the exercise of self-restraint by public officials must not only be non-rivalrous, so far as its beneficiaries are concerned, but also non-excludable. In other words, public officials should not treat a public good like self-restraint as if it was a 'pool resource'. Complying with the obligation to support such a view, sustaining self-restraint (along with the other relevant public goods) as a pure public good, is, as I have been suggesting, at the core of what it means to be a dutiful public sector worker.

Of equal theoretical significance is the fact that, whether or not a public good may become impure by being made exclusive, it is non-rivalrous so far as the un-excluded are concerned. There is no such thing as a 'quantum' of (say) official self-restraint, of discretion, of openness, or of accountability to be shared out between potentially rival claimants to the benefits. Naturally, one reaches the limits of, for example, accountability when one is fully accountable for all that one does. The benefits of full accountability can, however, be shared by all to an equal extent, however many seek to enjoy those benefits. There is no need to adjudicate between potentially competing claims to the benefits. To use a different example of the non-competitive nature of public goods the users of the justice system, however numerous, will all benefit from judicial impartiality and integrity, as public goods, even those subject to (an *ex hypothesi* fair) exclusion from the system, such as vexatious litigants. No one has to compete against others for the benefit therefrom. By contrast, as a common pool resource, the limits of the tax-take are the limits of what can 'go around'. The more people there are wishing to enjoy the benefits of public spending from taxation, the more consumption is liable to become rivalrous. Accordingly, on the one hand, to fail in one's duty to pay tax is to set back the interests or potential interests of—to harm or risk harming—those with legitimate claims on these benefits. On the other hand, as a public official, to fail in one's public duties respecting self-restraint, openness, discretion, integrity, impartiality, or accountability is not primarily to harm or risk harming anyone in such a way (although in some cases this may be involved).[130] Instead, failing in that way is primarily to detract from a valuable feature of the public culture of officialdom, diminishing its moral or ethical quality. Where such a failure comes in the form of an abuse of public position, power, or duty, perfectly

[128] We encountered this phenomenon in discussing self-restraint and civility earlier.

[129] See text at n 105 above.

[130] I have conceded that such an explanation is theoretically feasible as an auxiliary justification for criminalization.

consistently with the main tenets of the harm principle, it may be justified to treat such a failure as criminal misconduct in office.

2.9 The Role Theory and Misconduct in Public Office

The role theory is not a bespoke theory designed solely to account for crimes unique to public officials. For example, it is the best explanation of the need for company directors to declare an interest in an existing transaction or arrangement entered into by the company, or face a criminal sanction.[131] The role of company director involves a commitment to the good of transparency, in this respect, and is hence inconsistent with keeping such interests hidden in these circumstances. The existence of such offences could be perhaps explained, at a very considerable stretch, by the harm principle. In the United States of America, courts have spoken of a failure to declare a personal interest, or a failure to make full disclosure, as instances in which:

> the public is deprived of its *right* either to disinterested decision-making itself, or, as the case may be, to full disclosure as to the official's potential motivation behind an official act.[132]

As John Coffee has said of this individualist, violation-of-interest (harm-based) approach: 'The point is simply that "actual harm" does not work in the context of public decision-making... [W]e cannot meaningfully measure "harm" in this context'.[133] The role theory provides a better explanation.

Further, the role theory provides a basis for suggesting that, in this respect, company directors may have been unfairly picked out for criminalization, when those in non-corporate professional roles, who may do as much or more damage through similar forms of misconduct, do not face the same possible consequences for wrongdoing. In relation to avoiding conflicts of interest, for example, the Law Commission observes:

> Many people who are not considered to be public office holders are, or would be considered to be, under specific duties not to act in a biased or prejudiced manner or under the actual or apparent influence of a conflict of interest. Examples are doctors, solicitors, barristers, trustees and company directors.[134]

In most of these examples, a failure to live up to, or even a betrayal of one's role, will lead to disciplinary proceedings or civil action, rather than to criminal sanctions. The role theory provides a powerful explanation for the existence of such proceedings, even if a part of the burden of explanation is taken by the harm principle: without prohibitions on acting in situations where there is a conflict of interests, the incidence of wrongful set-backs to the well-being of those placing their trust in professionals

[131] Companies Act 2006, s 183(1).

[132] *United States v Sawyer* 83 F 3rd 713 (1st Cir 1996), 720–21 (my emphasis). Although this case concerned a public official, a similar 'right' has been found to be violated in cases of corporate misconduct: *United States v Wallach* 935 F 2d 445 (2d Cir 1991).

[133] John C Coffee Jr (1997–98), at 451.

[134] Law Commission, *Reforming Misconduct in Public Office* (n 2) para 6.57.

would doubtless increase. However, the role theory also provides a possible justification for extending the scope of criminal liability to cover the worst examples of bias and prejudice amongst professionals.

Nonetheless, the role theory is of particular importance in explaining the misconduct offence. That is because the role of public officials (or of those more broadly exercising public powers) in maintaining certain public goods, as a feature of the performance of their functions, is one of constitutional significance. Someone who suffers at the hands of a crooked or incompetent solicitor has a choice in the marketplace of other solicitors (even if it also is essential that some kind of disciplinary proceedings can be taken against that solicitor). By contrast, as argued in Chapter 1.1, when faced with a corrupt police investigation, an aggressive social worker, or a racist benefit officer, and perhaps also in each case an internal system that turns a blind eye to these kinds of deficiencies, to whom does the aggrieved citizen turn? There is no marketplace, choice-based solution. In the latter cases, however, the problem is not just that the citizen lacks a choice (unlike the victim of poor legal advice), and thus not simply that the citizen in question is more likely to suffer a set-back to his or her interests. The problem is a broader one: that the behaviour of the officials undermines, threatens, or casts a blight on the health of the constitutional relationship between the state and the citizen. Such a betrayal of a role, through abuse of public position, power, or duty, is rightly open to criminal sanctions, and no offence better labels it than misconduct in a public office.

3

Republican Foundations: Holding Officials to Account in Criminal Law

[T]he Crown-law ... gives the prince no power, but of doing good, and restrains the people from no liberty, but of doing evil.[1]

3.1 Accountability from the Top-down and Bottom-up

Historical treatments of the offence of misconduct in a public office have hitherto failed adequately to bring out two of its key features. First, there was an important difference between the theory and the practice. In practice, the offence developed largely, if not solely, as a 'top-down' projection of authority, a means of punishing lower-level officials for their misdeeds. A classic example is the leading case of *R v Bembridge*,[2] in which an accountant in the office of HM Paymaster General of the Forces was convicted of misconduct when he concealed from the public auditors no less than £48,000,[3] in the hope of profiting himself.[4] In theory, however, the offence carried a strong republican element to it, of accountability from the 'bottom-up'. The passage from Hawkins concerning the obligations of the prince, cited above, was a reflection of a long-standing view that, as one seventeenth-century lawyer put it:

The word Trust is frequent in the Kings Papers, and therefore I conceive the King does admit that his interest in the Crowne is not absolute, or by a meere donation of the people, but in part conditionate and fiduciary.[5]

On this view, what was wrong with misconduct was that it was a betrayal of the people's trust, not (or not solely) a betrayal of someone further up in the chain of command. As Mark Knights has observed,[6] that kind of analysis was also applied

[1] William Hawkins (1824), vol i, at xi.

[2] (1783) 3 Doug 327. For fuller historical treatment see Jeremy Horder (2017).

[3] Over £5 million in 2016, when multiplied by the percentage increase in the RPI: House of Commons Library (2012).

[4] Bembridge's conduct would now be regarded as fraud by abuse of position, or false accounting.

[5] Henry Parker (1642), at 4, cited by Mark Knights (2016), at 12. See further Howard Nenner (2009).

[6] Mark Knights (n 5), at 4.

in some quarters to the behaviour of members of Parliament (MPs), as well as to holders of public office more generally:

all Majesteriall Power in England whatever, are but Offices of trust, and bound up with this limitation, to be executed for the good of the trusters . . . the same doe we aver of a Parliament, and Parliament-men . . . when they cease to execute the end of their trust, which is as themselves say, to provide for the peoples weales, but not for their woes, and doe meerly indeavour to make themselves tyrants over the people.[7]

Such 'leveller' opinion may have been heretical in the seventeenth century, as a basis for holding government to account in general. Even so, as we will see, the language became familiar to much more orthodox accounts of the most serious form of misconduct in office. In Chapter 1, I implicitly drew on it to explain a distinction between issues respecting which we should put our absolute trust in MPs to behave with propriety, and issues respecting which our trust, in that respect, should be merely conditional. In the latter cases, when the conditions are violated, the courts should intervene to provide 'for the people's weales' (to use the words of Lilburne and Overton, in the passage just cited).

It has always been rare for someone in high office themselves to be prosecuted for misconduct, although it has happened.[8] In practice, the predominant view of the offence has been a top-down one, according to which high-level officials are regarded primarily as the victims of the misconduct offence, at the hands of their inferior officials, rather than the perpetrators. Accordingly, the bottom-up justification was deployed mainly as an additional justification for prosecutions of lower-level officials. Today, there is still a reluctance to use the misconduct offence to target wrongdoing by high public officials. Moreover, there is still a contentious understanding that where misconduct is systematically endorsed or tolerated at the highest political level, that takes it outside the realm of what may legitimately be subject to criminal prosecution.[9]

A second point commonly overlooked about the history of the misconduct offence relates to the two main forms it took, before being merged into one crime in recent times. The top-down account of the offence predominated in the development of both common law and statutory forms of 'wilful neglect' of office, as a form of misconduct. The strengthening of this version of this offence reflected an important eighteenth-century development. This was the need to exercise control over burgeoning legions of officials conducting the state's business in an ever-increasingly bureaucratic state.[10] The importance of the development of this offence was twofold. First, it cemented the role of the misconduct offence, in theory as well as in practice, as a top-down measure to ensure that lower-level officials did the bidding of higher-level ones. Secondly, this development shifted the emphasis in the misconduct offence from a judge-controlled (breach of common law) remedy to a parliamentary (breach of statute) remedy for official misconduct.

[7] John Lilburne and Richard Overton (1646), at 17–18, cited by Mark Knights (n 5), at 13.
[8] For some examples see Mark Knights (n 5), at 13.
[9] See the discussion in chs 4 and 5.
[10] See John Brewer (1988).

3.2 An Outline of the Two Misconduct Offences

What is now regarded as a single offence of misconduct[11] was in fact for centuries regarded as two offences (buttressed by some further, related crimes that will not be discussed here[12]).[13] This was the 'pre-merger' position that obtained before the decision in *Attorney General's Reference (No 3 of 2003)*.[14] The most serious of these offences was the one charged in *Rex v Bembridge*,[15] whereby:

> [A] man accepting an office of trust, concerning the public, especially if attended with profit, is answerable criminally to the King for misbehaviour in his office.[16]

The fault element in this offence would vary, depending on the nature of the misbehaviour. Bembridge's misbehaviour in engaging in false accounting was treated as a dishonesty offence. Bembridge was charged with 'wrongly, unjustly, and fraudulently contriving to conceal' the relevant sum.[17] In other instances, the misbehaviour might take the form of the misuse of power, the display of bias in decision-making, or other deliberate wrongdoing such as destroying records or covering up mistakes.[18] What was required was 'a dishonest, oppressive or corrupt motive'.[19]

Fault elements of these kinds involve what might be called 'attitudinal' states of mind, states of mind which in themselves carry an implication of wrongfulness.[20] They can be contrasted with 'cognitive' states of mind, such as intention, knowledge, or awareness of risk. These states of mind do not in themselves carry an implication of wrongfulness when they accompany a piece of conduct. In relation to a given piece of conduct, one has to know more about what was intended, known, or considered possible, before one can say whether having the state of mind in question makes someone worthy of blame respecting what they did. The cognitive forms of fault were more central to the offence of wilful neglect. However, in practice, there was no hard-and-fast rule that only proof of one kind of fault (attitudinal or cognitive) would suffice for proof of guilt of either offence. In certain circumstances,

[11] I put on one side here the evolution of the offence of cheating the public revenue, the roots of which also lie in the *Bembridge* case: see David Ormerod (1998).

[12] An example being extortion.

[13] I agree, on this point, with the argument of Terence F Williams (2010).

[14] [2004] EWCA Crim 868.

[15] (1783) 3 Doug 327.

[16] ibid at 332 (Lord Mansfield).

[17] ibid 328–29. With considerable plausibility, some argue that this manifestation of the offence was not confined—or came not to be confined—to those occupying public offices, but extended to members of the public cheating public funds, giving rise to the offence of cheating the public revenue. See Law Commission (2016a), at paras A36–A42.

[18] Sir James Stephen treated such instances as a separate misconduct offence from the offence of misconduct manifested by fraud: Sir James Stephen (1887), at arts 119 and 121. There is, however, no authority for this separation. They were traditionally treated simply as different ways of committing the same offence.

[19] *R v Borron* (1820) 3 B & Ald 432, (Abbott CJ); C S Greaves (1843), at 136.

[20] I use this term, instead of the more familiar 'affective' state of mind, because the latter concerns (more or less high intensity) emotions. Dishonesty is not an emotive state, but it does involve a certain (wrongful) attitude or disposition towards dealing with others, something that it shares with partiality or corrupt motives.

intention, knowledge, or awareness would suffice as proof of fault in relation to what—for convenience's sake—we can call the 'attitudinal offence'. Even so, as we will see, the attitudinal element to the attitudinal offence was highly significant, constitutionally, in terms of the justification given for treating it as a serious offence.

The wilful neglect version of the offence can to some extent be contrasted with the attitudinal offence.[21] Offences involving neglect of office have a long history, mainly associated with a top-down concern about failure to carry out royal commands (whether in the form of individual orders or laws).[22] An Act of 1437 provided that:

> If any coroner be remiss, and not make inquisition upon the view of the body dead, and certify not, as ordained by statute, he shall, for every default, forfeit to the King a hundred shillings.[23]

Albeit with one eye on codification, rather than mere statement of the common law position,[24] Sir James Stephen aptly summarized the neglect offence thus:

> *Neglect of Official Duty*: Every public officer commits a misdemeanour who wilfully neglects to perform any duty which he is bound either by common law or by statute to perform, provided that the discharge of such duty is not attended with greater danger than a man of ordinary firmness and activity may be expected to encounter.[25]

This offence required 'wilfulness' in the form of a knowledge or awareness of what the duty was (cognitive forms of fault), and neglect shown in the non-performance of that duty. Long-standing offence at common law though it was, this offence played a less prominent part than the judge-controlled attitudinal offence as the embodiment of republican constitutional virtues. As indicated above, far more important was the fact that it became the model for a number of offences created by statute from the seventeenth century onwards. As we will see, these offences embodied a quite different constitutional ethos: top-down parliamentary control over the country's expanding officialdom. These offences stood for the view that Parliament, not just the higher courts, could and should exercise authority over nonfeasance on the part of officials.

Today, these two forms of the misconduct offence are treated as one offence: the 'post-merger' position.[26] Merger has been achieved by stipulating that—whether what is in issue is dishonesty, oppression, corruption, bias, 'wilful neglect', or some other fault element—the offence will only be committed if the conduct (act or omission) in question amounts to 'conduct so far below acceptable standards as to amount to an abuse of the public's trust in the office holder'.[27] The theoretical basis of the offence in its merged form was considered in Chapter 2. I will concentrate in this chapter on the two forms (attitudinal and wilful neglect) that the offence took in the eighteenth century. What we find is that the common law offences of misconduct were treated as offences at the top or at the apex of a hierarchy of

[21] *Mackalley's Case* (1611) 9 Co Rep 656; *Crowther's Case* (1600) Cro Eliz 654.
[22] Law Commission (n 17) paras A83–A93. [23] ibid para A93.
[24] Law Commission (n 17) paras A25–A26. [25] Sir James Stephen (n 18) art 122.
[26] *Attorney-General's Reference (No 3 of 2003)* [2004] 3 WLR 451.
[27] ibid 467 (Pill LJ).

sanctions to deal with misconduct in public office. In the eighteenth century, the misconduct offence was used in such an 'apex capacity' in relation to the handling of misconduct by Justices of the Peace (JPs). In Chapter 5, we will consider how the modern misconduct offence today plays that apex role in relation to officials in the political sphere, such as MPs.

3.3 The Public Law Role of Criminal Law

> And it is true, that the life of a man is much favoured in law, but the life of the law itself (which protects all in peace and safety) ought to be more favoured, and the execution of the process of law and of the offices of conservators of the peace, is the soul and life of the law, and the means by which justice is administered and the peace of the realm kept.[28]

As the passage cited at the start of this chapter from Hawkins' *Pleas of the Crown* implies, the criminal law was as much about facilitating the punishment of public officials when they strayed from the path of public duty as it was about punishing private citizens for harm wrongfully done or risked. The increasingly exclusive focus on the latter as the proper domain of criminal law scholarship, from the nineteenth century onwards, obscured almost completely the nature and significance of the former to generations of earlier lawyers and legislators.[29]

For those earlier generations, Crown law had a significant public law role. Crown law was certainly not regarded, as it is in so many modern theoretical analyses, simply as the punitive counterpart of civil law liability in tort,[30] where both are seen as centrally concerned with wrongdoing by private citizens. Key elements of the criminal law were instead viewed as a counterpart to powers of judicial review in civil law. Together, these were concerned with preventing, punishing, or negating the effects of officials' abuse or neglect of public power. As Louis Jaffe explains, speaking of the pre-nineteenth-century period:

> Local officials were subject to the direct control and discipline of the Privy Council; they could be proceeded against by criminal presentment; and they could be sued at common law. These suits could be brought without [royal] consent.[31]

The misconduct offence constituted one edge of a two-edged sword available to the courts to prevent and deter the misuse of public power, the other edge being provided by judicial review. It is helpful to think of the criminal edge to this sword in terms of the 'common law model' of judicial review.[32]

Under the common law model, powers of judicial review are relatively flexible and context-specific powers, developed by the courts. They are powers to apply principles of fair procedure (including the principle that no one should act in their own cause), respect for human rights, and so on, to other power-exercising bodies,

[28] *Mackalley's Case* (n 21) 68b. [29] See Jeremy Horder (2016), at 42.
[30] See eg amongst a forest of such articles and books, Kenneth W Simons (2008).
[31] Louis J Jaffe (1963), at 9. [32] Paul Craig (2008), at 16–18.

including lower courts.[33] The common law model differs from the so-called 'ultra vires' model of review, in that the latter sees the authority of the relevant principles as derived from (general) parliamentary intent and not from the courts in their capacity as law-makers.[34] In relation to the application of the ultra vires model, the difficulty with it in this context is that it is not easy to determine general parliamentary intent in relation to the self-regarding actions of MPs, or of the Houses of Parliament as corporate bodies, when they are acting in a non-legislative capacity. It is, of course, in that non-legislative capacity that they act when deciding on such matters as whether to employ family members as part of their constituency team, whether to appoint friends to the House of Lords, or whether to grant themselves more generous pensions or daily allowances. We consider such issues in Chapter 4.

An early example of the public law role of the criminal law (not just the misconduct offence) concerned the exercise of powers by the Sewer Commissioners.[35] Some Sewer Commissioners, such as those in nineteenth-century London, were honest and efficient in seeking to improve public health;[36] but in earlier times, Commissioners were known to go beyond their restricted powers and duties, for profit-related reasons. Commissioners' traditional powers and duties involved maintaining existing drainage facilities, by imposing a levy confined to properties reliant on those facilities. Commissioners sometimes tried to expand their remit by funding new drainage projects—projects that would benefit their own land—and then having those projects paid for by a levy on whole local districts.[37] The Justices of Common Pleas declared that such a use of the levy system was not lawful.[38] For Coke, the actions of the Commissioners in pursuit of their powers:

> ought to be limited and bound within the rule of reason and law. For discretion is a science or understanding to discern between shadows and substance ... not to do according to their wills and private affections.[39]

So, when the Commissioners for Northampton later imposed a levy on an entire town (rather than just on the affected property owners), they were fined and committed for having acted contrary to the court's judgment.[40]

At common law, thus, public authorities might find themselves committing a kind of contempt of court, by going beyond their powers when the court had already ruled that so doing would be unlawful. As Ashurst J put it, in *R v Holland and Forster*:[41]

> [W]hat the law says shall not be done, it becomes illegal to do, and is therefore the subject of indictment, without the addition of any corrupt motives. And though the want of corruption

[33] ibid 17. [34] Chris Forsyth (1996).
[35] See eg the discussion in David Chan Smith (2014), at ch 3.
[36] See David Sunderland (1999). [37] See the discussion in Louis J Jaffe (n 31) 10–12.
[38] *Case of the Isle of Ely*, 10 Co Rep 141a, 77 Eng Rep 1139 (CP 1611).
[39] *Rooke's Case* (1599) 5 Co Rep 99, at 100.
[40] The precise authority they were said to have disregarded was *Rooke's Case* (n 39), in which the court had struck down an attempt to impose levies other than on a property-by-property basis: see Louis J Jaffe and Edith Henderson (1956), at 352–53. Following this incident, the Privy Council moved swiftly to issue a prerogative order forbidding further judicial interference in the work of the Sewer Commissioners.
[41] (1787) 1 Term Rep 692.

may be an answer to an application for an information . . . yet it is no answer to an indictment, where the judges are bound by the strict rule of law.[42]

We consider below the procedure by way of criminal information, in cases of corrupt (or other bad faith) motives. Contempts of court, and other offences against justice, were then, as now, a serious matter. In *Rex v Watson*,[43] D had been found to have launched a malicious prosecution. He persuaded the corporation of Yarmouth to enter an order in its books saying that, in taking the prosecution, he 'was actuated by motives of public justice'. This was held to be a contempt. Buller J remarked that:

When a person has recourse . . . to calumniate the proceedings of a Court of Justice, the obvious tendency of it is to weaken the administration of justice, and in consequence to sap the very foundations of the constitution itself.[44]

We will consider other cases in which officials were held to account by the criminal law in a later section. Before considering that issue in more depth, some explanation must be given of the theoretical basis for the public law nature of such pleas of the Crown.

3.4 Republican Theory and Law: Challenging Authority

On 27 January 1649, the High Court of Justice meeting in Westminster Hall announced its death sentence at the end of the king's trial:

he, the said Charles Stuart . . . *trusted within a limited power to govern* by, and according to the law of the land and otherwise; and *by his trust, oath and office, being obliged to use the power committed to him for the good and benefit of the people*, and for the preservation of their rights and liberties; yet, nevertheless, *out of a wicked design to erect and uphold in himself an unlimited and tyrannical power to rule according to his will*, and to overthrow the rights and liberties of the people, and to take away and make void the foundations thereof, and of all redress and remedy of misgovernment, which by the fundamental constitutions of this Kingdom were reserved on the people's behalf in the right and power of frequent and successive Parliaments; he, the said Charles Stuart . . . hath traitorously and maliciously levied war against the present Parliament, and people therein represented . . .[45]

This judgment embodies key elements of a 'republican' critique of government. Republican theories generally reject monarchical bases for supreme authority. More significantly, they also reject any other bases for authority that do not include a means by which that authority can be challenged or held to account and, if need be, put out of power. As the judgment indicates, the substantive foundations for

[42] ibid. [43] *Rex v Watson* (1788) 2 TR 199.

[44] ibid 207. To similar effect, Lord Chancellor Hardwicke had said in 1747 that: 'I look upon the administration of justice, as the principal and essential part of all government. The people know and judge of it by little else': William Cobbett (1803), vol xiv, at 20.

[45] 'The Charge Against the King' in Samuel R Gardiner (1906), vol iv, at 399 (my emphasis).

challenge are 'the rights and liberties' of the people, that a supreme authority is trusted and obliged to use his or her power to preserve.

In that regard, a core element of republican theory is the rejection of 'domination'.[46] Someone lives under domination if the way in which she conducts some aspect of her life[47] is subject to the discretionary power of another person. Philip Pettit describes domination as meaning that:

> the dominating party [here, the state] can interfere on an arbitrary basis with the choices of the dominated: can interfere, in particular, on the basis of an interest or an opinion that need not be shared by the person affected. The dominating party can practice interference, then, at will and with impunity: they do not have to seek anyone's leave and they do not have to incur any scrutiny or penalty ... [Domination involves] ... exposure to another's power of uncontrolled influence.[48]

Unlimited domination in this extreme form may be relatively rare. Moreover, a certain amount of domination can sometimes be justified. Prisoners are subject to a significant degree of domination during their sentences, even in benign prison regimes. More pertinently, domination may be manifested not only through a regime of control, but through the way, even on a single occasion, that an official uses his or her office. A classic instance of domination is an official's use of a public position, to use Coke's words, 'to do according to their wills and private affections' in the way another person is treated,[49] rather than using their authority to further the public good. Even when a public official is not acting in such a clearly arbitrary or self-serving way, domination may be manifested when officials are willing to put their own conception of the 'public good' ahead of compliance with the law. We will consider the higher courts' republican attack on such instances of domination in detail in the next section.

The importance of overcoming domination is equated by modern republican theorists with the importance of nurturing citizens who, rather than being cowed by or automatically deferential to authority:

> can speak their minds, walk tall among their fellows, and look others squarely in the eye. They can command respect from those with whom they deal, not being subject to their arbitrary interference.[50]

46 See Philip Pettit (1999), at 20.

47 Or, as in cases of slavery, all aspects of their lives.

48 Philip Pettit (2012), at 22 and 28. We should note Thomas W Simpson's critique of this account as a conception of lack of 'freedom', but it is the understanding of the kind of power the dominant party has that is of importance in this context. See Thomas W Simpson (2017).

49 *Rooke's Case* (n 39) 100.

50 José Luis Martí and Philip Pettit (2010), at 38. Republican theorists such as Pettit commonly seek to contrast republicanism with liberal political theory, on the grounds that the latter is said to be concerned only with guarding against unwarranted interferences with people's lives, and not with the ongoing capacity to engage in such interference at will. This supposed contrast is not soundly based. Liberalism is concerned with the protection and promotion of autonomy in people's lives, as those lives are lived not so much in competition with others as in common with others, without whose dedication to joint endeavours and commitment to 'individual' autonomy would scarcely be worth having. 'Domination', in Pettit's sense, is as much of a threat to liberalism, in this sense, as it is to republicanism.

In this final respect, the impact of republicanism in eighteenth-century England was, to say the least, patchy. Nonetheless, in a republican state, 'the citizenry [are and] should be ever vigilant of public power and be ready to contest and challenge it at the slightest suspicion or sign of abuse'.[51] Throughout a good deal of British history (and still occasionally today), people sometimes resisted domination through riot and rebellion, aiming to force through solutions to social, economic, and political problems.[52] However, republican theory is not primarily focused on the politics of disorder. Indeed, it has always placed a great deal of emphasis on the use of certain forms of the law—customary law, local law, or common law rights ('the principles of a free Government'[53])—to resist domination.

F W Maitland captures the spirit of this idea well, when speaking of local or customary law administered by the justices, as compared with law promulgated and adjudicated upon centrally:

> Englishmen have trusted the law; it were hardly too much to say that they have loved the law; but they have not loved and do not love lawyers, and the law that they have loved they did not think of as lawyers' law ... [it was] the voice of law [in the mouth of] many a country squire whose only juristic attainment was the possession of a clerk who could find the appropriate page in *Burn's Justice*.[54]

This kind of republican conception of law is *gemeinschaft* in character. That is, it is an approach in which there is no clear distinction between the demands of natural law, people's sense of community, and the scope and spirit of positive law.[55] So, for example, paradoxical as this might seem to lawyers accustomed to think of law in Weberian terms as the imposition of rational legal authority, even when engaged in civic disorder in the face of some supposed infringement of 'their' rights, Hanoverian people would have 'one eye on the Justices'.[56]

In the eighteenth century, alongside this *gemeinschaft* understanding of republicanism was a different conception, centred on 'lawyers' law'. This was a more *gesellschaft* conception,[57] in which the responsibility for controlling and punishing one kind of public officer was lodged with another kind of public official (judges in the higher courts and, in the end, Parliament as well). As Philip Pettit puts it:

> the state which guards citizens against private domination should also guard against their public domination, accepting the constraints—the checks and balances—imposed in a 'mixed' constitution.[58]

[51] Philip Pettit (2014), at 136.

[52] See eg John Walter (2006). There were even riots by footmen (successful in their aim, as things turned out) at the Drury Lane Theatre to preserve their customary privilege of attending their masters in their boxes.

[53] PRO, Adm.1/2309 (Hyde Parker) (2 September 1791), cited by Nicholas Rogers (2002), at 74 n 34.

[54] F W Maitland (1911), vol i, at 476–77.

[55] For an excellent general discussion see Eugene Kamenka and Alice Tay (1975).

[56] Randall McGowen (2002), at 148–51. An illustrative example involved popular resistance to the practice of impressment: see Rogers (n 53), and the discussion in section 3.9.

[57] See Eugene Kamenka and Alice Tay (n 55) ch 6.

[58] Philip Pettit (n 51) 136.

In that regard, the judgment of state officials is to be shaped and determined by a Weberian demand for consistently rational legal authority, and not by local custom or by popular conceptions of rights and freedoms. As we will see in the next section, during the eighteenth century, this Blackstonian[59] way of understanding how 'public domination'—misconduct in office—should be tackled became predominant, although in the case of the courts, the need for such rational legal authority was itself justified by an appeal to natural law.

3.5 Supporting the State's Foundations: The Attitudinal Offence

> But though discretion does mean (and can mean nothing else but) exercising the best of their judgment upon the occasion that calls for it; yet, if this discretion be wilfully abused, it is criminal, and ought to be under the control of this court.[60]

In pre-nineteenth-century criminal jurisprudence an important theme, highlighted by Coke CJ, in the passage from *Rooke's Case* cited above,[61] was the need to deter and punish instances in which public officials put aside the obligations of public duty, and acted 'according to their wills and private affections'.[62] Of central importance, amongst the values protected by the prosecution of such conduct, was liberty. As Blackstone put it:

> Of great importance to the public is the preservation of this personal liberty; for if once it were left in the power of any the highest magistrate to imprison arbitrarily whomever he or his officers thought proper (as in France it is daily practised by the Crown) there would soon be an end of all other rights and immunities.[63]

Blackstone, like Bentham, was a stern critic of the criminal law's indiscriminate threats to use the death penalty for low-level crimes by private citizens.[64] Even so, Blackstone highly valued the role that he saw the criminal law performing, in sustaining the legitimacy of the transfer to a sovereign power of key rights of every man in the state of nature. This was the role the criminal law played in punishing the kinds of crime, such as inter-personal violence, that violated rights in the state of nature.

However, the criminal law also played that legitimating role when it deterred or punished those who, in purporting to carry out official duties transferred to them out of the state of nature, acted as judges in their own cause, or who for private reasons, ill-temper, or other improper motive, did otherwise than their duties required. That role was linked, in Blackstone's mind, to what he regarded as

[59] See Sir William Blackstone (1765), vol i, 149–50.

[60] Mr Justice Denison giving the judgment of the Queen's Bench Division in *Rex v Young* (1758) 1 Burr 556.

[61] *Rooke's Case* (n 39): see text at n 39.

[62] ibid at 100.

[63] Blackstone (n 59) vol i, at 98.

[64] On the similarities between Blackstone and Bentham, in this respect see Gerald J Postema (1986), at 263–65.

an aspect of Western (and in particular, English) cultural superiority. In 'despotic Eastern' countries, says Blackstone, the 'true principles of government' are never understood, and 'it is imagined that there is no obligation from the superior to the inferior, no relative duty owing from the governor to the governed'.[65] By contrast, in Blackstone's account, it is English criminal law that serves in part to maintain what he took to be England's cultural superiority in this respect, through its concern for accountability under law. How so?

For Blackstone, everyone may rightfully claim to punish crimes that violate rights in the state of nature;[66] but, that being so, a problem about doing justice will arise. If each were to be judge and jury in his or her own cause, when deciding on punishment, it would be impossible to achieve the ideal that the criminal law should be:

> Founded upon principles that are permanent, uniform and universal; and always conformable to the dictates of truth and justice, the feelings of humanity, and the indelible rights of mankind.[67]

The overwhelming majority of English criminal law scholars since Bentham have understood, and expanded upon this ideal in terms of the principles of criminal liability as they relate to wrongdoing by private citizens. Blackstone was himself concerned with some of these matters, and there is obviously much of importance in such a concern. Even so, in the last 150 years, that focus has become too exclusive. Overlooked, in consequence, has been the role the criminal law has played, and continues to play, in deterring and punishing official wrongdoing: wrongdoing committed whilst someone is acting in an official rather than in a private capacity. Yet, this is a vital role for the criminal law. It is such wrongdoing that undermines or threatens the integrity of the very state institutions charged with establishing the emerging liberal principles of criminal law—'the soul and life of the law'[68]—as they apply to private citizens.

In that respect, for Blackstone, to make the ideal criminal law a possibility, the right to criminalize and punish must be transferred to a single power, capable not only of claiming authority over all, but also of governing in the interests of all. As Blackstone puts it:

> In a state of society this [natural] right [to punish] is transferred from individuals to the sovereign power; whereby men are prevented from being judges in their own causes, which is one of the evils that civil government was intended to remedy ... [The magistrate] ... bears the sword of justice by the consent of the whole community.[69]

[65] Blackstone (n 59) vol iv, at 149.

[66] This theory is challenged by, for example, those who would justify punishment by reference to the individual right of self-defence, rather than by reference to an individual right to punish: see eg Victor Tadros (2011). For present purposes, it is not important to adjudicate on the merits of each theory.

[67] Blackstone (n 59), vol iv, at 3.

[68] *Mackalley's Case* (n 21) 68b.

[69] See Blackstone (n 59) vol iv, at 7–8.

Accordingly, alongside bribery of public officials, extortion by public officials, and the criminalization of 'the negligence of public officers' (wilful neglect),[70] Blackstone lays heavy emphasis on:

> Yet another offence against public justice, which is a crime of deep malignity; and so much the deeper, as there are many opportunities of putting it into practice ... This is the oppression and tyrannical partiality of judges, justices, and other magistrates, in the administration and under the colour of their office. However, when prosecuted, either by impeachment in parliament, or by information in the court of King's Bench (according the rank of the offenders) it is sure to be severely punished.[71]

In an anonymous case at the end of the seventeenth century, Holt CJ recorded that:

> The Mayor of Herford was laid by the heels [i.e. imprisoned], for sitting in judgment in a cause where he himself was the lessor of the plaintiff in ejectment, though he by the charter was the sole judge of the Court.[72]

When Sir Joseph Mawbey, a JP, falsified a document to say that the highway for which he was responsible had been repaired, when he knew it had not (or was reckless as to whether it had), he was prosecuted for obstructing and perverting the course of justice. Of this offence Ashurst J said:

> It seems to me that a greater offence can hardly be stated than that of obstructing or perverting the course of justice, on which the lives and properties of all the subjects depend.[73]

In a similar vein, Sir Matthew Hale expressed the view that 'at the common law the undue razure or embezzling of a record was a great offence, for which even a judge himself was punishable by fine and imprisonment'.[74]

It was not only judges who might find themselves punished for acting in bad faith or corruptly, and in particular for acting in their own cause *(in sua causa)*. For Sir Edward East, 'the abuse of a great public trust from corrupt motives'[75] was a wrong capable of being regarded as the basis for the creation of an offence at common law applicable well outside a judicial context.[76] A late seventeenth-century example is *R v Burdett*.[77] In this case, a criminal information was laid against a Newgate farmer for extortion, in that he had unlawfully insisted on payment of fees by those wishing to use stalls at the market, as well as extracting excessive fines for transgressions. He was found guilty at *nisi prius* (although the verdict was later set aside on grounds not relevant here). When James Gibson, a lawyer and partner to the deputy solicitor of

[70] ibid 140–41. We will consider the wilful neglect offences in the next section.

[71] Blackstone (n 59) vol iv, at 140–41. The passage is relied on successfully by counsel for the prosecution in *R v Mawbey and Others* (1796) 6 TR 619, at 631. Justices proceeded against by way of criminal information were prosecuted for misdemeanour in their office. The criminal information procedure was abolished by s 12 of the Administration of Justice (Miscellaneous Provisions) Act 1938. Prosecutions on indictment, as opposed to criminal informations, were rare: see Douglas Hay (2002), at 22 n 7.

[72] *Anon* (1699) Salk 396. Mayors were often also JPs.

[73] *R v Mawbey and Others* (n 71) 635.

[74] Sir Matthew Hale (1736), at 646.

[75] East, *Pleas of the Crown* (Butterworths, 1803) 35.

[76] The example he had in mind was the common law offence of simony, the corrupt presentation to a benefice.

[77] (1697) 1 Ld Raym 148.

the Treasury, forged a document purporting to be 'an office copy of the accountant general's certificate of paying into the bank the sum of £437 13s 7d', he was hanged for the offence in 1794, as a warning against the betrayal of trust and of a public office.[78]

An allegation of 'malversations in office' would also be valid when laid extra-territorially against officers employed in positions of trust in the East India Company. In *R v Hollond*,[79] such an allegation was made against a member of the Council of Madras, under statutes relating to East India Company operations. Hollond was charged under 24 Geo 3 chapter 24, section 49, which stated:

> Every wilful breach of the trust and duty of any office or employment under the said United Company by any of the officers or servants of the said United Company in the East Indies shall be deemed and taken to be a misdemeanour at law . . .

This offence was defined in such a way as to straddle the attitudinal and wilful neglect varieties of misconduct. We turn to a consideration of the role of statute in creating misconduct offences in section 3.8.

Other early writers laid similar emphasis on the role of the criminal law in punishing the abuse of office. Serjeant Hawkins, speaking of the King's Bench, described its jurisdiction as being not merely over capital offences, but also over misdemeanours of 'a public nature', tending to (inter alia), 'any manner of misgovernment'.[80] In that regard, falling within the jurisdiction of the High Court was misconduct on the part of JPs, on which much of the case law is focused. That is hardly surprising, given the central role of the JPs, not only in taking part in local governance, but also in ensuring the legitimacy of that governance as it appeared to the governed. As F W Maitland famously put it:

> It is indeed very difficult to tell how much of the English respect for law . . . is centred on the amateur justice of the peace. If we had to name the institution that had most to do with its growth, we should long hesitate between the Commission of the Peace and trial by jury . . . The most learned barrister of seven years' standing will find it hard to get so high a reputation [as that of a justice] among country folk for speaking with the voice of the law . . .[81]

In his account of the powers and duties of the JPs, Hawkins considers it important to discuss not only the crimes that fall within the justices' jurisdiction, and their powers more broadly, but also their duties to avoid conflicts of interest and other abuses of authority. In relation to conflicts of interest—so important to Coke and Blackstone, as we have seen—Hawkins makes it quite clear how strict was the duty on justices to avoid them:

> The general rule of law certainly is, that justices of the peace ought not to execute their office in their own case; and even in cases where such proceeding seems indispensably necessary, as in being publicly assaulted or personally abused . . . while in the execution of their duty, yet if another justice be present, his assistance should be required to punish the offender.[82]

[78] *Newgate Calendar* (1824), vol v, at 229–32, discussed in McGowen (n 56) 136.
[79] *R v Hollond* (1794) 5 Term Rep 607.
[80] Hawkins (n 1) vol ii, Bk 2, at section 3.
[81] F W Maitland (n 54) vol I, at 476–77.
[82] Hawkins (n 1) vol ii, Bk 2, at section 68.

At common law, where an order for the removal of a pauper from the parish was made, the order would be 'illegal and bad' if one of the justices was an inhabitant of the parish from which the pauper was to be removed, because the justice would be 'interested, as being liable to the poor's rate'.[83]

In *R v Davies*,[84] the Penryn justices had refused to grant licences to publicans who voted against the justices' own recommendations concerning who should stand as an MP. Lord Mansfield granted an application for a criminal information against the justices in the light of 'the corrupt motive of such refusal; for the oppressive and unjust refusing to grant [the licences]'.[85] In another case also called *R v Davies*,[86] D was a collector of customs and a JP with forty years' service. He had sat as one of the justices to estimate the salvage of a vessel, when he was entitled to a part of the salvage as a Customs-House officer. Although the award of salvage was found to be reasonable, a criminal information was nonetheless issued against him, in the light of what the court called 'the great impropriety and irregularity of his sitting as a judge, who, as a Customs-House Officer, was to take benefit of the value of the salvage'.[87]

The potential liability for judicial acts breaching the principle of *nemo iudex in sua causa* was founded on a public law-style contrast with mere error or ignorance of law. In cases where an official had acted in bad faith, or for some other improper motive, the very integrity of public office was at stake. Accordingly, only in such cases would the intervention of the criminal law be warranted, to punish the betrayal of trust. Hawkins writes:

> Justices of the Peace are not punishable civilly for acts done by them in their judicial capacities, but if they abuse the authority with which they are entrusted, they may be punished criminally at the suit of the King by way of information.[88]

Hawkins here gives his own version of Blackstone's crime of 'deep malignity', namely acts manifesting the 'oppression and tyrannical partiality' of judges.[89] Hawkins continues:

> The court of King's Bench . . . will never grant an information against a Justice of the Peace for a mere error in judgment; for even when a Justice does an illegal act, yet although the judgment was wrong, if his heart was right, if he acted honestly and candidly, without oppression, malice, revenge, or any bad view or ill intention whatsoever, the court will never punish him by the extraordinary course of information . . . but if they act improperly knowingly, an information shall be granted.[90]

An error of judgment might, then, render an official act null and void (illegal, in that sense). However, if partiality, oppressiveness, dishonesty and secrecy, spite, and so forth, crept into the making of judgments, such acts would be criminal: examples of the attitudinal offence. In *R v Mather*,[91] the justices ordered a woman to be whipped,

[83] ibid at section 69. This strict approach was relaxed by 16 Geo 2, c18.
[84] (1762) 3 Burr 1317. [85] ibid 1317–18. [86] (1772) Lofft 62.
[87] ibid 63. [88] Hawkins (n 1) vol ii, Bk 2, at section 74.
[89] Blackstone (n 59) vol iv, at 140–41.
[90] ibid, citing *Rex v Jackson* (1737) 1 Term Rep 653. See also *Groenvelt v Burwell* (1697) 1 Salk 378.
[91] (1733) 2 Barn 249, cited by Graham McBain (2014), at 56.

when (as the Court concluded), they must have been aware that they had no legal power to make such an order. The justices were found guilty of misconduct, on the basis of 'oppression in the execution of their authority'.[92] As indicated above, in Blackstone's terms, judgments reached on such a basis undermine the foundation on which rests the legitimacy of the transfer of people's individual rights in the state of nature to public authorities. Such judgments betray the trust of the people in the justification for authority, in a way that mere official error will not.

For Lord Mansfield, giving judgment in *Rex v Bembridge*, public offices were offices of 'trust and confidence concerning the public'.[93] He gives a similar analysis in *Rex v Young*.[94] An information was laid against justices who were alleged to have 'arbitrarily, obstinately and unreasonably' refused to renew a licence to run an inn.[95] Whilst the justices were cleared of that allegation on the facts, Lord Mansfield was reported as saying:

> [I]f it clearly appears that the Justices have been partially, maliciously, or corruptly influenced in the exercise of [their] discretion, and have (consequently) *abused the trust reposed in them*, they are liable to prosecution by indictment or information . . . If their judgment is wrong, yet their heart and intention be pure, God forbid that they should be punished![96]

A case in which the justices were found to have transgressed in this way is *R v Brooke*.[97] In this case, a personal disagreement between justices at the tower led to two justices deliberately releasing men on bail, even though the justices knew the men had been correctly denied bail by a different justice, under the Vagrancy Act 1744. The two justices denied any impropriety, on the grounds that their conduct was 'common practice'. The court granted an information against the two justices. Ashurst J said that the justices had been guilty of 'a palpable and gross abuse of their office,' and had 'made themselves parties in the business and associated themselves with the persons who had been convicted'. That being so, this was no mere error of law or example of ignorance of law:

> And though they have denied generally that they acted from any interested motives in this business, this is not sufficient; for if they acted even from passion or opposition, that is equally corrupt as if they acted from pecuniary consideration.[98]

Eighteenth-century governance was 'an extraordinary patchwork—of old and new, useless and efficient, corrupt and honest—mixed in together'.[99] In spite of many

[92] (1733) 2 Barn 249.

[93] *Rex v Bembridge* (n 15) 155–56. See also the reference to abuse of trust in *Rex v Young* (n 60).

[94] *Rex v Young* (n 60).

[95] Such cases might at that time have political implications. As in *R v Davies* (considered above), a refusal to grant a licence might relate to the applicant's refusal to back a political candidate favoured by the Justices: Douglas Hay (n 71) 32.

[96] *Rex v Young* (n 60) 561–62 (my emphasis in italics). See *Windham v Cleers* (1588) Cro Eliz 130: 'If a man be accused to a Justice of the Peace for an offence, for which he causes him to be arrested by his warrant, although the action be false, yet he is excusable; but if the party never be accused, but the Justice of his malice and own head cause him to be arrested it is otherwise'. See also *R v Palmer and Baine* (1761) 2 Burrows 1163, and *R v Cozens and Another* (1780) 2 Douglas 426.

[97] (1788) 2 Term Rep 191.

[98] ibid 195 (Ashurst J).

[99] Brewer (n 10) 71.

abuses, there was, for example, an understanding in the early eighteenth-century Parliament that MPs should abstain from voting in divisions which affected them personally.[100] A similarly nuanced view should be taken of the role of the courts. The fanaticism of Jeremy Bentham—the 'arch-philistine ... the leather-tongued oracle of the bourgeois intelligence'[101]—saw to it that generations of lawyers came to believe that the role of eighteenth-century judges in developing offences at common law had led (as he presumptuously wrote to the President of the United States):

> Instead of compliance and obedience ... [to] the evil of transgression, mixed with the evil of punishment ... and in the hands of the judge, power everywhere arbitrary, with the semblance of a set of rule to serve as a screen to it. Such are the fruits of this species of mock law even in the country which gave it birth.[102]

This is largely bombast, because the law governing the accountability of public officials that we have considered was no mere 'semblance of a set of rules'. Further, the judicial power to develop those rules was not 'power everywhere arbitrary', or an attempt to undermine the authority of other state officials; far from it.

Bentham ignores the fact that Parliament had considerable faith in the judiciary. Judges could be MPs themselves, but were also expected to attend the House of Lords to advise on the drafting of legislation.[103] Lord Mansfield was a member of the cabinet under Newcastle (1757–62) and Bute (1762–93).[104] Parliament clearly trusted judges with criminal law reform in important areas, even as Parliament itself began increasingly to replace the common law of crime with statutory provisions (however curiously drafted). For William Pitt, matters of criminal law reform could often adequately be 'fully weighed and settled by those learned and able men [the judges] who filled the highest station in the Law Department'.[105] This opinion is hardly surprising. Commonly drawn from the ranks of law officers to the Crown, judges had considerable experience in drafting legislation; indeed, Mansfield CJ actively assisted George III with legislative strategy.[106] So, why should judges not have been trusted with the discretion to develop and apply the criminal law to state officials? This is a theme pursued in greater detail in Chapter 4.

3.6 The Attitudinal Offence at the Apex of Sanctions

There is, thus, an impressive body of eighteenth-century law and commentary supporting the application of the attitudinal version of the misconduct offence to public officials of different kinds. That support was given in the interests of maintaining public confidence in the integrity of legal decision-makers, and hence in the authority of the state. It has been argued, however, that what I am calling the

[100] D W Hayton (2002), vol 1, at 361–62; Lemmings (n 100) 170.
[101] Karl Marx (reprint, 2007), vol i, at 668.
[102] Cited by Philip Schofield and Jonathan Harris (1998), at 20.
[103] Stuart Jay (1997), at 196.
[104] He also attended cabinet under the Grenville ministry (1763–65), along with the Chancellor.
[105] Cobbett (n 44) vol 26, at 1058.
[106] Jay (n 103) 193–96.

republican basis for holding public officials to account in criminal law was more apparent than real. Almost needless to say, Bentham was one such critic of this system of accountability. Consistent with the analysis given above, for Bentham:

> The trading Justices had judges over them: Judges by whom,—if haply, in an extreme case, money could be raised sufficient to buy a hearing for a cry for punishment,—they might be punished:—Judges who, though not fond of punishing any man with a King's commission in his pocket,—might thereon, by fear of shame, be peradventure driven to do so, if the case were flagrant.[107]

This view might be thought to do scant justice to the High Court's painstaking efforts, reviewed above, to strike a difficult balance between the need to give JPs (acting without pay) scope to err without fear of adverse consequences, against the need to punish those who gave judgment in bad faith. It is the attempt to strike this balance in the right place, rather than complacency or servility, which does some work in explaining why suits successfully alleging the latter kind of betrayal of trust were rare, and only reluctantly entertained by judges wary of undermining the authority of the justices.

However, it would be wrong not to acknowledge some force in Bentham's view. Lord Mansfield, for example, was of the opinion that he 'should always lean towards favouring [the justices]; unless partiality, corruption or malice shall *clearly* appear'.[108] An illustration of such reluctance is provided by *R v Justices of Sleaford*.[109] In this case, the justices had refused to put a substantial householder upon the poor's rate (which was necessary, to give a vote for MPs), and refused to amend the rate. In spite of the suspicion of political motivation for the justices' actions, the court said:

> As [the justices] were acting in a Court of Record, with powers entrusted to them by the constitution ... it must be a very strong case indeed, with flagrant proofs of their having acted from corrupt motives, that would warrant a rule for an information.[110]

Whilst, in Westminster and Middlesex, challenges to justices may have been more common,[111] Douglas Hay's study of cases in Staffordshire shows that, in the last six decades of the eighteenth century, there were only thirteen applications for a criminal information against magistrates for misdemeanour in the exercise of their office.[112] Quite apart from the fact that such proceedings were undertaken so rarely, they were also being preferred to the more normal way of taking a criminal case, by prosecution on indictment. The latter was avoided by would-be litigants against JPs. Apart from anything else, the grand jury at the Assizes, which had to accept the bill of indictment, would itself be comprised overwhelmingly of fellow-justices.[113] In

[107] Jeremy Bentham (1825), at 429. The reference to 'trading' justices is a derogatory reference to the system of paying justices through fees per case, rather than through a fixed salary.

[108] *Rex v Young* (n 60) 561–62 (my emphasis).

[109] (1763) 1 Blackstone W 432. [110] ibid.

[111] William Holdsworth (1938), vol x, at 249–50.

[112] Douglas Hay (n 71) 23–27, where he discusses the procedure in cases of criminal information. In addition, there were eleven proceedings for writs of *certiorari*.

[113] Some 80% of the members of the Grand Jury would be justices: Douglas Hay (n 71) 26.

any event, as one late eighteenth-century justice acknowledged, a justice would be well aware that:

> the objects whom he may be tempted to aggrieve are usually too humble, ignorant and timid, to think of seeking redress except in very palpable and flagrant cases, and frequently too poor to be able to undertake the task of seeking it in any.[114]

It should, further, be acknowledged that Hay's painstaking research suggests that, even in the few cases that were taken against JPs, the JPs in question were not gentlemen—who could safely ignore the King's Bench—but tradesmen holding offices such as mayor or alderman. JPs facing a criminal information in Hay's study included a maltster, a tanner, and an apothecary.[115] Hay concludes that criminal information proceedings against magistrates commonly did not amount to much more than a reflection of local animosities harboured by those of the magistrates' own social class, who had the money, time, and motive to bring proceedings.[116] For Hay, the requirement that there be proof of 'actual corrupt interest' was, in effect, a conferral of immunity from legal retribution for wrongdoing.[117]

Is this conclusion unduly cynical? As we have seen, the insistence on evidence of bad faith or gross impropriety of some kind, if proceedings by way of information were to go ahead against a JP, had a sound moral justification. It is only in such cases that one finds a genuine *betrayal* of citizens' trust, a point still of some importance to modern legal theorists' discussion of the role of judges and arbitrators.[118] Moreover, Hay perhaps overlooks the possibility that the misconduct offence was not the only sanction available to discipline errant justices, and was already operating at the apex of hierarchy of sanctions. Norma Landau has argued that when corrupt or otherwise wrongful conduct was engaged in by the justices, non-criminal means of expressing disapproval or sanctioning were common. One procedure for less serious cases (such as mistakenly bailing an alleged felon) involved inviting the errant justice to dinner with the other justices. A post-prandial apology, and if need be a promise not to engage in further misconduct, would then be required.[119] Alternatively, in more serious cases (commonly involving illegal conduct), following a quasi-formal investigation, representation could be made by the Sessions to the Lord Chancellor to remove the errant justice from his post.[120] Between 1716 and 1792, the Middlesex Sessions made such representations to the Lord Chancellor in fifteen cases, resulting in twelve removals from office.[121] Dismissal—not prosecution—was normally the remedy, even in cases where there had been corruption or other deliberate misconduct,[122]

[114] Reverend Thomas Gisborne (1794), at 286, cited by Douglas Hay (n 71) 22–23.

[115] Douglas Hay (n 71) 41. The deployment of the criminal law only against those of the less politically influential 'middling sort' is something encountered in *Rex v Bembridge* (n 15). See Jeremy Horder (n 2).

[116] Douglas Hay (n 71) 42. [117] ibid 43.

[118] See Joseph Raz's discussion of the 'service' conception of authority in Joseph Raz (1995), at ch 10.

[119] See Norma Landau (2002), at 47 (she calls this the 'post-prandial reprimand').

[120] ibid 47–48. [121] ibid 49. [122] ibid 55.

because dismissal from public office was regarded as, in itself 'a degradation and . . . an imputation of bad morals'.[123]

What this analysis demonstrates is that the eighteenth century witnessed the emergence—weak though it might have been—of a (partly informal) hierarchy of reprimands, sanctions, and punishments to deal with judicial misconduct. At the apex of this flexible system of holding justices to account stood the criminal information, alleging misconduct in office, as described by Blackstone and Hawkins. Even so, there is substance in Hay's 'class-based' analysis of the instances in which the aggrieved were willing to prosecute, and in which higher court judges felt able to entertain such prosecutions. As we will see in the analysis of the current state of the law in Chapter 4, in modern times what might be called the 'political class' (overlapping with but not identical to a social or economic class) has considered itself—and largely been treated—as immune from prosecution for its misconduct. We consider the modern remedies lying beneath the misconduct offence in Chapter 5.

3.7 Wilful Neglect: The Political Evolution of Misconduct (1)

That brings us to consideration of the changing role of the monarch, Parliament, and the courts in relation to the task of holding public officials to account in criminal law for wrongdoing in office. Consideration of this changing role provides the background to discussion of the 'wilful neglect' variety of the misconduct offence, as it was employed by Parliament rather than by the courts.

We have seen that the republican understanding of criminal law was first associated with an assertion of (common law) 'people's' rights against the arbitrary or oppressive exercise of power by the Crown and its agents.[124] That simplistic picture became more complex as Parliament began to assert its authority to legislate in the national interest on ever greater numbers of occasions, especially from the middle of the eighteenth century onwards.[125] For Blackstone, drawing inspiration from Locke,[126] 'prudently framed' laws impartially and fairly administered increase people's 'civil liberty'—republican freedom under law—even as such laws reduce people's natural liberty—the freedom to do as one pleases.[127] However, increasingly, in a period of nascent regulation, Parliament more often sought to govern through officials possessed of delegated powers, rather than directly through law.[128] A case in point, at a time of considerable war-generated fiscal pressure, was that of the ever-increasing discretionary powers granted to HM Customs and particularly to HM Excise, in relation to search and seizure.[129] The introduction of such flexible powers challenged older notions of the need for a (literal) rule of law. As one newspaper put it, in this new era:

[123] The words of the Duke of Northumberland, Lord Lieutenant of Middlesex and Westminster 1763–86, cited by Norma Landau (n 119) 55.

[124] See section 3.5.

[125] See generally Lemmings (n 100).

[126] John Locke (1690), at 125–26.

[127] Blackstone (n 59) vol i, at 120.

[128] Lemmings (n 100) 7–8.

[129] See generally Brewer (n 10).

it is difficult for the most cautious Man, who leads an active Life, to avoid offending innocently against some penal Statute; to which perhaps he is as great a Stranger as he may be to the laws of the Koran.[130]

These developments were aspects of the war-generated and ministry-led 'growth of government bureaucracy, especially in its revenue branches'.[131] From 1760 until the early Victorian period, between 73 per cent and 93 per cent of parliamentary Bills were sponsored by ministries rather than being private members' Bills,[132] a striking new development.[133] It is against this historical setting that we should examine the role of Parliament in holding public officials to account by creating offences of wilful neglect of office.

Neglect of office was a long-standing offence at common law, which operated alongside another old rule (no longer extant) that failure to fulfil a statutory duty could amount to criminal 'contempt' of statute.[134] A number of early cases involved failures by constables or officers of the peace to perform their duties. In *Crowther's Case*,[135] a contempt of statute case, a constable had wrongfully refused to make hue and cry following a burglary. He was indicted for his refusal, as this was held to be a breach of duty. In *R v Wyat*,[136] D was a constable who had failed to levy a fine, in accordance with a warrant, on someone convicted of deer stealing. So, he was himself fined. The court said that: 'where an officer neglects a duty incumbent on him, either by common law or statute, he is for his fault indictable'.[137]

In the Law Commission's detailed survey of the history of the misconduct offence, these cases are treated as 'top-down' in character: yet further illustrations of offences against the authority of the Crown.[138] However, their true significance is that they illustrate the 'bottom-up' republican character of the public law dimension to the criminal law at this time, and to the offence of misconduct in particular. Whether or not technically appointed in the name of the monarch, officials such as parish constables or market holders were beholden primarily to the communities in which they lived. Local, small-time tenure of office was the way in which respectable citizens participated in (self-)government, a republican alternative to reliance on voting at lengthy intervals for national parties as the primary means of such participation:[139]

For here in the country with us, if a man's stock of a few beasts be his own, and that he lives out of debt, and pays his rent duly and quarterly ... [he] ... is able to do the king and country good service. We make him a constable, a sidesman, a Head-borough and at length a church warden ... here is the great governor amongst us, and we wonder that all others do not respect him accordingly.[140]

130 *The Newcastle Intelligencer* (30 November 1757).
131 See McGowen (n 56) 132.
132 Peter Jupp (2006), at 150–51.
133 Courtney Ilbert (1913), at 62.
134 Law Commission (n 17) paras A.97–A99. See also section 3.3.
135 *Crowther's Case* (n 21).
136 *Rex v Wyat* (1705) 1 Salk 380.
137 ibid 381. See also *R v Gould* (1705) 1 Salk 381, in which D was indicted for refusing to provide for an apprentice.
138 Law Commission (n 17) para A.114.
139 For an excellent essay on this dimension to the historical picture see Mark Goldie (2001), at ch 6.
140 Godfrey Goodman (1616), at xi. Goodman was vicar of Stapleford Abbots.

By 1689, there were 180 incorporated boroughs in England and around 9,700 parishes. In every parish were innumerable minor officials and office-holders—surveyors of the highways, clerks, sextons, beadles, reeves, haywards, and so on—just as in each borough there was a mayor, aldermen, a chamberlain, a recorder, clerk, coroner, stewards, bailiff, tithing men, ale tasters, porters, wardens of the poor, and officers of the night watch.[141] Goldie has estimated that, at any one time, there were around 50,000 parish officers of one kind or another in 1700, and as many as 100,000 by 1800.[142]

In that regard, people did not 'run' for office in the way they do now. Instead, it was simply expected that one would take up the burdens (while enjoying some benefits) of office when one's turn came around;[143] and office 'dodgers' could be fined (£10 in the case of constableship). Bearing in mind the very considerable range of duties involved in some of these offices, perhaps especially regarding JPs and constables,[144] the temptation to engage in neglect (alongside corruption and other forms of misconduct) was very considerable.[145] Complaints were made about the way in which strict rotation of offices inevitably resulted not merely in incompetent but also in idle office-holders.[146] So, the misconduct offence, along with other offences such as extortion and contempt, thus stood at a vital intersection of local custom, local politics, and state policy. The importance of such offences was as much to ensure principles of local or parish accountability were not betrayed as it was to secure compliance with royal commands. In taking up offices, small as well as great, men 'paid homage to the concept of voluntary self-government'.[147]

So, in that regard, the criminal law set its face against back-sliding, as well as against corruption, fraud, and other forms of knowing malfeasance. It did so, because good office-holding was at the foundation of good citizenship, and good citizenship was at the heart of the theory of government in the age of Blackstone. For Sir William Hawkins, the role of the criminal law—and of the neglect offence in particular—was in this respect founded simply on natural law as right reason:

> I take it to be agreed, that in the grant of every office whatsoever, there is a condition implied by common reason, that the grantee ought to execute it diligently and faithfully ... [F]rom consideration of the general rules ... and the various circumstances of every case, [a man] will easily discern how far each offence deserves to be punished.[148]

An offence symbolizing this approach was the common law (and possibly still extant[149]) offence of refusal to take up public office. Unnecessary, even eccentric, as this offence might now seem, its important eighteenth-century function was to underpin a republican system of governance, in which it was vital that citizens took responsibility for the discharge of their public roles (however minor).

141 Goldie (n 139) 159–60. 142 ibid 161. 143 ibid 168.

144 For the extraordinarily varied list of the duties of a constable, from apprehending vagrants to exterminating vermin see ibid 160.

145 See Steve Hindle (2000), at 1. 146 Goldie (n 139) 171.

147 Landau (n 119) 359. 148 Hawkins (n 1) vol 1, at 66.

149 W Archbold (2014), at para 25-406. McBain claims that the offence is now obsolete: McBain (n 91) 68.

In *R v Denison*,[150] D had refused to take up the office of Mayor of Leeds. D claimed that his mercantile interests required him to be abroad for long periods of time, meaning that he was unable to reside in Leeds for any length of time. In the circumstances, it was found that D had not had adequate opportunity to respond to the demand that he be sworn in as mayor. However, Lord Mansfield confirmed that 'an information will lie for a refusal to accept an office of this nature',[151] and Denison J added that: 'If the defendant was a person who knew he was to be elected, and had contemptuously gone away to avoid being chosen, then it would be a proper case for the court to interpose'.[152] In this respect, as David Eastwood puts it, 'the Hanoverian political system embodied institutions the character of which might best be described as republican, participatory and communitarian'.[153]

Parliament would itself frequently employ a version of the neglect-of-office offence in statutes creating or modifying regulatory regimes. Such regimes typically depended, for their effectiveness, on action in relation to (say) inspection or enforcement, by public officials. An early example is an Act of 1627, 'for the better suppressing of unlicensed alehouse keepers'. Under the Act:

> [I]f any Constable or inferior officer shall neglect to execute [a] ... precept or warrant or doe refuse or doe not execute by himselfe ... upon the Offendor the punishment limited by this statute, that in that case it shall and may be lawful ... to commit the Constable or other inferior officer so refusing or not executing the said punishment ... to the common gaole ... until he or they so neglecting or refusing shall have paid the somme of fortie shillings of lawfull money of England ... for their said contempt.

Such offences applied further up the social scale to, for example, clerks of the market. An Act of 1640, 'for the better ordering and regulating of the Office or Clarke of the Market', made it an offence for a clerk of the market, 'upon reasonable request and warning [to] refuse to seal or give allowance unto such ... measures as are according to the said standard of the Exchequer'. The penalty for such a refusal was a £5 penalty for each offence. On some occasions, a statute would specify the different penalties that were to be imposed, depending on the neglectful officer's place in the regulatory hierarchy. In an ordinance of 1643, 'for the speedy rising and leavying of moneys, set by way of charge or new impost on severall commodities', excise commissioners were established to oversee the collection regime, with 'collectors, clerks, and other subordinate officers' beneath them. Under the ordinance, the commissioners had the power:

> XXII To punish all such subordinate officers ... as shall be found wilfully negligent, remisse, or refractory in the said service, by fine, not exceeding the double value of the yearly wages which he is to receive ...

The Commissioners themselves, although men of influence such as aldermen or sheriffs, were made subject to higher-level censure:

150 (1758) 2 Lord Kenyon 259. 151 ibid. 152 ibid.
153 David Eastwood (1987), at 9.

XXIII And if the said Commissioners and Treasurer, or any of them shall offend in their respective Offices, they shall be lyable to such censure as shall be imposed on them by both Houses of Parliament.

It is noteworthy that here, and, indeed, in almost all early examples of regulatory crime, there is no taint of the 'bloody code'. Punishments are broadly proportionate to the wrong, and rationally related to the nature of the offence and the status of the offender. Here, then, is further evidence of the distorted picture of seventeenth and eighteenth-century criminal law handed down to us by Victorian opinion-makers. Reading Bentham and Blackstone on the state of the criminal law in the eighteenth century, one would never guess that, between 1660 and 1800, statutes broadly concerned with 'law and order' went from 9 per cent of all statutes in 1660–1688 to 2.7 per cent in 1760–1800. By contrast, statutes concerned with the economy (such as that just considered) went from 11.9 per cent of all statutes between 1660 and 1800, to 30 per cent between 1760 and 1800.[154]

3.8 Wilful Neglect: The Political Evolution of Misconduct (2)

As the scale of government regulation increased from the mid-eighteenth century onwards (with Parliament meeting more regularly), we find the same reliance on the neglect offence to hold public officials to account. In 1735, we find an Act for the public registering of all deeds, conveyances, wills, and other incumbrances that shall be made of, or may affect, 'any Honors, Manors, Lands, tenements or hereditaments with the north riding of the county of York'. By section xxix of that Act:

if any registrar or his deputy, shall neglect to perform his or their duty, in the execution of the said office ... or commit or suffer to be committed any undue or fraudulent practice in the execution of the said office ... then such registrar shall forfeit his said office, and pay treble damages with full costs of suit to every such person or persons who shall be injured thereby.

Another example from 1735 is an Act, 'for the amendment of the law relating to actions on the statute of hue and cry'.[155] Under this Act, officers were obliged to collect money owed under a bond (a 'penal sum' of £100) entered into by the complainant when a complaint of robbery was made to the hundred. The bond was to cover costs in the event that the complaint was unsuccessful or abandoned. Should that occur, the amount due for costs would be taxed or assessed. In relation to this process, section x of the Act stipulated that:

[154] Julian Hoppit (1996), at 119. In the same period, statutes concerned with the regulation of communication went from 4.1% to 18.3%.

[155] See also 'An Act for rendering the laws more effectual for punishing such persons as shall wilfully and maliciously pull down or destroy turnpikes for repairing highways, locks, or other works erected by act of Parliament' (1735). Section XIII provided for a penalty for refusing to issue a warrant: 'If any constable or constables, who are hereby required to execute all warrants ... concerning turnpikes, shall refuse to execute any warrant or warrants ... for apprehending any person or persons that shall be guilty of any offence against this Act ... then such constable or constables ... shall forfeit and pay the sum of five pounds ...'.

If any such officer or officers who are to levy such taxations and assessments ... shall refuse or neglect to levy and collect the same ... or shall refuse or neglect to pay over the sums of money so levied and collected ... every offence shall, for every such refusal or neglect, forfeit double the sum appointed to be by him levied and collected as aforesaid.

Section xi went on to say:

If any constable, borsholder, headborough or tythingman, shall offend ... by refusing or neglecting to make [a] fresh suit and hue and cry ... every such offender shall for every such refusal or neglect forfeit five pounds.

A later example is the Order in Council, made on 22 March 1748, in relation to measures to prevent the spread of distemper in cattle.[156] This provided inter alia that:

In case any chief Magistrate ... High Constables, Clerks of the Peace, church wardens, Overseers, Constables, and other person or persons appointed ... shall be guilty of any neglect or failure of his or their duty, in all or any of the matters hereby required of them, they shall be liable to ... penalties.[157]

Under an Act of 1761, churchwardens and overseers of the poor were required to keep accurate registers of all 'parish poor' infants under a certain age. Section xvii of the Act supported this duty through the creation of a fixed penalty offence:

[I]f any churchwarden, overseer of the poor [or the like] ... shall neglect his duty as directed in and by this Act ... [he] shall, for every offence, forfeit and pay to the informer the sum of forty shillings.[158]

Below, I will consider whether there is more to this parliamentary usage of an old common law offence than plain borrowing of its form.

How many prosecutions for neglect of office were there? David Lemmings gives some figures for the Cheshire Quarter Sessions between 1678 and 1818.[159] Out of a total of 144 presentments, six were for official neglect of some kind, with a further forty-nine presentments for failures in point of obligation to repair bridges, roads, and waterways. The latter obligations were increasingly important, as trade increased during the eighteenth century,[160] as we saw earlier in the case of *R v Mawbey*.[161] The Highways Act 1691 had made compulsory a meeting of JPs every four months to ensure 'the execution of ... their authority' in relation to their administrative (as opposed to judicial) duty to ensure that the highway surveyors were doing their job. Out of a total of 124 presentments between 1729 and 1731, thirty-one were for official neglect, and ninety-one for failures to repair bridges, roads, waterways, and the

[156] *London Gazette*, issue 8730 (22 March 1748); and see John Broad (1983).

[157] In that regard, one clergyman, chafing at the obligation to read out in church the new restrictions and duties, fulminated: 'An Act, longer than a sermon, was ordered to be read ... relating to the killing, slaughtering &c, of cattle, more fit for a butcher than a clergyman; and which manifestly took off the attention of the congregation from the rest of the service ... one may venture to say, that however well acquainted the compilers of the Act were with the spirit of the laws, they were ignorant of, or not attentive to, the spirit of the gospel': Charles Lind (1769), at 3.

[158] For further discussion in a closely related context see Anthony Ogus (1992), at 11–12.

[159] Lemmings (n 100) 29.

[160] See Hoppit (n 154) and Dan Bogart (2005).

[161] *R v Mawbey and Others* (n 71). See section 3.5.

like. These figures are significant, in spite of the judicial reluctance (explored earlier) to use the criminal law against 'amateur' JPs.

At a theoretical level, what is important about this use of the official neglect offence in regulatory statutes is that it symbolizes a changing view of how accountability in criminal law should be understood.[162] To begin with, 'regime Whigs' grew more confident in exercising their parliamentary authority in a top-down way inimical to traditional rights, not least to meet their fiscal and war aims, along with the aggressive promotion of commerce.[163] Parliament increasingly entrusted the achievement of those aims to a growing army of salaried state officials:[164] a development criticized a century later by one commentator—political theorist and lawyer, Joshua Toulmin Smith—as marking the emergence of the 'pseudo-liberalism of modern times'.[165]

This prompted a change in the understanding of the basis for the accountability of state officials, and of law more generally. Their accountability is no longer seen solely in terms of the kind of accountability at common law discussed above. The latter kind of accountability—at common law—we could call 'downward-responsive' in character. As we have seen, higher court judges, acting in Mansfield-like fashion, often saw themselves as exercising their royal authority on behalf of the people,[166] just as paternalistic lower level justices applied the law more generally in a context-sensitive way sensitive to local customs and traditional rights.[167] By contrast, the later eighteenth century saw a rise in a very different kind of thinking. Law enforcement was placed in the hands of public officials—such as excise men—without local influence or connections, whose authority was granted wholly by the Crown and Parliament. Their duty was to apply the law without fear or favour, as agents of and in the interests of the central state.[168] As Lemmings concludes:

> As in the case of the general statutes that gave extra powers to magistrates, specific Acts frequently created authorities with wide powers and relative immunity from correction by the courts ... these authorities generally exercised power in ways that superceded the quasi-republican culture of governance associated with the common law.[169]

This recognizably Weberian development had implications for the accountability of such officials. Accountability was increasingly 'upward-responsive'.[170] Following a model of bureaucratic rationality, officials' accountability was to the body—Parliament—that had granted them express legal authority to exercise discretion and imposed on them a duty to act. Accountability was no longer to the ordinary people over whom that discretion was exercised.

[162] See Lemmings (n 100) 171.
[163] Lemmings (n 100) 132; Linda Colley (1992), at ch 2.
[164] Officials empowered by unprecedented discretionary powers beyond (at that time) the review jurisdiction of the courts: Lemmings (n 100) 7–8.
[165] Joshua Toulmin Smith (1851), at 10.
[166] See *Rex v Bembridge* (n 15), and the discussion in section 3.4.
[167] See the discussion of the law governing press gangs in section 3.9.
[168] Lemmings (n 100) 7–8; Brewer (n 10) 83.
[169] Lemmings (n 100) 171.
[170] As Lemmings puts it, 'On the face of it, the massive increase in law-making from Westminster might seem to constitute part of a general transformation from common law traditions of self-government towards rule from above': Lemmings (n 100) 126–27.

In an important sense, this change reflected the perception that Parliament was, constitutionally speaking, 'in the saddle', and (in relation to its legislative activity) riding hard. It is, surely, not just a point of constitutional theory, but a reflection of regime Whig legislative confidence, that leads Blackstone to claim that in government there must be:

> A fupreme, irrefiftable, uncontrolled authority, in which the *jura summi imperii*, or the rights of sovereignty, reside. And this authority is placed in thofe hands wherein ... the qualities requifite for fupremacy, goodnefs and power are the most likely to be found.[171]

For Blackstone, this body was, of course, Parliament, and not the Crown or the courts; but it is noticeable how Blackstone is immediately drawn to remark how it follows that Parliament may 'put the execution of the laws into whatever hands it pleases, and all the other powers of the ftate must obey the legiflative power in the execution of their feveral functions ...'.[172] No longer are state officials to draw directly on external normative sources, such as natural law, local customs, or traditional rights to affirm their (or any other official's) authority. In the new era of parliamentary sovereignty, it is the trust of the supreme legislature that is betrayed by official misconduct, and only through the betrayal of the legislature is the trust of the people thereby betrayed. It is no longer directly the trust of the people and their customs that have been betrayed.

3.9 Republican Values and Resistance to Legislative Authority

To set in context this transformation of the way in which the wilful neglect offence was understood, we can briefly consider the constitutional battle over the legality of press ganging.[173] In relation to this issue, tension between the two ways (bottom-up; top-down) of understanding the accountability of officials acting under delegated authority boiled over, in the streets and in the courts.[174]

There had been objections to press ganging since the seventeenth century.[175] It was frequently condemned in republican terms as a violation of Magna Carta and hence of the 'native liberty' of Englishmen,[176] and as a practice equivalent to—indeed, a form of—slavery. Between 1738 and 1805, there were no less than 602 affrays, mostly in London, involving clashes between crowds and press-gang officers and their men.[177] Even so, whilst admitting its controversial character both morally and legally, Sir Robert Walpole had made it clear that the need to protect 'our dominions of greatest value' in his view trumped 'ill-timed regard for the case of particular persons [press-ganged sailors], or a popular affectation of tenderness for liberty'.[178] The question of legality was shortly thereafter resolved in the courts. In

[171] Blackstone (n 59) vol i, at 49. [172] ibid.
[173] See Rogers (n 53); Bernard Capp (1989); Paul A Gilje (2013).
[174] The following account is taken from Rogers (n 53). [175] See Capp (n 173).
[176] James Oglethorpe (1728), at 10; and *Mist's Weekly Journal* (18 May 1728), both cited by Rogers (n 53) 73.
[177] Paul A Gilje (2002), at 76, citing Rogers (n 53).
[178] Cobbett (n 44) vol vii (1739–41), at 428–38, cited by Rogers (n 53) 74.

the momentous case of *Rex v Broadfoot*,[179] Foster J upheld the legality of the practice of impressment, at a time when criticism of impressment coming from all quarters was becoming vociferous.[180]

Broadfoot was a merchant seaman who, in resisting impressment, shot dead a member of a press gang as the gang sought to seize him (some 1 in 4 of such affrays ended in a death or in serious injury at that time[181]). The question arose whether Broadfoot was guilty of murder or manslaughter. The issue turned on whether Broadfoot had a right to resist, on the grounds that the impressment was illegal, even if he overreacted in the manner his resistance took (making him guilty of manslaughter only).[182] Foster ruled that Broadfoot was guilty of manslaughter only, because the warrant in question had required an officer to be present at the impressment, and none had been present at the time. At a more general constitutional level, however, Foster J found that the practice of impressment was grounded in a royal prerogative 'of immemorial usage ... inherent in the Crown, grounded upon common law'.[183] In itself, that justification for 'state necessity' was controversial. Some years later, Granville Sharp scathingly criticized it:

> It is a doctrine without bounds when once admitted, for it insensibly declines to every evil, like a High Road to Hell. It is better for a Nation to risk even its very existence in the world, trusting in God's providence, than to set aside the administration of equal justice & righteousness in order to subsist by a manifest oppression of any particular part of the community.[184]

Perhaps unsurprisingly, thus, Foster also bolstered this justification (subsequently endorsed by Blackstone[185]) by relying on the proposition that the legality of press ganging had also been 'recognised by many Acts of Parliament' that dealt with various aspects of press ganging.[186] This point was also emphasized by lawyers for the City of London, when the City sought in 1770 to obtain exemption from impressment for its freeman. In the City's lawyers' opinion, impressment was 'founded on that Universal Principle of Laws, that private interest must give way to public Safety, being well established by ancient and continued Usage' but, most importantly, was also 'recognised and regulated by the legislature'.[187] Appeals to long usage and the authority of the common law might no longer be sufficient, in themselves, to uphold the legality of such powers.

Rex v Broadfoot might in some respects be considered a forerunner of the opinion established in *Entick v Carrington*,[188] that, when agents acting under ministerial (Crown) authority invade the rights of the subject:

[179] *Rex v Broadfoot* (1743) 2 Salk 31.

[180] Daniel A Baugh (1965), at 147.

[181] See Gilje (n 173) 77, citing Rogers (n 53).

[182] See the discussion in Jeremy Horder (1992).

[183] *Rex v Broadfoot* (n 179) 84.

[184] Granville Sharp, writing as 'Maynard', *London Public Ledger* (7 January 1777).

[185] Blackstone (n 59) vol i, at 267–68.

[186] *Rex v Broadfoot* (n 179) 78. For the statutes in question see eg 4 Anne c19; 4 and 5 Anne 6. See further *Rex v Tubbs* (1776) Foster's Crown Cases 155, and the discussion in Rogers (n 53) ch 4.

[187] *Annual Register* (1770), vol xvii, at 232, cited by Rogers (n 53) 76.

[188] (1765) 19 Howell's State Trials 1029.

The justification is submitted to the judges, who are to look into the books; and if such a justification can be maintained by the text of the statute law, or by the principles of common law. If no excuse can be found or produced, the silence of the books is an authority against the defendant, and the plaintiff must have judgment.[189]

Foster, however, unwittingly laid the foundation for popular and magisterial resistance to press ganging, especially in the city of London, in the legalistic basis that he gave for finding that the warrant in *Rex v Broadfoot* was defective. In the later case of *Rex v Tubbs*,[190] Lord Mansfield warned impress officers not to abuse their position, and to act 'with the greatest moderation and only upon the most cogent necessity'.[191] Accordingly, taking a mile having been given an inch, magistrates would discharge impressed men brought before them on the slightest of pretexts.[192] Press gangs might find themselves imprisoned by magistrates when (following Foster's lead) the gangs engaged in the practice of impressment in the absence of a regulating officer.[193] Alongside popular street resistance to the impress, local traders who were affected, such as publicans subject to a 'hot press' not infrequently resisted the officers on legal grounds, if the officers had not given notification of an impending raid, or if the warrant was not shown or was not in order.[194]

Such bottom-up republican resistance to press ganging did not weaken the official view that the practice could be wholly justified in a top-down manner. When the navy impressed all and sundry, even those with exemptions, in reaction to the threat posed in 1779 by the combined forces of America, France, Spain, and Holland,[195] it was granted an ex post facto exemption for its actions when the manning crisis had passed.[196] Lord Chancellor Thurlow took the view that he (as Lord Chancellor) 'was to judge of the necessity, and as to the warrants ... pronounce them *legal*'.[197] Such a top-down understanding of the power to confer discretionary authority on press-gang officers was, of course, controversial, with one critic complaining about legality being conferred:

Merely because a minister of the country may perhaps from motives of corruption, or views of ambition, chuse to enter into a war, and by an unjust exercise of power, force those honest fellows to become the instruments either of his villainy, or his vengeance.[198]

The importance of this passage is that it illustrates the link, in critics' minds, between the existence of overly broad powers of authority and the corrupt misuse of those powers. On a republican account, opposition to overly broad powers is part and

[189] ibid. [190] (1776) Foster's Crown Law 155. [191] ibid.

[192] Magistrates, perhaps especially mayors, were also concerned to maintain good relations with important merchants, who, like the Navy, relied on an adequate supply of men to serve as merchant seamen. That concern militated against giving press officers any more scope than was absolutely necessary to force men into the Navy.

[193] See Rogers (n 53) 80–82.

[194] ibid 82–83. It should be noted that resistance to the impress was not always so nobly motivated. There was, for example, a thriving trade in exemptions granted by the Admiralty to those working in 'reserved occupations': Rogers (n 53) 88.

[195] ibid 92. [196] ibid 72–74.

[197] *Whitehall Evening Post* (9–11 October 1787), cited by Rogers (n 53) 78.

[198] *Newcastle Chronicle* (24 November 1792), cited by Rogers (n 53) 77.

parcel of an opposition to corruption and official misconduct more broadly, a theme I will pursue in Chapter 5. It was not to be seen (as Thurlow and Walpole saw it) as nothing more than the raising of obstructive difficulties to ministers seeking bona fide to exercise such powers in the public interest.

By the end of the eighteenth century, Parliament—and ministers acting in their ministerial capacity—had become much more powerful politically, and the Crown—the body responsible for judicial appointment—politically too weak, for meaningful challenges to parliamentary legislative authority to be launched with judicial approbation. However, an important question that arises from this chapter concerns the lesson that we should draw from the long pre-Victorian tradition of republican thinking and practice in relation to the deterrence and punishment of official misconduct. Albeit at different levels of court, and in a variety of contexts, that tradition consisted of a concern for natural rights, a strong sense that official misconduct and corruption betrayed those rights, and, accordingly, a willingness to confine authoritarian activity such as press ganging within the strictest legal bounds.

In Chapter 4, a case is made for just such an approach, on the part of prosecutors and the higher courts, towards the (mis)use of parliamentary privilege as it bears on MPs' non-legislative parliamentary activity. I will argue for a much more restrictive approach to be taken by the courts towards the immunity from suit given to MPs' exercise of parliamentary privilege, when the exercise of that privilege in non-legislative contexts involves corruption. The courts still have an important right and duty to champion republican values, in relation to the non-legislative activity of Parliament, even if, for sound democratic reasons, they do not have the right to question Parliament's legislative activity. The misconduct offence is capable of application to non-legislative activity, and in no field is the application of the offence more needed than when such activity involves, or may involve, corruption.

4

MPs' Criminal Liability: Tackling Personal Corruption

> People didn't just tell us what to do, but how to go about it. They want their politicians to uphold the highest standards of propriety. That means being transparent in all we do. It means rooting out any form of misconduct.[1]
>
> Now this [the Bill of Rights] is a charter for freedom of speech in the House. It is not a charter for corruption.[2]

4.1 Defining Corruption

In the United States of America, allowances (expenses) levels for individual Members of the House of Representatives are authorized in statute, but are regulated and adjusted by the Committee on House Administration pursuant to 2 USC 4313, and House Rule X(1)(j).[3] The mean amount for each Member was US$1,255,960 in 2015. Some 70–75 per cent of this sum is spent by members on staffing.[4] However, such spending is subject to a crucial ethical constraint. The relevant part of Rule 8 of the Code of Official Conduct governing the House reads:

> (A) a Member, Delegate, or Resident Commissioner may not retain the relative of such individual in a paid position; and
>
> (B) an employee of the House may not accept compensation for work for a committee on which the relative of such employee serves as a member.[5]

Similarly, Federal law 5 USC § 3110 prohibits a federal official, including a Member of Congress, from appointing, promoting, or recommending for appointment or promotion any 'relative' of the official to any agency or department over which the official exercises authority or control. The rule is relatively strict. For example, should a Member marry a member of his or her staff, during the course of the latter's

[1] The Right Honourable David Cameron MP, in the forward to the Ministerial Code (15 October 2015).

[2] Lord Salmon, Hansard, HL Debs, col 631 (6 December 1976).

[3] Ida Brudnick (2015), at 3.

[4] ibid at 12.

[5] Rules of the House of Representatives (2015), rule XXIII(8).

employment, the employee must leave the Member's employ.[6] The clarity of this position contrasts sharply with the ethical mire into which United Kingdom (UK) parliamentary practice had sunk until 2017, with regard to these issues, the courts having failed to force Parliament to remain on the moral high ground. Part of the task of this chapter is to explore this contention.

More broadly, I will argue that there is currently inadequate accountability to the courts, through the criminal law governing misuse of public office, when high state officials institute or connive at illegitimate policies or systems to benefit themselves personally, their families, or their favourites. I will suggest that, so far as the immunity of Members of Parliament (MPs) from prosecution is concerned, the courts have wrongly sought to draw a line between misconduct at what might be called an 'operational' level (where there is no immunity), and misconduct at a 'policy' or systemic level (where immunity applies). To draw the line in that place is to leave an important gap in the assurance given to members of the public that officials will not seek to benefit themselves and their families from their tenure of public office. The current rules permit MPs collectively to take unchallengeable decisions concerning the extent to which they may engage in corrupt use of office, because the courts have approached the constitutional status of such rules from a 'top-down' perspective (involving, by and large, accountability to oneself, as the rule-maker). The rules are hence beyond accountability or scrutiny from the 'bottom up', through the application to them of the ethical standards understood and observed by ordinary honest people: standards that are the lifeblood of the criminal law (and of the offence of misconduct in particular).[7] There is a case for saying that the criminal law should play a primary role in tackling personal corruption in politics, even if it is of course important to provide for some civil or public law process by which the ill-gotten gains of personal corruption are recovered.[8] There is a very simple reason for this. To exploit public office for personal gain is *intrinsically* wrong. So, a substantial part of this chapter will be devoted to arguing that the courts' current approach to this issue, embodied in the decision in *R v Chaytor*,[9] is too generous to MPs and to the top-down perspective on accountability.

There are worse things that one can do through the use of public office than line one's own pockets. Using one's official position to commit torture is an obvious example.[10] Even so, a special kind of betrayal of office is involved when an official—and perhaps especially an MP—engages in personal corruption. The point and purpose of public office is to act for public benefit, and not for oneself or one's family and friends. It is a legitimate function of the criminal law to be at the forefront of efforts to deter and punish the betrayal involved when officials cross the line from one use of public office to the other. Indeed, the availability of the offence of misconduct in a public office, to deter and punish such impropriety in public life, can

[6] ibid. [7] See the discussion of these issues in chs 2 and 3.

[8] By way of contrast, the right approach to 'political' corruption more broadly should be more subtle, because the issues are more complex. As we will see, civil remedies such as negation play a primary role here, although the criminal law is still important. For this role see ch 5.9.

[9] [2010] UKSC 52. [10] See the Criminal Justice Act 1988, s 134.

be regarded as a pillar of the constitution. To recall a distinction made in Chapter 1, when MPs create rules to govern their own conduct, our trust in them to get this right is only conditional, not absolute. Accordingly, when that trust is broken, and MPs engage in personal corruption, the criminal law can and sometimes should be used to punish and deter such conduct. In this respect, the criminal courts have a constitutional role to play as guardians of public trust that integrity amongst the highest level officials will be maintained.

Before setting about these tasks, I will try to set the issues briefly into a historical context. In terms of opportunities for corruption, the picture is one in which the perceived value of political office changes in nature. In the eighteenth century, it is treated by office-holders as a means by which directly to increase income (and sometimes to amass a huge fortune). In contrast, by the end of the nineteenth century, election as an MP had increasingly become a means by which wealthy businessmen sought to entrench or enhance their influence and affluence indirectly (known as 'revolving in'[11]). A place in the political system was becoming the ultimate mark of success in commerce or industry, laying the foundations for the close relationship between business and politics. Arising out of that relationship also came the possibility of 'revolving out', a significant problem of personal corruption in parliamentary politics today. Revolving out occurs when someone who already holds a public position, such as a politician, seeks to use his or her position to gain personal financial advantages in the private sector (such as a position on a board of directors, or employment following the termination of a period in public office), through contacts in the world of business.[12] I will then go on to analyse the problem of personal corruption in general, before moving on to the question of immunity from suit. In section 4.2, we begin with an analysis of the Law Commission's proposals for reform of the criminal law governing corrupt misconduct in public office. Before doing so, however, it is worth offering a brief account of what is meant by 'personal' corruption, as opposed to 'political' corruption (addressed in Chapter 5), although in legal terms nothing hangs on the distinction.

In very broad terms, corruption involves using one's position to act improperly, with regard to the distribution or exercise respectively of some benefit or influence.[13] Acting 'improperly' involves acting in a way that, bearing in mind the context in which the corrupt person acts,[14] an honest and reasonable person of moral and political integrity would regard as improper.[15] This is an open-ended test, reflecting

[11] For the phrase 'revolving in' see the discussion in Stuart Wilks-Heeg (2015), at ch 10.

[12] We will return to this issue in ch 5, in discussing the wider picture of political corruption.

[13] The phrase 'with regard to' the distribution of benefit or influence is used in order to reflect the fact that someone may act corruptly even though they are not in possession or control of the benefit or influence in question. So, for example, X might improperly seek to influence Y in the distribution of assets controlled by Y. In such an example, X acts improperly 'with regard to' the distribution of the benefit.

[14] This rider about 'context' is meant to reflect the fact that there is an element of context specificity to all analysis of corruption. In some jurisdictions, for example, it would be quite proper as a matter of political ethics for a monarch to seek to influence the course of political developments, whereas in other jurisdictions this would be regarded as improper, as liable to corrupt politics.

[15] This test is analogous to the test employed by the Bribery Act 2010 to define improper conferrals of advantages: Bribery Act 2010, s 5.

the fact that the nature of impropriety in the distribution of resources and influence varies greatly, in both public and private sector contexts. Moreover, in every society, there will inevitably be disagreement and tension between what are to be regarded as the practices and processes that merely set the context in which corruption should be understood, and what are to be regarded as the practices and processes that are in themselves (potentially) part of the corruption problem.[16] Further, the test may appear to have an element of circularity about it; but that is not a weakness. Attempts to escape completely from circularity end up arbitrarily excluding important categories of corrupt conduct.

For example, one important feature of the test is that it does not tie the existence of corruption to a failure to follow existing rules or practices. Someone may properly be described as acting 'corruptly' even when intentionally *following* a rule or custom, where that rule or custom is itself the root of the problem. In some circumstances, someone may have to deviate from a rule or custom in order to maintain his or her integrity and avoid corruption. Tests for corruption that focus on departures from rules tend to distort the analysis in favour of those, like MPs, with the power to make rules or create customs. I will come back to this point below. Related to this is another important feature of the test. It is indifferent to where someone is placed, on the scale of officialdom or in society more generally. A refuse collector who insists on cash tips from householders is as liable to be found to be corrupt as an MP who says that, in using public funds to employ his or her spouse or daughter (say) as an assistant, he or she is only doing as other MPs have granted themselves the power to do. In both examples, the individual may be found to have used his or her position[17] to seek or obtain benefit improperly, if that is—in the relevant context—the view taken by people of moral and political integrity.

More specifically, I will divide corruption into two forms: 'personal' corruption and 'political' corruption. A distribution of benefit or influence can be regarded as improper if the distribution or the exercise in question[18] reflects the *personal value* of the action to the corrupt person, when that is at odds with the criteria by which the benefit or influence should respectively be distributed. I shall treat such cases as ones of 'personal' corruption. Additionally, benefit or influence may be improperly distributed, even when its personal value to the corrupt person is not a factor behind the distribution. This can happen when the benefit or influence is given or denied through the use of a conception of what is 'good' that is preferred, as a distributive principle, to principles that ought to be applied. I will treat the latter kinds of cases as ones of 'political' corruption. For example, suppose that, when distributing social security benefits in the UK, an official gives preference in the exercise of his or her discretion to those who are religious believers. This would be to engage in political corruption. I will frequently refer

[16] This particular issue will come to the fore in ch 5.

[17] It follows that, by 'position', I do not have in mind a narrow conception concerned only with the performance of a formal bureaucratic function: the refuse collector is using his or her 'position', even though it does not involve such a function.

[18] Including a failure to distribute benefit, or to use influence or to be open to influence, when that would have been appropriate.

to political corruption cases like this as ones in which the corrupt person acts in a 'partisan' way. In such cases, the grant or denial of a public benefit is being distorted by the partisan use of a conception of what is right or acceptable, as a distributive principle, which is at odds with distributive principles appropriate (within the UK[19]). Clearly, the two categories may overlap in some instances, but it is helpful to separate them for the purposes of analysis. Falling within the category of political corruption are cases in which benefit or influence, flowing from state institutions, improperly redounds to non-state bodies such as companies or political parties (or vice versa), and from companies to political parties. We will spend a good deal of time discussing such cases in this chapter, and in Chapter 5. This is because, at least in the case of political parties, there may in fact be a substantial element of what they do that is integral to furthering public benefit, and is thus not properly described as corrupt.

It is very common amongst corruption theorists to define corruption in terms of the use of a position of trust for 'private' gain.[20] A foundational modern analysis is that of J S Nye, who defined corruption as:

> Behaviour which deviates from the formal duties of a public role because of private-regarding (personal, close family, private clique) pecuniary or status gains; or violates rules against the exercise of certain types or private-regarding influence.[21]

I have already suggested that it is distorting to tie the definition of corrupt behaviour to deviation from formal duties or rules. Moreover, Nye seems narrowly concerned with what I am calling personal corruption rather than with what I would call political corruption; but how helpful is it to understand corruption in terms of action that is 'private-regarding'? I suggest that this is a useful rule of thumb, but no more than that, especially where political corruption is in issue. Suppose (as is customary) that an incoming government appoints only members of its own party to ministerial positions, overlooking much better qualified and experienced candidates from other parties. Is that a 'private-regarding' (and hence, *ex hypothesi* corrupt) policy, favouring party interests over the national interest, or is it an ethically acceptable course of conduct motivated by public benefit, in that it brings greater unity of political purpose to government (or, perhaps both of these things)? I will consider such issues in greater depth in Chapter 5. For now, we can answer the question by going back to the test given earlier. In order to determine whether such a course of conduct is corrupt, one must ask whether it involves distributing benefit or influence in accordance with a conception of what is good that, bearing in mind the political context, a person of moral and political integrity would regard as improper. Whether or not the action can be described as 'private-regarding' can at best provide only a partial answer to that question.

[19] In a theocratic country, perhaps the use of religious test for the distribution of social security benefits would not be regarded as corrupt, because it would fall within what is regarded as ethically permissible.

[20] See eg Transparency International, 'What is Corruption?' (2016).

[21] J S Nye (1967), at 419.

In the kinds of examples of personal and political corruption just given, I have been concerned with substantive questions about inappropriate criteria bearing on a corrupt person's decision. However, cutting across the distinction between personal and political corruption cases are instances in which the impropriety or corrupt element is more procedural than substantive in nature. For example, an excessive regard for secrecy in decision-making might be regarded as corrupt(ing),[22] as might an insistence that one remains unaccountable for one's actions. Both of these indicia of corruption were in issue in the expenses scandal that haunted the so-called 'rotten' Parliament of 2005–2010,[23] discussed in section 4.7. Similarly, when making official decisions, the reliance by a public officer on the advice of a personal 'guru' might be regarded as a corrupt practice, even if the official is motivated solely by considerations of what he or she believes to be in the public interest. So-called 'noble cause' corruption usually falls into this category: where law enforcement agencies bend or ignore some kinds of rules of due process to secure arrests and convictions.[24] We will consider some procedural defect cases of corruption in due course.

The most important kinds of personal corruption (improperly putting one's personal values ahead of appropriate criteria, in distributing benefit or influence) involve either self-preference, or preference for someone with whom the corrupt person enjoys a close relationship.[25] A 'close' relationship will often be a relationship with, say, a spouse, a son or daughter, another relative, a lover, or a friend; but personal corruption may also be involved when someone behaves improperly by benefiting someone such as a work colleague, a mentor, or a family firm. The corrupt person's relationship can still be described as 'close', in these cases, even though they may appear to be more arm's length relationships. To give two different examples, an MP's relationship with his or her constituents, or the prime minister's relationship with MPs in his or her party, is not necessarily close, although it may become so in individual cases, depending on the nature and extent of the interpersonal dynamic between them. Nonetheless, either of the two relationships just mentioned could still involve personal corruption. They will involve corruption, if benefit or influence is given or received in a way that is improper because it wrongly reflects the personal value of the relationship to the corrupt person rather than being explicable in terms of public benefit. With this background in mind, we can turn to the Law Commission's proposals for reform of this area of the law.

4.2 The Scope of Personal Corruption

Under the present law, in deciding whether someone is guilty of criminal misconduct, the question is whether D had (without reasonable excuse or justification)

[22] See the discussion in ch 5.2.

[23] http://www.telegraph.co.uk/news/election-2010/7573025/General-Election-2010-Good-riddance-to-the-Rotten-Parliament.html.

[24] For further discussion see John Kleinig (2002).

[25] Where a close relationship can include a relationship with a company. On the economic and political significance of family ties see eg Alberto Alesina and Paola Giuliana (2013).

wilfully misconducted him or herself, to such a degree as to amount to an abuse of the public's trust in the office holder.[26] A definition in these terms, albeit supplemented by guidelines, was defended in Chapter 2. How much of an improvement is the Law Commission's proposed redefinition of the misconduct offence, in cases of corruption?[27] I will be analysing the test provisionally proposed in the Commission's Consultation Paper.[28] D's conduct would be judged in the light of the following test:

(1) D commits the offence if he or she abuses his or her position, power, or authority.
(2) That is to say, if:
  (a) he or she exercises that position, power, or authority for the purpose of achieving:
    (i) a benefit for himself or herself; or
    (ii) a benefit or a detriment for another person; and
  (b) the exercise of that power, position, or authority for that purpose was seriously improper.

The Law Commission's definition is not a piece of statutory drafting, and that must be kept in mind in any analysis of the precise terms used. The definition is meant to improve the law, in point of certainty. This is to be achieved principally by confining the offence to instances in which an official exercises his or her position[29] with the specific purpose of benefiting him or herself, or another, or of causing detriment to another. So, our principal focus must be this purposive element.

Let me begin with some brief remarks about the inclusion of purposefully causing detriment to another person, within the scope of the revised offence. Clearly, an official may misconduct him or herself by purposely causing detriment to another person. Here is an example: the so-called George Washington Bridge lane closure scandal.[30] During the week of 9 September 2013, traffic gridlock was created in Fort Lee, New Jersey through the rush-hour closure of two lanes on the bridge, the busiest motor vehicle bridge in the world. The decision to close the lanes was taken by one or more of the New Jersey governor's officials. The motivating factor was the desire for political retaliation, following a failure on the part of the Fort Lee Mayor to back the governor (Chris Christie) in the gubernatorial election.[31] There might be a number of permissible reasons for closing a vehicle bridge; but such a basis for

[26] *Attorney-General's Reference (No 3 of 2003)* [2004] EWCA Crim 868, [2005] QB 73, para 61.

[27] The Law Commission proposes a differently defined offence to deal with misconduct outside the field of corruption. That other definition is not relevant here.

[28] Law Commission, *Reforming Misconduct in Public Office* (2016b), at para 6.50 (Provisional Proposal 28). The proposals were examined more broadly in ch 2.

[29] On which see the discussion in ch 2.

[30] Discussed by the Law Commission, *Reforming Misconduct in Public Office* (n 28) paras 5.154–5.155.

[31] http://www.nytimes.com/2016/11/05/nyregion/bridgegate-conviction.html?_r=0; 'Two indicted in George Washington Bridge Case; ally of Christie pleads guilty', *New York Times* (1 May 2015). In this case, a conspiracy to defraud was the preferred charge, rather than a more recognizably corruption-focused offence.

doing so ought to be excluded from consideration. For officials to be motivated purely and simply by a desire for political revenge on the Fort Lee Mayor is certainly misconduct in a public office, and any definition of the offence must cover such cases.[32] Even so, although misconduct is unquestionably involved, would it also be right to call the action 'corrupt'? This is more problematic. The central case of corruption is more naturally thought of in terms of intending to benefit improperly,[33] rather than in terms of intending purely to set back another's interests—cause them detriment—improperly.

There is an analogy here with the distinction between the proper moral scope respectively of theft and of criminal damage. Theft is essentially an acquisitive crime, and criminal damage a destructive crime. So, if I smash your valuable vase, it is natural and proper to think of that action as criminal damage. However, if my intention in smashing the vase was to deprive you of it permanently, then it is possible—albeit artificial—to think of my action as a dishonest appropriation of the vase, with an intention of permanent deprivation, and hence as theft. It is simply that this would be a peripheral case of theft. Similarly, cases of misconduct involving the intention (purpose) of causing detriment are peripheral cases of corruption, even if they fall four-square within the scope of the misconduct offence. Suppose D fails to appoint V to a post because V is black. Such an action is undoubtedly wrongful discrimination, but is it also corrupt? The answer to that question might be thought to depend on what D intended. If D's intention was to preserve the *ex hypothesi* all-white character of D's workplace, then there is an intention to benefit a group in a partisan and hence corrupt way.[34] By contrast, suppose that D intended solely to set back V's interests, as a black person, irrespective of any other effect his or her (D's) action might have. Equally discriminatory though such a motivation is, it makes the action at best a peripheral case of 'corruption', in much the same way that breaking a vase with the intention of permanent deprivation is a peripheral case of theft. Nonetheless, a peripheral case is a still 'a case' and we should not rule out a corruption analysis in cases of intending to cause detriment (perhaps especially where some malicious pleasure is derived from the action). So, if D wrongfully denies V promotion because D resents the rapidity with which V's career has progressed, such an abuse of power may be called 'corrupt' even though D gains nothing by the action.

Putting aside the issue of detriment, the focus on acting for the purpose of benefiting must be subjected to significant scrutiny. We now need to look more closely at the case where the allegation is that someone has used their position improperly to benefit another person. A question arises about the exclusive focus on acting with the purpose of achieving 'benefit' for another, in the Law Commission's proposals.

[32] Under the Law Commission's proposals, the case would in fact fall to be considered under their proposal for an offence of breach of duty posing a risk of serious harm to public order or safety: see Law Commission, *Reforming Misconduct in Public Office* (n 28) para 5.156.

[33] Where 'benefit' is understood to extend beyond financial or material benefit to include, for example, sexual favours. I will shortly turn to the question of whether an intention 'to benefit' improperly is a sufficiently broad notion, without the addition of an intention 'to influence' improperly.

[34] 'Partisan' actions, as a form of corruption, are considered in ch 5.2.

The Commission speaks of benefit involving an 'advantage'.[35] This term recalls the language used under the Bribery Act 2010 to describe the focus of a corrupt transaction. However, if it is to amount to an abuse of position for a public official to act in order to 'benefit'—or to cause detriment to—another person, then it ought equally to be an abuse of position for a public official to seek to exercise improper *influence* on someone:[36]

EXAMPLE: A Civil Servant (D) knows that a leading UK business is thinking of moving an industrial plant employing thousands of people from the UK to mainland Europe. D writes to the Managing Director saying that the present Prime Minister is known to be minded to recommend for knighthoods industry leaders who remain loyal to the UK.

In this example, D should be regarded as guilty of misconduct, albeit perhaps not of a very serious kind. It is not for any public official to seek to influence business decisions by holding out the prospect that the business managers may gain public honours, if they act in a certain way. However, in finding misconduct on D's part, it should not be necessary to show that D had as his or her purpose the conferring of a benefit on any person. It should be enough to show that D intended to exercise the wrong kind of influence over the managing director. In its Report and draft Bill on bribery,[37] the Law Commission took pains to ensure that the offence of bribery was not confined to cases in which P offered, and R accepted, a benefit that P knew it was wrong for R to accept.[38] The offence was extended to capture cases in which P sought improperly to influence R's conduct in the performance of a relevant function.[39] It would seem that the importance of that extension has not been appreciated, in relation to reform of the misconduct offence. Although the conferral of benefits was also involved, an important example of influence-based personal corruption gave rise to the impeachment and removal from office of former South Korean President, Park Geun-hye.[40] Over many years, Park had improperly allowed a friend and confidante, Choi Soon-sil, access to public documents and substantial influence over public decisions.

That brings us to the question of 'impropriety' in cases of corrupt misconduct. Let us first consider cases in which the purpose is to benefit another or others. In one way, the treatment of such actions as on a par with cases of benefiting oneself is baffling, because using public office to benefit others is what public office is *all about*. So, in such cases, it is not enough to ask whether a public official who has acted with the purpose of benefiting another has thereby acted in a way that is 'seriously improper'. One needs to identify which instances of acting to benefit another are improper for a public official, before one comes on to the question of whether they

[35] Law Commission, *Reforming Misconduct in Public Office* (n 28) para 6.72. An 'advantage' clearly ought to include sexual favours as well as financial gain or (say) promotion. The Commission does appear to suggest this: Law Commission, *Reforming Misconduct in Public Office* (n 28) paras 1.21 and 8.2.

[36] Or, indeed, by one's conduct to show oneself open to improper influence. See the recent decision of the Hong Kong judiciary in *HKSAR v Rafael Hui* (2017) http://legalref.judiciary.hk/lrs/common/ju/ju_frame.jsp?DIS=109907.

[37] Law Commission (2008).

[38] Bribery Act 2010, s 1(3) and s 2(3).

[39] ibid s 1(2) and s 2(2).

[40] http://www.bbc.co.uk/news/world-asia-37971085.

might be 'seriously' improper. Otherwise, how are public officials to know which of their many actions intended to benefit others fall, in principle, within the scope of wrongdoing (that may be adjudged serious)?

To address this problem, in some jurisdictions the 'intention to benefit another' criterion is supplemented by a requirement for proof of dishonesty. For example, under section 142.2(1) of the Australian Criminal Code Act 1995, abuse of public office is committed when:

> (1) A Commonwealth public official is guilty of an offence if:
> (a) the official:
> (i) exercises any influence that the official has in the official's capacity as a Commonwealth public official; or
> (ii) engages in any conduct in the exercise of the official's duties as a Commonwealth public official; or
> (iii) uses any information that the official has obtained in the official's capacity as a Commonwealth public official; and
> (b) the official does so with the intention of:
> (i) *dishonestly* obtaining a benefit for himself or herself or for another person; or
> (ii) *dishonestly* causing a detriment to another person (my emphasis).

What difference does the addition of the requirement to prove 'dishonesty' make to the nature and scope of the misconduct offence as defined above? It certainly provides a basis, lacking in the Law Commission's proposals, for distinguishing between proper and improper instances of benefiting others, in one's capacity as a public servant.[41] However, in this instance, the inclusion of dishonesty as a fault requirement can only forge the important distinctions in an incomplete way, without an additional focus on the conduct element. Accordingly, the provision remains coy about the kinds of actions benefiting others in which it is improper for officials to engage.

A better alternative is to identify at least some of the 'other' people respecting whom acting on an intention to benefit constitutes a wrong in itself: where the nature of the official's purpose changes his or her normative position, making the act itself improper. Consider, for example, the treatment of 'politically exposed persons' (PEPs) by the Financial Action Task Force (FATF).[42] PEPs are people performing prominent public functions.[43] FATF expects appropriate risk-management procedures to be in place to ensure that countries do not facilitate the laundering of the proceeds of crime by such people.[44] So far as FATF is concerned, these risk-management procedures must be in place to prevent not only laundering on behalf of a PEP him or herself, but also on behalf of:

[41] In that regard, I will come back later to the use of dishonesty as a fault term in the misconduct offence.

[42] Financial Action Task Force (2013).

[43] See the definition in the Money Laundering Regulations 2007, Sch 2, s 4.

[44] Financial Action Task Force (n 42) para 4.

Family members [who] are individuals related to a PEP either directly (consanguinity) or through marriage or similar (civil) forms of partnership.

Close associates [who] are individuals closely connected to a PEP, either socially or professionally.[45]

Where a PEP employs public funds in order to benefit a family member or close associate, that act may *in itself* constitute a kind of misconduct, just as if the PEP had used the funds to benefit him or herself. In a similar vein, the 8th and 9th amendments to the Chinese Criminal Code (respectively, enacted in 2009 and 2015) together made it an offence (a) to give a bribe to state functionaries, to close relatives or other persons closely related to them, or to former state functionaries, their close relatives, or other persons closely related to them, and (b) for such persons to receive a bribe.[46]

The Independent Parliamentary Standards Authority (IPSA) now operates with an analogous category of 'connected persons', in setting out restrictions on MPs' expenditure. Noticeably, by way of contrast with the definitions just given, it extends the definition to connections through corporate activity:

For the purposes of this Scheme, a connected party is defined as: (a) a spouse, civil partner or cohabiting partner of the MP; (b) parent, child, grandparent, grandchild, sibling, uncle, aunt, nephew or niece of the MP or of a spouse, civil partner or cohabiting partner of the MP; or (c) a body corporate, a firm or a trust with which the MP is connected, as defined in section 252 of the Companies Act 2006.[47]

There was a need, in the Law Commission's proposals, to tie the notion of 'benefit to another' to clearer categories of cases to be covered by the offence, and the use of these examples would have assisted to that end.

However, it is clear that 'benefit to another' cannot be confined to the kinds of cases just mentioned. It might, for example, be equally improper for a minister to use his or her position to benefit a powerful or important constituent. How, then, can further light be shed on the notion of benefit—or influence—such that we will have a basis for identifying impropriety in the conferral of the benefit or in the use of the influence? As indicated at the end of section 4.1, a key point is that corruption is linked not simply with 'benefits' conferred through the occupation of public office or through the use of public power, but with benefits *improperly* thereby conferred.[48] A chancellor of the exchequer might decide to lower income tax rates for those earning more than £50,000 a year. As he or she is numbered amongst such people, the chancellor must be intending to benefit him or herself—as a member of the relevant group—through this use of public office and power. Clearly, however, the decision is not corrupt. That is because—or so we may assume—the Chancellor's purpose is to confer on the group (which includes him or herself) a benefit furthering the public interest: a public benefit. The Chancellor does not improperly adopt the

[45] ibid para 11. [46] For analysis see Covington & Burling (2015).

[47] Independent Parliamentary Standards Authority, *The Scheme of MPs' Business Costs and Expenses 2017–18* (2017b), at para 3.19.

[48] See generally Transparency International, 'What is Corruption?' (n 20).

policy because of its personal value to him or her, to use the terminology introduced in section 4.1. That is the key to understanding why the decision is not corrupt, even if it is regarded by the Chancellor's opponents as misguided, as a matter of public policy. The importance to a corruption analysis of acting in the public interest is addressed further in Chapter 5.2.

However, as indicated in section 4.1, even when a public official purports to act in the public interest, their conduct may still be corrupt for procedural rather than for substantive reasons. This point can be illustrated using the example of influence. It is fully within the remit of public officials—indeed, it is frequently central to their function—to seek to influence other people (and to be influenced by them), as well as to benefit them. What makes the role of influence exercised on or by a public official improper? There are at least two kinds of case. First, influence might be simply undemocratic, or (in societies that are not democratic) in some other way contrary to the political processes that ought to be followed in a particular society, rather than corrupt. Consider an example in which the UK prime minister is found to have relied, when taking a key decision, solely on the merits of advice given to her by the Queen. That might open the prime minister (as well as the Queen) to criticism, because the prime minister's actions undermine what is supposed to be the democratic basis for decision-making. Even so, although it is undemocratic (and hence improper in that sense), without more, the action does not seem to be corrupt (and hence improper in that sense): the decision was one purportedly made on the merits. To move to the second kind of case, such an action would in addition be more likely to be regarded as corrupt, in the UK context, if the prime minister were found to have relied on the Queen's advice not because the advice was considered to have merit, but simply because (right or wrong) it was the Queen's advice. Such a surrender of political judgement to the Monarch is, of course, undemocratic. Beyond that, however, such a surrender of judgement—unrelated to the merits of the issue—lacks political integrity, and hence should be regarded in the UK context as corrupt. This example does illustrate, however, that there is almost inevitably a good deal of intuitive judgment at work—shaped by one's political and cultural assumptions—in deciding what counts as (political) 'corruption'. We will come back to the issue of influence in section 4.5 and Chapter 5.11, when discussing the practice of 'lobbying'.

The corruption-focused version of the misconduct thus needed to be extended to cover an intention on the part of a public official to influence others improperly, and intending to be or being influenced improperly. One significant advantage of leaving the definition of misconduct in office as it is—an argument made in Chapter 2—is that such cases are in theory already covered by the offence. Although section 142.2 of the Australian Criminal Code Act 1995 (cited above) addresses the case of influence, it does so only in order to cover instances in which D uses his or her influence dishonestly to secure a benefit for another; but this is too narrow. It can be improper—a misuse of office—to exercise influence, or to allow oneself to be influenced, irrespective of whether there is also an intention to benefit thereby. The role of dishonesty in the misconduct offence is further considered below.

Finally, we should note an important gap in the Law Commission's proposed definition, albeit a gap deliberately created. The gap concerns instances in which D does not have the bringing about of a benefit (or detriment) as his or her purpose, but is nonetheless aware that he or she will or might by his or her action or omission (wrongfully) obtain a benefit or detriment. Here is an example illustrating the potential significance of confining the corruption species of misconduct to gaining benefits purposively:

D is a prison doctor who is (as he knows) a beneficiary under V's will. V is a prisoner with an incurable and excruciatingly painful illness. With V's consent, D administers a pain-killing treatment for V that will incidentally have the effect of shortening V's life. The treatment alleviates V's pain, but also shortens V's life, with the result that D inherits under V's will earlier than might otherwise have been the case.

In this example, D (*ex hypothesi*, someone performing a public function) will not be guilty of misconduct under the Law Commission's 'purposive' approach to the obtaining of advantages. This is because D did not intend his action to result in a personal benefit, even though he knew it would. This holds true, even if there were—as D should have known—treatments available that would have alleviated V's pain without shortening his life, making D's conduct unjustified. Doing something wholly unwarranted, knowing full well—but without having this as one's purpose—that the action will confer a benefit on oneself, does not fall within the scope of the Law Commission's revised offence. That is an important omission, even if in some cases it is possible that a jury might infer purpose from D's knowledge and the nature of his or her conduct. The omission stems from the decision to abandon a focus on 'abuse' of one's position or powers as the essence of misconduct, a decision criticized in Chapter 2. Perhaps, in the example just given, D's conduct is not all that serious, as an example of misconduct, in virtue of lacking a purposive intent to act corruptly; but it was argued in Chapter 2 that it is wrong to exclude cases from the scope of the offence purely on the grounds of lack of seriousness.

The example just given might seem far-fetched; but the issue it raises—'indirect corruption'—is highly significant in political contexts. The potential for indirect corruption arises when someone in business enters politics knowing that this is likely to enhance their private business (or the business of a friend or relative) in some way: 'revolving in'.[49] It also arises in some cases of 'revolving out': when someone already in politics agrees to become involved in a private business concern, knowing that this will or might—but not necessarily intending to—improve their finances.[50] More broadly, by confining the corruption-focused offence to cases involving a purposeful gain (or causing of detriment), a much broader swath of wrongful acts in political contexts are excluded from the scope of the offence. An important example arises when someone in politics falsely claims not to have a conflict of interest. These kinds of example, connected to the rise of close associations between politics and

[49] See section 4.1.

[50] Naturally, most cases of revolving out do involve an intention to secure a financial benefit. We consider revolving out in greater detail later in this chapter.

corporate activity, are discussed in ensuing sections of this chapter. For, it may be a disputed matter whether all such examples involve 'corruption'.

We must now turn our attention to an important historical shift in the way that the highest officers of state tended to commit misconduct, through corrupt acts. In broad terms, the dramatic rise of corporate activity during the nineteenth century, following a sharp fall in the income directly at the disposal of the state following the end of the Napoleonic wars, entailed a change in the way that politics provided a path to personal enrichment. Increasingly, that path involved links between the political and the commercial world, links that continue to pose ethical problems in politics today. I will begin in section 4.3 with a discussion of the use of office in a direct and purposive way (to employ the Law Commission's favoured approach) to secure enrichment, before moving to the more complex issues raised by indirect corruption and conflicts of interest in later sections.

4.3 MPs Increasing their Private Resources: Eighteenth-Century Lessons

> The sudden and great rise in stocks has made me richer than I ever intended or desired to be ... I have, as Paymaster, great sums in my hands which, not applicable to any present use, must either lie dead in the Bank or employed by me ... I sell out and gain greatly.[51]

There is a long tradition in the UK of regarding the holding of public office as either or both of an opportunity to increase one's own wealth, prestige, or influence, and a chance to further the careers of one's relatives. In the eighteenth century, having attained high office, the former was commonly achieved—as Lord Holland indicates in the passage just cited, unashamedly discussing his own case—through the use of largely unfettered discretion to employ public money to increase personal gain. There was a 36-fold increase in the state's revenue during the eighteenth century, to meet the cost of wars and service the ballooning national debt.[52] This meant that the state was sopping up some 24 per cent of gross national product (GNP) by 1815, providing ample opportunities for unchecked and conspicuous consumption by the unscrupulous office-holders into whose hands it came,[53] the consequences of which still reverberate today.[54] It is instructive to consider the detail

[51] Henry Fox (1902), 72. Lord Holland is referring to the eighteenth-century custom of investing public money in order to make personal profit, when the money was not immediately required for public purposes.

[52] W J Ashworth (2004).

[53] Indeed, for some scholars, the personal profligacy of high office holders at this time was what necessitated the imposition of taxation on the colonies to meet the costs of war, a viciously circular policy that led to further rebellion and additional wars: Victor L Johnson (1954).

[54] The wealth accumulated by one Paymaster General of the forces, Richard Rigby (in office from 1768 to 1782) ultimately paid for the Pitt-Rivers museum in Oxford in 1884. One property investment made by another Paymaster, Lord Holland (in office, 1757–65), using the proceeds of office, was in an estate now known as the Holland Park area of London, significant parts of which are still owned and managed by the related Ilchester family: http://www.waellis.com/Ilchester-Estates.

of such consumption by one such office-holder, the aforesaid Lord Holland, whose accounts were the subject matter of the swindle that led to the landmark prosecution of Charles Bembridge for misconduct.[55]

Lord Holland was a leading politician identified with the Whigs, who had been Secretary for War, a Lord of the Treasury and Leader of the House of Commons, and was thought by some to be prime minister material. A protégé of Sir Robert Walpole, he started adult life in traditional fashion, quickly squandering his share of his father's fortune and fleeing to Paris to escape his creditors. Becoming friends there with a wealthy woman who became his patron, he was able to return to England. In 1744, he eloped with and married a much younger woman, the daughter of the 2nd Duke of Richmond (one of the purposes of Lord Hardwicke's Marriage Act of 1753 was to prevent such runaway marriages). Holland had briefly tasted power when the Duke of Newcastle, as prime minister, entered into an alliance with him in 1755, but their government fell. When Newcastle entered into an alliance with Pitt in 1757, Holland accepted the position of Paymaster-General of the Forces. The benefits of office allowed Holland to go on a veritable spending spree. In their analysis of his accounts, Sutherland and Binney found expenditure (listed as sundries or extras) on shares in turnpikes, on a privateer, and on an Indiaman called—inevitably—the *Lord Holland*.[56] Holland also not so much dabbled as made a splash in the stock market. In 1761 and 1762, he spent some £1,000,000 of public money on subscriptions to government loans, including perpetual stock, long annuities, lottery tickets, and other stock market purchases. Such subscriptions might be purchased in a public-spirited way, to assist the government in financing the war effort; but by the end of 1761 (probably as a result of insider trading), Holland had sold most of the property in the loans.[57] Lord Holland also made private loans of public money to members of his family, or to friends (including £500, concerning an East India speculation, to William and Edmund Burke in 1766), sometimes concealing the nature of the loan by the use of a family member as nominee.[58]

Like any self-respecting MP then, or in the late twentieth century,[59] Lord Holland invested considerable sums of public money in acquiring real estate. He gave his name to Holland House, formally known as Cope Castle—and hence to Holland Park (the house came with 200 acres of land)—in London. Lord Holland bought the estate in 1768 for £17,000 (using some £4,000 of Pay Office funds) with some of the profits earned as Paymaster-General, although he had been living there as a lessee since 1746.[60] In total, his spending of public money on real estate rose to £193,000. That sum included the use of some £14,615 to buy a house for himself on the north-east coast of Kent that, after Holland's death, his son

[55] For a full discussion see Jeremy Horder, '*R v Bembridge* (1783)' (2017).

[56] Lucy Sutherland and J Binney (1955), at 244.

[57] ibid 244. The authors give much more detail of Holland's extensive dealings in the market, at 247–49.

[58] ibid 241.

[59] The power that MPs granted themselves to purchase property through the use of tax payer-funded mortgages lasted from 1985–2010: see Sir Thomas Legg (2010), at paras 16–17.

[60] Lord Holland died there in 1774.

Charles James was forced to sell (to none other than the Pay Office cashier, one John Powell).[61] Holland lived well, spending some £6,000 per annum from 1758 under the heading of 'housekeeping', and no less than £20,620 on expenses incurred when travelling in France between 1763 and 1765.[62] He commissioned pictures of himself from Hogarth and Ramsey, at twenty guineas each.[63] He paid another £341 to Reynolds for paintings in 1765, making appear positively modest the modern sum of £85.35 that disgraced Liberal Democrat MP Chris Huhne paid with public money for the mounting and framing of, and inscription on, a photograph of himself for his constituency office.[64] Holland spent £2,600 to ensure that his son, Stephen, was elected to Parliament for New Sarum, and another £3,000 to see the more famous son, Charles James, elected as MP for Midhurst. Further, and finally, he spent as much as £185,718 from public balances on debts incurred by these two sons, mostly due to gambling.[65] We should note that Lord Holland was not exceptional, in his free-spending habits. One of his successors, the notorious Richard Rigby,[66] was a reckless spendthrift.[67] In 1784, the Attorney-General went so far as to call on him to return a very substantial balance of public money still in his hands, after he had demitted office as Paymaster in 1782. Even so, by 1791, three years after his death, the balance owing was still £150,000: tens of millions in modern-day money.[68]

The other common form of eighteenth-century corruption—similarly revived in the late twentieth century—involved nepotism, which was commonly achieved in different ways. For example, the use of rotten boroughs ensured that nearly 20 per cent of MPs were the sons of peers by the end of that century.[69] Hans Stanley MP's advice to new MPs was:

> Get into Parliament, make tiresome speeches; you will have great offers; do not accept them at first, then do: then make great provision for yourself and family, and then call yourself an independent country gentleman.[70]

[61] Sutherland and Binney (n 56) 249. Powell was originally charged with misconduct in a public office, alongside Charles Bembridge, but Powell committed suicide before the trial: see Horder, '*R v Bembridge* (1783)' (n 55) 85.

[62] Sutherland and Binney (n 56) 249–50.

[63] ibid 250.

[64] http://www.telegraph.co.uk/news/newstopics/mps-expenses/5314093/Chris-Huhne-a-multi-millionaire-but-you-buy-his-chocolate-HobNobs-MPs-expenses.html.

[65] It has been remarked of Charles James that: 'He once gambled from Tuesday night until Friday with no sleep, taking time off one evening to debate in the House of Commons. He played hazard from Tuesday evening until five Wednesday evening, covering £12,000 he had lost, but losing that and £11,000 more before going to Parliament': Cheryl Bolen (2006).

[66] Mortal enemy of Edmund Burke, as well as co-witness for the defence, along with Burke, at Bembridge's trial: see Horder, '*R v Bembridge* (1783)' (n 55).

[67] F P Lock (2008), at 508. When Edmund Burke succeeded Rigby as Paymaster-General of the Forces, he found the kitchens in the Pay Office in Whitehall far too large for his more modest needs. There were, moreover, no bookshelves: *Morning Herald* (20 April 1782).

[68] http://www.historyofparliamentonline.org/volume/1754-1790/member/rigby-richard-1722-88. Sir George Trevelyan wrote of Rigby that his only virtue was that 'drank fair': see the discussion in Sir GO Trevelyan (1880), at ch 3. That seems a harsh judgement: at least, it was said of Rigby by his son that 'by his gallantry and attention, he made a tender impression upon some of the proudest female hearts in either Great Britain or Ireland': Richard Rigby (1788), at 23.

[69] John Brooke (1964), at 148.

[70] Cited by Jesse Norman (2013), at 52.

Another outlet for nepotism came through the power to appoint relatives to posts, an example being appointment as a salaried deputy working alongside what we would now call 'civil servants'.[71] When he was prime minister, Lord North secured the appointment of his half-brother as Dean of Canterbury at the age of 29, as Bishop of Lichfield at the age of 30, and as Bishop of Winchester, aged 40.[72] Edmund Burke, perhaps the most famous anti-corruption campaigner in English political history, was himself an indulger in the opportunities for nepotism afforded by appointment to high office. For a few months in 1782, and then again in 1783–84, he had (like Lord Holland and Richard Rigby) been appointed Paymaster General of the Forces, probably the most lucrative Crown sinecure at that time, in a hotly competitive field for that title. About his appointment, he said:

> It [fell] ... to my lot to do something for what I considered as the improvement and reformation of that office – the principal fault of which I considered to be, that it had been rather like a private office of account, than a public administration.[73]

Even so, this high-minded commitment to reform did not prevent Burke from using his own appointment as Paymaster to appoint his son as a Deputy Paymaster in London on £500 per year, his cousin Will to a new post of Deputy Paymaster in India (£5 per day), or from using his influence to secure for his brother a position as Secretary to the Treasury at £3,000 per year.[74] He met the inevitable allegations of hypocrisy by narrowing the scope of the moral high ground: his was a constitutional objection to the 'secret influence' of the Crown in making appointments,[75] and not to the more general use of office as a source of powers of patronage to advance the careers of favourites.[76]

That argument was controversial, even then. At his trial for misconduct in office (the sale of offices in Chancery) in 1725, Lord Macclesfield had argued that:

> The Publick is concerned only in the Goodness of the Officer, not how advantageous to him the Grant of the Office is, nor in the Inducement to which he that appointed him had to put him in: whether Friendship, Acquaintance, Relation, Importunity, great Recommendation or a Present.[77]

This claim was rejected, Macclesfield was found guilty, and fined the enormous sum of £40,000 (which he nonetheless paid off within six weeks[78]). Even so, the modern UK Parliament has inexcusably resurrected Lord Macclesfield's argument, as a force

[71] See Horder, '*R v Bembridge* (1783)' (n 55) 88. [72] Roy Porter (1991), at 59.

[73] Said as part of his evidence as a character witness at the trial for misconduct in public office of his accountant in the Pay Office, Charles Bembridge: *R v Bembridge* (1783) XXII State Trials 1, 66. Coming back into office as Paymaster in 1783, Burke had rashly expressed his confidence in the fraudster Bembridge's abilities as office accountant, only to be seriously embarrassed (in the House of Commons itself) shortly thereafter by the latter's conviction for misconduct. He subsequently described Bembridge as a 'wild, precipitate senseless and ... desperate wretch': see Lock (n 67) 5.

[74] Lock (n 67) 508–509; Horder, '*R v Bembridge* (1783)' (n 55) 99.

[75] Influence described by no lesser figure than Sir William Blackstone as 'most amazingly extensive': Sir William Blackstone (1765), bk 1, at 336.

[76] See the discussion in Lock (n 67) 509.

[77] William Cobbett (1803), vol xvi, at 1274, cited by Mark Knights (2016), at 11.

[78] See Roy Porter (1991), at 59. Porter gives the fine as £30,000.

to be reckoned with. Parliamentarians decided, in the late twentieth century, that they should be able to use public money to employ staff to assist them with Parliamentary duties, and that there should be no barriers to the employment of their own relatives as staff members for this purpose. The matter is considered in section 4.7.

In that regard, a final lesson from eighteenth-century practice concerns the temptation to engage in corruption created by the opportunity to augment one's salary through additional fees and expense claims. The claim sometimes made that 'generous' use of expenses allowances by modern MPs justifiably compensates for the allegedly low salaries they receive had its own analogy in the eighteenth century. Salaries payable to office-holders at that time were sometimes still at levels set in medieval times. Accordingly, far more important to an office-holder's income were the opportunities office-holding presented to make money through fees, gratuities, poundages, and a luxuriant variety of other official prerequisites.[79] Part of the background to the case of *Bembridge*[80] is that Bembridge himself was able to augment his annual salary of £150 many times over, as an accountant in the pay office of the Paymaster-General of the Forces, by charging fees for making good the accounts of former paymasters. For example, following his conviction, he (inter alia) was fined £2,600, this being the sum he had received for making up (in more than one sense of that phrase) Lord Holland's accounts. Of this system of discretionary perks, Willes J sententiously remarked, in relation to Bembridge's milking of the system:

> I cannot help lamenting the unhappy state of this country, that in these times of necessity and public distress, the passing the accounts [sic] of a paymaster should cost the state, in fees paid to its officers, the enormous sum of £14,900, as appears by the warrant read. The right to these extravagant fees ought to be, and I hope will be hereafter, a subject of parliamentary enquiry.[81]

Unsurprisingly, when the Accounts Commissioners came to review the system towards the end of the eighteenth century, they recommended that:

> [I]n place of all these . . . Fees, and Gratuities, there should be substituted and annexed to each of these offices, of whatever Rank and Denomination, one certain Salary . . . [which] should be an ample Compensation for the Service required; and the Quantum estimated by the various Qualifications and Circumstances necessary for the Execution, and which together form the Title to Reward.[82]

The recommendation still has resonance today, especially when we come on to consider the 2009 MPs' expenses scandal in section 4.7. It is in effect a recommendation for a shift away from the reliance on discretion in the setting of kinds and levels of remuneration (a system vulnerable to corruption), to a system of fixed benefits less easily undermined by corrupt influence.

In the case of MPs, the shift from the one system to the other was not properly settled for well over 200 years. In setting, on a discretionary basis, their own salaries

[79] These additional benefits 'were, therefore, cultivated assiduously in almost every government department': John R Breihan (1984), at 60.

[80] *R v Bembridge* (1783) 3 Doug 327; (1783) XXII State Trials 1.

[81] ibid. [82] Commissioners of Public Accounts (1780–82), at 712–14.

and the growing list of 'gratuities' (benefits) that went with their salary, MPs were largely exempt from the application of the criminal law of corruption.[83] The only thing preventing the emergence of a much more significant disconnect between the public commitment to clean government, and the private financial practices of MPs, were internal customs relying for their force on 'personal honour and group pressure'.[84] Yet, the potency of such rules was never tested, due to the emergence of a parliamentary myth of the incorruptibility of MPs. No longer able, unlike their eighteenth-century predecessors, openly to admit to favouritism and profiteering from their position, UK politicians created the self-serving myth of selfless devotion to public service, right up to and during the 2009 expenses scandal. As late as July 2008, the Leader of the House, Harriet Harman, was still responding to allegations of abuse of expense allowances by saying:

> [T]he overwhelming majority of hon Members carry out their duties with probity, energy, dedication and commitment, the media reporting that includes expenditure on the salaries of our staff and on our office costs and which says that they are part of our salary is misleading and often malicious.[85]

Notoriously, in January 2009, Harman—a former legal officer at the National Council for Civil Liberties—had sought to exempt MPs' expenses from disclosure under the Freedom of Information Act 2000.[86] Her complaint in this passage that the media were confusing office salaries and costs with an MP's salary is, of course, completely disingenuous but very revealing. The problem has always been understood to be the abuse of a virtually unchallengeable discretion to increase not only salaries but in particular office costs (fees and gratuities). The problem has never been a technical confusion on the media's part resulting in a failure to distinguish expenses and salaries. We consider the direct corruption involved in MPs' use of expenses in section 4.7.

4.4 MPs Increasing their Private Resources: Nineteenth-Century Lessons

The much-vaunted cleaning up of politics during the Victorian period, following the great reform of 1832, probably had a good deal to do with the simple fact that, after 1815, the 24 per cent figure for gross domestic product (GDP) absorbed by

[83] Alan Doig (2006), at 3. [84] ibid.

[85] Hansard (3 July 2008), col 1066. A similar view about the virtue of almost all MPs was expressed by a number of Parliamentarians at the time, along with more express threats to use legal action to close down media interest in the affair: see Martin Gainsborough (2011), at 23.

[86] Hansard (22 January 2009) col 900. See also Hansard (3 July 2008) col 1105: 'I can tell the House that the Government intend to introduce a statutory instrument under section 7(3) of the Freedom of Information Act, which will exclude Members' addresses or any material that could lead to the identification of Members address'. In December 2010, it became public knowledge that Harman was one of the MPs who secretly paid back expenses wrongly claimed between 2008 and 2009: *Daily Telegraph* (9 December 2010). In November 2010, Harman's parliamentary private secretary, Ian Lavery, had blocked a motion that would have put the repayments in the public domain.

government expenditure on wars in the eighteenth century had dwindled to 12 per cent by 1830, and to a mere 6 per cent by 1870. So, the opportunities for truly large-scale plundering—political 'asset stripping'[87]—were severely diminished.[88] In consequence, the nature and manifestation of personal corruption changed. Big spending abuses by Crown appointees ('bedchamber janissaries'[89]) disappeared, so that the focus became the financial gains made possible by ethically problematic associations between political and corporate activity. Before looking at this in more detail, it would be helpful to consider how the insufficiently regulated relationship between corporate power and political power or influence led to one of the most notorious English political scandals, not long after the end of the Victorian period now under discussion, the Marconi scandal of 1912.[90]

Care must be taken in assessing the true significance of this scandal, as there is no doubt that the controversy was in part whipped up by the political right wing, to demonstrate—as they saw it—the unfitness of Liberal Party arrivistes to govern.[91] Even so, the events are instructive. The government had agreed in 1911 to set up a chain of wireless stations throughout the empire. The Marconi Wireless Telegraph Company was chosen by the Postmaster General to undertake the building of 6 out of 18 such stations. The Postmaster General, Herbert Samuel, was a close friend of the company's managing director, Godfrey Issacs, who was the brother of Attorney General, Sir Rufus Issacs. Although the existence of the contract was not made public at the time, Marconi's shares rose from over £2 to £9 between August 1911 and March 1912.[92] Whilst the shares were still valued at £2, Sir Rufus Issacs bought 10,000 shares in Marconi and sold some to other ministers, including Lloyd George (the chancellor of the exchequer), and Liberal chief whip Lord Murray. In spite of this admission of direct profiteering from government policy, the appearance of allegations to that effect in French newspaper, *Le Matin*, during February 1912, led to a libel action against the paper taken by Sir Rufus Issacs and Herbert Samuel. This resulted in the paper withdrawing its allegation and apologising. Although Issacs admitted buying shares in Marconi at the trial, it was not publicly disclosed that the shares had been made available to him at a low price by his brother, the Marconi managing director. A charge of criminal libel was also pursued by Godfrey Issacs over similar allegations made in the British press by Cecil Chesterton. Chesterton was fined £100 on conviction, but continued to print the allegations against ministers, who chose not to sue.[93]

The Parliamentary Select Committee looking into the matter in early 1913 divided in its conclusions along party lines. Opposition members judged that the ministers

[87] Roy Porter (1991), at 61: 'The state at their disposal, grandees pioneered the art of political asset-stripping'.

[88] See the discussion in Paul Seaward (2010).

[89] Charles James Fox's memorable phrase: Commons debate on the influence of the Crown (1783), in William Cobbett (n 77) vol xxiv 197–225.

[90] The following account is taken from W J Baker (1998).

[91] See Seaward (n 88) 46.

[92] The decision was eventually made public in April 1912.

[93] It should be noted that Lord Birkenhead, who had acted for the prosecution in the libel case, considered Chesterton to have been in part motivated by anti-Semitism: Lord Birkenhead (1926), at 274.

involved had acted with 'grave impropriety', but Liberal members of the Committee cleared ministers of all wrongdoing. This 'whitewash' came in spite of the admissions that shares had been purchased in Marconi by Sir Rufus Isaacs, Herbert Samuel, and David Lloyd George, and the fact that Lord Murray (who subsequently disappeared to Bogotá) had purchased additional shares for the Liberal Party itself.[94] *The Times*, in its leading article of 19 June 1913, said of the scandal:

> A man is not blamed for being splashed with mud. He is commiserated. But if he has stepped into a puddle which he might easily have avoided, we say that it is his own fault. If he protests that he did not know it was a puddle, we say that he ought to know better; but if he says that it was after all quite a clear puddle, then we judge him deficient in the sense of cleanliness.

Perhaps predictably, the scandal did not lead to legal changes in the obligations of ministers or MPs concerning the probity of their earnings. However, G K Chesterton, at least, was clear in his own mind that the scandal exposed by his brother had undermined ordinary people's trust in the honour of MPs:

> I believe it is almost ... essential to divide [recent history] into the Pre-Marconi and the Post-Marconi days. It was during the agitations upon that affair that the ordinary English citizen lost his invincible ignorance; or, in ordinary language, his innocence ... it [the scandal] will be seen as one of the turning-points in the whole history of England and the world.[95]

To understand why Chesterton takes this view, we need to consider the rising political significance of corporate activity in the nineteenth century, and (albeit, perhaps, with the benefit of hindsight) the failure on the part of Parliament—still relevant today—to do enough to ensure that this development did not have a corrupting influence on politics.

In very broad terms, the Victorian period saw a struggle—albeit one not always articulated as such—between two rival conceptions of civic virtue, and hence of the locus of corruption. On the one hand, there was an older idea that only the landed gentry, secure in both their income and their place within the ruling elite, could reliably and disinterestedly devote themselves to the public good. This elite brand of 'republicanism', if such it can truly be called, had for a century or longer involved looking down on the political aspirations of the nouveau riche, on the basis that these aspirations involved the corruption of politics through the influence of 'the monied interest'.[96] On this view, social mobility is itself a potentially corrupting force in society and politics.[97] On the other hand, the rise of men of industry and finance brought to prominence a new perspective on corruption, one that turned the tables on the old elite. This new, Protestant work ethic perspective 'depicts a polity of idle leisured men of privilege triumphing over a policy of equal opportunity where industrious hard-working men ...... are rewarded according to merit'.[98] The

[94] See Baker (n 90) 146.
[95] G K Chesterton (1943), at 205–206; see also Harris (n 95) 113–15.
[96] Henry St John, Viscount Bolingbroke (1794), at 165, cited by Shelley Burtt (2004), at 108.
[97] Burtt (n 96) 112.
[98] Isaac Kramnick (1994), at 59.

picture was muddied by economic cooperation between landed elites and parvenus, but the contrast is nonetheless a helpful one to keep in mind.

The rule that an MP should withdraw from debate in Parliament when he or she has a direct financial interest in the outcome is one of long standing.[99] The foundation of modern practice is a ruling by Gladstone in 1892 to the effect that the questions to be asked are:

> Is the benefit conferred by the Vote concentrated on the persons themselves, or some combination of persons, or is it diffused over a very wide field? Second, is it a direct or an indirect benefit?[100]

The questions were of some importance. In 1895, twenty-four members of the Conservative administration held between them some sixty directorships and trusteeships of private companies.[101] At that time, moreover, twenty MPs and three peers served on the Council of the London Chamber of Commerce.[102] By 1900, of the 586 peers, 435 were directors of companies.[103] By 1905, the directorships held by ministers in public companies had risen to 71.[104] On 18 April 1896, the *Economist* had critically observed:

> Notoriously, men are often placed upon boards of directors simply and solely because they are Members of Parliament, and are, therefore, believed to be able to exercise a useful influence. It would be well if the constituencies would take the matter up and let their Members understand that they do not confer the honour of membership of Parliament merely in order to raise a man's value in the guinea-pig market.[105]

Criticized here is what I have been referring to as the practice of revolving out, to which the rise of economically and politically powerful companies gave rise: a subject to which we will return. Of equal significance at that time was the developing practice of 'revolving in' at parliamentary level, whereby new would-be plutocrats (industrial barons, retailers, newspaper proprietors, financiers) such as Lever, Lipton, and Harmsworth entered politics.[106] Such people were increasing in numbers (especially in the Conservative Party).[107] By 1886, the aristocratic and landed class had fallen to 37 per cent of MPs, with business people up to 32 per cent (from 15% in 1859).[108] Indeed, businessmen constituted 46 per cent of MPs in the post-1832 new urban and industrial boroughs.[109]

There were tangible benefits not only for the individual but for the company in such developments. For 'new tech' firms, the election to Parliament of a director led on average to a 2–2.4 per cent increase in the firm's share price.[110] These

[99] See the discussion in D C M Platt (1961), at 269–70, discussing early seventeenth century precedents.
[100] 2 Parl Deb 4s 655 (1892). [101] Platt (n 99) 274.
[102] ibid 275. [103] ibid 274. [104] 144 Parl Deb 4s 148.
[105] *Economist* (18 April 1896) 481, cited by Platt (n 99) 276.
[106] See, for some examples, Paul Johnson (2010), at 10–11.
[107] Angus Hawkins (2015), at 362: 'During the 1880s and 1890s, business "interests", banking, shipbuilding, the railways, and manufacturing became well represented within the Conservative Party'.
[108] T A Jenkins (1996), at 104. [109] ibid.
[110] See the discussion in Fabio Braggion and Lyndon Moore (2013).

developments took place, of course, against a background of growing recognition of the significance of company activity in England. In 1856, there were about 700 companies in existence; by 1914, this had risen to 58,900.[111] In an associated development, the number of Englishmen leaving over £500,000 at death rose from seventy-four between 1809 and 1858 to 246 between 1880 and 1899, mainly owing to the increasing number of fortunes made in commerce and finance.[112] Whereas, before 1885, few people 'in trade' could expect to receive some kind of honour in recognition of their work, Lord Salisbury gave 23 per cent of his honours to business people, a trend increased under Arthur Balfour, at a time when party finances had begun to become an issue.[113] The trend did not pass without critical comment. The following remarks at the turn of the century are not untypical:

> We all know how insidious are the ways of corruption, how unconsciously motives of private gain may work upon virtuous resolves. Stringent, then, is the duty imposed upon men in office to live and move in a cleaner air far above the atmosphere of suspicion.[114]

One example of 'revolving in' is that of William Henry (WH) Smith, who entered Parliament in 1868, becoming First Lord of the Admiralty,[115] Secretary of State for War and Leader of the Commons. Dynastic examples include the Barings and Rothschild families,[116] and the Chamberlains. Joseph Chamberlain (1836–1914) was the Colonial Secretary, and father of the better known Neville Chamberlain. Joseph's brother Arthur was chairman of Kynoch's, a firm awarded a contract by the government to supply cordite (after the firm had been permitted to revise its bid during the tendering process),[117] even though Kynoch's products were shown to be inferior to those of its rivals.[118] A letter of introduction used by Kynoch's representatives had contained the words: 'You will be interested to know that the chairman of the company is Mr Arthur Chamberlain, brother of the present Colonial Secretary'.[119] Joseph falsely claimed in the House of Commons that his family had no interest in a company supplying war goods, but also—an argument still familiar today—that such situations were inevitable if successful business people were to become involved in politics.[120] Some 50 per cent of cabinet ministers still held company directorships in 1900, at a time when some 30 per cent of MPs were company directors.[121] As Harris puts it, in relation to developments in the Victorian period:

> For much of the nineteenth century, maintaining a generally non-corrupt executive proved less challenging than reining in members of the legislature, many of whom had no hope of (or, often, desire for) office. Elite corruption continued to be a major theme of popular

[111] See the discussion in Geoffrey Todd (1932).
[112] See the discussion in W B Rubinstein (1977).
[113] Harris (n 95) 113. The issue of party finance is discussed in ch 5.
[114] F Hirst, G Murray, and J L Hammond (1900), at 115.
[115] His lack of naval experience was satirized through the figure of Sir Joseph Porter in Gilbert and Sullivan's *HMS Pinafore*.
[116] Amongst a number of others: see Rubinstein (n 112) 610.
[117] Harris (n 95) 111.
[118] Platt (n 99) 281.
[119] Cited by Platt (n 99) 282.
[120] ibid.
[121] Seaward (n 88) 46; Rubinstein (n 112) 621.

newspapers well into the latter half of the nineteenth century ... corruption was generally regarded as undesirable but unavoidable by-product of a generally legitimate system.[122]

Following the Liberal Party election victory of 1906, there was reform; but the particular focus—and even then, only a limited one—became the position of ministers, rather than that of MPs more generally. Prime Minister Henry Campbell-Bannerman told the House:

The condition which was laid down on the formation of the Government was that all directorships held by Ministers must be resigned except in the case of honorary directorships ... and directorships in private companies.[123]

By the early twentieth century, there was more of an expectation that public life would be 'clean'.[124] But how clean has it become? The parliamentary practice of declaring an interest became commonplace in the inter-war years.[125] The matter is now governed by Paragraph 13 of the MPs' Code of Conduct, which indicates that: 'Members shall fulfil conscientiously the requirements of the House in respect of the registration of interests in the Register of Members' Financial Interests'.[126] An 'interest' is a matter that 'someone might reasonably consider to influence their actions or words as an MP'.[127] In the case of ministers, the level of duty to disclose is somewhat wider: ministers must ensure that 'no conflict arises, or could reasonably be perceived to arise, between their Ministerial position and their private interests, financial or otherwise'.[128]

In the case of the Conservative Party, in particular, there has been a long-standing connection between backbench MPs and the corporate world. For example, during the 1955–59 Parliament, 163 out of 270 (60%) of backbench Conservative MPs were employed in business and, by 1961, some 295 out of 360 were so employed.[129] A 2015 study found that MPs and peers in England were directors in 2,465 companies enjoying combined revenues of nearly £220 billion. About 40 per cent of

[122] Harris (n 95) 110.

[123] 154 Parl Deb 4s 234–45 (20 March 1906). The exception for private companies sounds wide in scope, but from 1939 it was confined to family firms that were not engaged in any substantial amount of trading. For example, in 1952, Harold Macmillan was not permitted to retain his interest in Macmillan's, because of the size of its trading interests: Phillip Murphy (1995), at 92. Even so, Campbell-Bannerman's ruling failed to deal with shareholdings, investments, and other interests in Government contracts.

[124] Some evidence for which is the passage of the Sheriffs Act 1887, Public Bodies Corrupt Practices Act 1889, the Prevention of Corruption Act 1906, and the Prevention of Corruption Act 1916. See further Tim Lankester (2007).

[125] Report of the Select Committee on Members' Interests (Declaration), 1969–70, vol xiv, at 159.

[126] The Register was established on 22 May 1974: see the discussion by Richard Kelly and Matthew Hamlyn in Horne, Drewry, and Oliver (2013).

[127] www.parliament.uk/mps-lords-and-offices/standards-and-financial-interests/parliamentary-commissioner-for-standards/registers-of-interests/.

[128] www.gov.uk/government/uploads/system/uploads/attachment_data/file/486508/List_of_Ministers_Interests_Dec_2015.pdf.

[129] Murphy (n 123) 91. Murphy suggests that this did not lead to much direct influence exercised by companies on government, but it did predispose Conservative Party MPs to favour commercial interests more generally. Experience in the business world might also mean one was more likely to be favoured for certain ministerial posts.

these directorships were not fully declared.[130] In such cases of revolving out, we need to attend to the availability of legitimate reasons for acting. This takes us back to the discussion of indirect forms of corruption.

4.5 Corporate Interests and Conflicts of Interests

The UK is not a 'pure' republican state, in which politicians are expected to give up all outside sources of income, and any other sources of potential conflict of interest, in order to devote themselves solely to furthering the public interest. It would obviously be possible to create such a state. Indeed, as indicated in Chapter 1, the pure republican ideal informs the approach currently taken to the judiciary. The *Guide to Judicial Conduct* for judges in England and Wales makes this abundantly clear.[131]

However, the cost of pure republicanism in politics would be financially high, as it is in the case of the judiciary. In the case of MPs, this is because MPs would have to be compensated for the lack of guaranteed tenure, a tenure enjoyed—along with a significantly higher salary—by judges. It is also possible that to provide such rewards for MPs might turn out to be self-defeating. It might increase to unacceptable levels the numbers of those seeking to enter or to remain in politics simply because of the financial rewards involved. Additionally, so far as both revolving in and (to a lesser extent) revolving out are concerned, there is a long-standing belief that politics benefits from the involvement of those who maintain significant outside interests, including financial interests, and for whom politics is not their whole (professional) life.[132] What is important is that, when MPs are permitted to retain outside interests that may conflict with their duty to serve the public interest, it remains an obligation on them to act only on public (interest) reasons, in their capacity as public office holders: their 'primary obligation'. Controversial though this is, an MP is hence regarded as in some circumstances justified in becoming or remaining involved in an activity that may conflict with their primary obligation, even by becoming a lobbyist on behalf of a commercial organization.[133] This issue is considered further below (so far as the potential criminal liability of MPs is concerned), and in Chapter 5.11. Nonetheless, Parliament has sought to reduce the extent to which such conflicts are liable to reduce MPs' commitment to their primary obligation. As indicated above, it does this by requiring disclosure of such interests, when they are financial in nature.[134] This is an obligation liable to deter MPs from entering into remunerative arrangements that will attract critical scrutiny on the grounds of their impropriety,[135] as well as providing a means for holding to account those who

130 Martin Williams (2016), at ch 1.

131 *Guide to Judicial Conduct* (2013).

132 See eg the discussion in Murphy (n 123) 92–94, speaking of expertise gained by MPs about West Africa in the course of pursuing business interests.

133 See eg https://www.theguardian.com/politics/2017/jul/31/labour-mp-barry-sheerman-first-serving-politician-registered-lobbyist.

134 https://www.parliament.uk/mps-lords-and-offices/standards-and-financial-interests/parliamentary-commissioner-for-standards/registers-of-interests/register-of-members-financial-interests/.

135 I explore the theoretical basis of such 'Fullerian' obligations in ch 5.

do act in a way that leads them to bring a private interest into conflict with their primary obligation. What, then, should be the role of the criminal law in this context?

As we have seen, under the Law Commission's revised definition of the criminal offence of misconduct in corruption contexts, there is a special normative focus on the purpose with which someone acted: the purpose of obtaining a benefit or of causing someone to suffer a detriment. That focus excludes the possibility that someone could be guilty of misconduct simply in virtue of having failed to disclose, even knowingly, a conflict of interest, unless that failure was accompanied by a purpose of the relevant kind.[136] Naturally, anyone in office may mistakenly fail to avoid a conflict of interest, and that should not be a matter for the criminal law, even in the case where there is some negligence involved. However, to go back to the issue raised at the end of section 4.2, is it right to confine the scope of criminalization narrowly to cases in which someone actually has as his or her *purpose* the exploitation of a conflict of interest to their own or another's advantage? The foregoing discussion suggests that this confines the scope of the corruption offence too narrowly.

The Law Commission's argument was that the creation of an undeclared conflict of interest is not, in itself, a sufficient basis for criminalization unless: 'D engag[es] in further wrongful conduct as a result of that conflict of interest'.[137] However, the Commission does not seek to identify any further wrongs that might justify criminalization beyond purposefully benefiting or causing a detriment. Yet, at least two candidate-wrongs emerged in the course of the discussion in sections 4.3 and 4.4. First, there is dishonestly making statements known to be false or misleading in relation to a conflict of interest (the Kynoch case[138]), or in relation to any other significant obligation of trust under a code of conduct. With regard to someone in public office, or exercising a public power, this ought to be sufficient in principle to justify criminalization, even in the absence of proof a purpose of benefiting or causing detriment. Secondly, there is dishonest breach of the Ministerial Code, both in so far as the Code relates to the making of gains from outside interests (the Marconi case),[139] or in relation to other significant obligations of trust. In that regard, it is helpful to focus on revolving out.

The issue of revolving out is a significant one in UK politics. The argument that politics benefits from the involvement of those with specialist knowledge and interests outside politics does not apply to revolving out, with the same force as it does to revolving in. When an MP revolves out, it is commonly his or her political knowledge or prestige on which the outside organization seeks to draw. It is the organization that seeks to benefit, in terms of knowledge, with the MP commonly benefiting financially. The purpose of revolving out is not normally and primarily engaged in with the main purpose of increasing an MP's knowledge or interests, although that might be so in a case where an MP works (unpaid) for an organization with that purpose in mind. For that reason, controls and restrictions on revolving out

[136] Law Commission, *Reforming Misconduct in Public Office* (n 28) para 3.224.

[137] ibid para 3.215. [138] See section 4.4.

[139] ibid. Perhaps most cases falling into the latter category will in practice have involved a purpose on the officer-holder's part of making a gain. Even so, the misconduct offence should cover the wider case.

ought to be strong and comprehensive. Perhaps predictably, the controls exercised over revolving out have proved to be weak and ineffectual.

The Ministerial Code provides that ministers are prohibited from 'lobbying'[140] government, on behalf of any new employer, for two years.[141] It is well known that breaches of the rule are hard to uncover, and that the prohibition is ambiguous and difficult to enforce.[142] Ministers are also required to take advice on any appointment they might wish to take up, within two years of leaving government, from the Advisory Committee on Business Appointments (ACoBA), a body first set up to provide such advice in 1975.[143] The advice given by ACoBA is centred on a set of rules designed to ensure that (a) an appointment is not made in exchange for previous favours, (b) no improper advantage is gained by the minister's new employer from information the former minister may have on government policy or on the employer's competitors, and (c) there is no exploitation of former contacts within government possessed by the minister. What happens if ACoBA finds cause for concern about a prospective appointment? ACoBA says:

> [If ACoBA] considers that public concern could be of such a degree or character, it may recommend a delay in taking up the appointment, or that for a specified period the former Minister should stand aside from involvement in certain activities, for example, commercial dealings with his or her former Department, or involvement in particular areas of the new employer's business.[144]

ACoBA was set up on a non-statutory basis, and has no power to prevent a minister from taking up an appointment involving a conflict of interest. Still less does ACoBA have a power to negate any financial benefit accruing to a former minister by taking proceedings to seize such benefits on behalf of the public (or to prevent them being provided beforehand).[145] Yet, the work that it does is of considerable constitutional significance. In 2010–11, ACoBA advised forty-two ministers respecting ninety-five applications to take up positions outside politics, and in 2015–16 it advised thirty-three ministers in relation to 123 such applications.[146] More broadly, between 2000 and 2014, 600 former ministers and top civil servants were appointed to over 1,000 business roles.[147]

ACoBA's limited powers were brought to the public's attention in 2017, by the decision of the former Chancellor of the Exchequer, the Rt Hon George Osborne MP, to become the editor of a leading daily newspaper whilst remaining an MP and Privy Councillor. Osborne informed ACoBA of his intention to take up the

[140] The exact scope of this notion is unclear. [141] Ministerial Code (n 1)s 7.25.

[142] House of Commons Select Committee on Public Administration (2016–17), at paras 44–47.

[143] https://www.gov.uk/government/organisations/advisory-committee-on-business-appointments.

[144] ACoBA, 'Business Appointment Rules for Former Ministers' https://www.gov.uk/government/uploads/system/uploads/attachment_data/file/579754/Business_appointment_rules_for_former_ministers.pdf para 7.

[145] See the discussion of the civil law remedy of 'negation' in ch 5.9.

[146] House of Commons Select Committee on Public Administration and Constitutional Affairs (2016), at para 22.

[147] High Pay Centre (2015), at 5.

position on 13 March 2017, but the decision was announced by the newspaper only days later, on 17 March 2017 (with a contract being signed on 20 March 2017). This gave ACoBA no time to consider the ethics of the appointment.[148] ACoBA pointed out that Osborne's conduct was a clear breach of the Code (as Osborne must have been aware), because ministers are required 'to abide by the advice of the Committee'.[149] All ACoBA felt able to do was express its 'regret' at Osborne's conduct, and say that it was 'not appropriate' for Osborne to have behaved in such a fashion.[150] It is hardly surprising, then, that in 2016–17, the House of Commons Select Committee on Public Administration found, when examining the work and powers of ACoBA, that:

> The regulatory system for scrutinising the post public employment of former Ministers and civil servants is ineffectual and does not inspire public confidence or respect ... ACoBA, in its current form is a toothless regulator which has failed to change the environment around business appointments.[151]

What are the key requirements of the Ministerial Code, in theory binding on ministers? There are general provisions that, as in the case of the standards applicable to MPs more generally, seem to have no real binding force, such as the obligation 'to behave in a way that upholds the highest standards for propriety', and the obligation to ensure 'that no conflict arises, or appears to arise, between [a minister's] public duties and their private interests'.[152] Potentially more significant is paragraph 7.7, which says that: 'Ministers' decisions should not be influenced by the hope or expectation of future employment with a particular firm or organisation'. Can breach of this provision have legal consequences? Such a breach of the Code would in many instances fall short of the Law Commission's requirement for the misconduct offence that someone has the making of a benefit as their 'purpose'. To act in 'hope' or in 'expectation' of gain is not necessarily to act with the 'purpose' of making a gain.[153] Nonetheless, breach of paragraph 7.7 might amount to bribery, contrary to section 2(5) of the Bribery Act 2010, if, to use the wording of the 2010 Act: 'in anticipation of ... R [the Minister] requesting, agreeing to receive or accepting a financial or other advantage, a relevant function or activity is performed improperly'. What is lacking in the Code is a focus on the avoidance of temptation, in an environment in which ministers—at least in some areas, such as defence[154]—are likely to be regularly exposed to lobbying once they take up office, and to lucrative possibilities when they leave office (with the attendant possibility of an improper link arising between the two). For that reason, the Public Administration and Constitutional Affairs Committee recommended in 2016 that all public servants must 'always

[148] ACoBA https://www.gov.uk/government/uploads/system/uploads/attachment_data/file/611805/2017-04-28_Advice_letter_to_GO_re_ES.pdf; https://www.theguardian.com/politics/2017/mar/17/george-osborne-named-new-evening-standard-editor-newspaper.

[149] ibid. [150] ibid.

[151] House of Commons Select Committee on Public Administration and Constitutional Affairs (n 146) summary.

[152] Ministerial Code (n 1) 1, 15. [153] See section 4.2.

[154] Transparency International, *Fixing the Revolving Door between Government and Business* (2012); https://www.theguardian.com/uk/2012/oct/15/mod-military-arms-firms.

report to your line managers any offers of jobs or other rewards, or any informal suggestions of such rewards, that may have, or be reasonably seen to have a bearing on your role as a public servant'.[155]

Such a requirement of transparency should be backed by the threat of enforcement through both the civil and the criminal law. The best way to ensure that this is done effectively is, first, to reduce the control that Parliament has over the content of the Ministerial Code. Its rules and principles should be determined by a body with a majority of independent members, perhaps chaired by a retired Supreme Court Justice. Secondly, suppose that a former minister has taken up a remunerative position outside government, in breach of the Ministerial Code. In such a case, there should be a civil liability to account for any salary or benefit that accrues, or a liability to pay a penalty equivalent to the estimated benefit in question ('negation'[156]). It should also be possible for breaches of the Code to lead to criminal liability. As suggested above, criminal liability could be established to cover a case in which a former minister has been dishonest, in committing a breach of a code concerning a matter of trust. In accordance with the settled understanding of dishonesty in law,[157] such liability might arise when a minister knowingly fails to report an offer of employment from a company, in circumstances in which he or she is aware that ordinary people would regard the failure as dishonest. Even in the absence of a specific offence of this kind, such dishonest breaches of the Ministerial Code should already be regarded as covered by the offence of misconduct in public office,[158] in so far as it continues to be defined in terms of 'abuse of position or power'.[159] As argued in Chapter 2, any vagueness in such a definition can be mitigated by ensuring that, as part of any future reform, there are non-exhaustive examples of what will be regarded as falling within the scope of 'abuse' in any given field of public activity, such as ministerial activity.

That brings me to the neglected obligations of MPs in relation to lobbying. In the field of private sector bribery internationally, it is right to place a heavy deterrent emphasis on supply-side activity by commercial organizations.[160] Such organizations frequently emerge from countries that respect the rule of law and have a low tolerance for corruption domestically. It follows that those organizations should be well adapted, culturally and structurally, to internalizing the costs of adopting high ethical standards when they operate, and to facing legal sanctions when they do

[155] House of Commons Select Committee on Public Administration and Constitutional Affairs (n 146) para 105.

[156] See the discussion of negation in ch 5.9.

[157] *R v Ghosh* [1982] 3 WLR 110 (CA). In this context, the *Ghosh* test is more appropriate than the test for dishonesty suggested in *Ivy v Genting Casinos UK Limited* [2017] UKSC 67.

[158] There has never been any doubt that the fault element for misconduct in office can be satisfied by proof of dishonesty. See eg *R v Borron* (1820) 3 B and Ald 432.

[159] See the argument in ch 2. It has long been clear that, in appropriate circumstances 'dishonesty' can form the main plank of the fault requirement for the misconduct offence: see eg *R v Borron* [1820] 3 B & Ald 432; *R v W* [2010] EWCA 372.

[160] See OECD (2006), at 6: 'The OECD has been addressing corruption first and foremost by developing various instruments targeting "active bribery", or the "supply side" of corruption – that is, the offering of bribes'.

not.[161] That may not be the case on the demand side, for the public sector bodies with whom international commercial organizations deal.[162] The countries in which those bodies operate may be poorly adapted to counter corruption and uphold the rule of law, and may in any event not be party to international anti-corruption agreements covering public sector procurement.

However, when the focus is public officials working in the very countries where respect for the rule of law is entrenched, and where there is (in theory) low toleration for corruption, there is no special reason to adopt a predominantly supply-side approach to regulation and criminalization. Yet, what we find is that whilst there is (rightly) ever-increasing pressure to subject those supplying private lobbying services to greater regulatory and criminal law intervention,[163] there is less attention paid in this respect—predictably enough, by politicians, in particular—to the public officials (including MPs themselves) targeted by private sector lobbyists. Evidence suggests that although 90 per cent of MPs overwhelmingly believe that charities are effective communicators with them, 57 per cent also believe that business interests are fairly or very effective communicators with them.[164] In rule of law states that have strong commitments to anti-corruption in the public sector, it is arguable that the regulation of *officials'* conduct, and (where appropriate) the criminalization of their wrongdoing, should be a main focus. In that regard, the absence of regulation to promote public goods has meant that too much activity in the field of lobbying remains a matter of top-down discretion and claim of right, rather than being regarded as subject of public duties respecting the promotion of public goods.

In criticizing the current position, Transparency International has observed that:

1. £3.4 million was paid to 73 MPs last year for external advisory roles—a significant risk of conflicts of interest.
2. Payments for parliamentary advice are still allowed in the House of Commons, but prohibited in the House of Lords, Scotland and Wales—a major loophole in the rules.
3. In practice, legislators across the UK are permitted to retain conflicts of interest so long as they are declared.[165]

Transparency International's concerns throw into relief a particularly glaring absence from the legislation on lobbying.[166] As we will see in Chapter 5.11, professional lobbyists must be registered in order lawfully to engage in lobbying, or face sanctions for doing so: the offences and civil penalties in both the existing and proposed UK legislation have lobbyists as their object. However, MPs, civil servants, or special advisers who deal with lobbyists face no sanctions, even for knowingly engaging with a lobbyist operating illegally. It is nothing short of self-serving hypocrisy for Parliament to have made it, for example, an offence for lobbyists to fail

[161] That is not to imply that the enforcement of such obligations, as compared with their imposition, will be an easy matter.

[162] Benjamin A Olken and Rohini Pande (2011).

[163] Considered in ch 5.11.

[164] Philip Pavin (2007), at 27.

[165] Transparency International (2015a), at 15.

[166] For MPs' rules on lobbying see House of Commons (2015).

to keep the registrar informed of their client lists, when MPs appear to be under no such threat in relation to many of their own dealings with those same lobbyists. Under the Australian Lobbying Code of Conduct, section 4 says that a government representative 'shall not knowingly and intentionally be a party to lobbying activities by . . . . . . a lobbyist who is not on the Register of Lobbyists'.[167] There was, and remains, a clear need to make such conduct an offence under lobbying legislation, or to see that it falls within the scope of the misconduct offence.

It was argued above that a dishonest breach of the Ministerial Code, and the dishonest making of false or misleading statements in relation to obligations under the Code, should be matters for the criminal law, either as specific offences or through application of the offence of misconduct in public office. A similar approach should be taken to MPs' more general code of conduct, in so far as it relates to conflicts of interests in general and to lobbying in particular. Codes of conduct governing MPs and ministers (as well as judges) are the republican heart of the constitution. It is appropriate that attempts to depart from or undermine them can be met with criminal sanctions.[168] In relation to lobbying, the MPs' Code of Conduct states, amongst other things, that:

> 10. Members shall base their conduct on a consideration of the public interest, avoid conflict between personal interest and the public interest and resolve any conflict between the two, at once, and in favour of the public interest.
> 11. No Member shall act as a paid advocate in any proceeding of the House . . . . . .
> 13. Members shall fulfil conscientiously the requirements of the House in respect of the registration of interests in the Register of Members' Financial Interests. They shall always be open and frank in drawing attention to any relevant interest in any proceeding of the House or its Committees, and in any communications with Ministers, Members, public officials or public office holders.
> 14. Information which Members receive in confidence in the course of their parliamentary duties should be used only in connection with those duties. Such information must never be used for the purpose of financial gain.[169]

These specific obligations should be unambiguously underpinned by criminal liability in the circumstances just mentioned.

In the section on lobbying, the Code of Conduct also makes MPs subject to a more general obligation:

> 16. Members shall never undertake any action which would cause significant damage to the reputation and integrity of the House of Commons as a whole, or of its Members generally.[170]

[167] Australian Government (2013), at 3. No sanction is attached to this prohibition.

[168] As I indicated, when speaking of the Ministerial Code, it follows that the contents of the Code of Conduct governing MPs cannot be solely a matter for MPs themselves. There must be majority independent input into it: see ch 4.6.

[169] House of Commons, Code of Conduct (2015) s 5.

[170] ibid.

Dishonestly engaging in such an action, in relation to lobbying activity, may also be a fit subject for a prosecution for misconduct. More broadly, a political party that seeks to evade, or knowingly tolerates breaches of, the Code of Conduct should itself be vulnerable to prosecution, in accordance with the principles to be discussed in section 4.13. A Crown Prosecution Service (CPS) and Court of Appeal determined to defend republican values and to deter and punish corruption amongst legislators would have the courage to use the misconduct offence in such circumstances.

To reinforce the importance of these points about the enhanced use of the criminal law of misconduct, we can turn to a comparison between attitudes and approaches to business corruption, and attitudes and approaches to corruption in politics.

4.6 Corruption in the UK: Business and the Political System

> The fact that we are all known to each other is the best safeguard of all against improper conduct.[171]

In the UK, corruption in the form of bribery (including extortion) has now properly been addressed by the criminal law, through the Bribery Act 2010. However, other forms of corruption have not been tackled by the criminal law on a systematic basis to anything like the same extent. The UN has provided a helpful guide to such other forms of corruption.[172] Some, such as embezzlement, theft, fraud, insider trading, and money laundering, are not normally considered part of UK law dealing with corruption, as such. In the UK, such crimes are treated as part of a broader picture constituting the field of so-called 'white-collar' crime or, perhaps more accurately, crimes arising from a breach of (public or corporate) trust.[173] Crimes of corruption are, of course, an important part of that broader picture, because they typically constitute breaches of corporate or public trust. In that regard, the UN mentions as significant threats and wrongs: conflicts of interest and interest 'peddling', nepotism, favouritism, clientelism, and illegal political contributions.[174] The list is not a complete one. For example, Transparency International has identified the 'revolving door' problem, discussed above, as a corruption risk in the UK.[175] As Transparency International puts it:

> Conflicts of interest related to the revolving door can take many forms, for example:
>
> - Public officials might allow the agenda of a previous private-sector employer to influence their government work, being overly sympathetic to a sector that they have a responsibility to regulate.
> - Public officials might abuse their power while in office to favour a certain company, with a view to ingratiating themselves and gaining future employment.

[171] Michael Clark Hutchinson MP, HC Debs (22 May 1974) col 441.
[172] United Nations (2001).
[173] See Susan Shapiro (1990).
[174] United Nations (n 172) 1.
[175] Transparency International (2010), at 7.

- Former public officials who accept jobs in business might influence their former government colleagues to make decisions in a way that favours their new employer.
- Former public officials might use confidential information to benefit their new employers – for example, during procurement procedures.[176]

What are the values by reference to which such practices are regarded as corrupt? The UN Convention against Corruption commits its signatories, including the UK, to universal governance standards for the public sector (Article 7), including efficiency, transparency, merit, equity, and objectivity. Article 1(c) commits the signatories to the promotion of 'integrity, accountability, and proper management of public affairs and public property'.[177] In significant respects, UK politics does not live up to these ideals.

How important is it that the criminal law should be available as a measure to target corruption in these broader senses? One way of answering this question is to compare the drivers behind reform (or the lack thereof) of bribery, on the one hand, and other forms of corruption, on the other. The primary motivation behind the comprehensive reforms instigated by the Bribery Act 2010 was to tackle business corruption, not corruption in politics.[178] In that regard, many of the practices that form part of the UN's broader picture of corruption—such as nepotism or the peddling of influence—may be corrupting in politics, but are not necessarily risks or wrongs at all in the marketplace. On the contrary, for example, nepotism in appointments within a company may not only be cost-efficient but also reinforce trust amongst those running the company, in circumstances where this is of greater market value than merit-based recruitment. In academic terms, nepotism—or patronage more broadly—may constitute 'a risk-reduction mechanism through which high-trust relationships and control capacity can be manufactured and sustained'.[179] In the context of law reform, a focus on market practices, rather than political practices, may give rise to the perception that, if the criminal law is needed at all to tackle corruption in the UK, it is indeed needed mainly to address bribery, as bribery is no longer internationally accepted as a legitimate market practice.[180]

In this respect, however, there is a yawning gap between criminal law reform priorities in the UK, and survey evidence concerning perceptions of corruption. A 2013 Global Corruption Barometer (involving 114,000 participants from 107 countries) showed that only a minority, albeit substantial—27 per cent—had paid a bribe over the course of the previous year. By contrast, 67 per cent considered that favouritism was what got things done in the *public* sector, and over 50 per cent thought that the influence of vested interest groups explained government actions

176 Transparency International, *Fixing the Revolving Door between Government and Business* (n 154) summary.

177 See Alina Mungiu-Pippidi (2015), at 3–4.

178 See eg, https://www.gov.uk/government/news/bribery-act-comes-into-force--6.

179 Matthew Flinders and Felicity Mathews (2010), at 642. Flinders and Mathews are actually concerned with political rather than with business patronage, but I will return to that point.

180 See generally http://www.oecd.org/corruption/oecdantibriberyconvention.htm.

better than the public interest.[181] Following this pattern, in the UK, it is not only illegal but also rarely necessary to pay a bribe to secure access to services,[182] but that is not the end of the matter. Corruption in the UK may not have left people generally economically poorer, but it has nonetheless left them with a sense of political impoverishment. Transparency International's 2010 survey of over 2,000 UK residents revealed that nearly 60 per cent had never personally been affected by corruption (as by being asked to pay a bribe), and only 13.7 per cent claimed to have been so affected, with the remainder unsure.[183] Even so, 53.4 per cent believed that corruption in the UK had increased either a little (30.9%) or a lot (22.5%). As the Transparency International survey makes clear, the explanation for this is people's belief that it is the body politic that is most infected by corruption. When asked what might be a plausible or possible example of corruption in the UK, some 86 per cent mentioned a seat in the House of Lords being given to a business person who has made large donations to a political party, 79.9 per cent mentioned the 'revolving door' issue of a public official taking a job with a company that he or she was previously responsible for regulating, 67.3 per cent pointed to MPs employing family members, and 63.7 per cent brought up the influence of political lobbying by companies.[184] Lest this evidence be dismissed as distorted by the 2009 post-expenses scandal, it is important to emphasize that it reflects broader international trends. As Mungiu-Pippidi explains:

> [E]vidence in recent years from multiple sources would be contradictory and incomprehensible unless we were to accept that the general population when asked to assess corruption offers its assessment of its society's capacity to enforce public integrity and fairness, rather than reporting on individual experiences of corruption as legally defined in criminal codes.[185]

It might easily be claimed that the reason for the public focus on corruption in politics is that it is this species of corruption that obsesses the media, whilst (so the argument runs), business corruption goes unreported and hence ignored. Not so. The survey discussed above demonstrated a high level of public awareness of the potential for corruption in the marketplace. 74.2 per cent of those surveyed mentioned, as a plausible risk of corruption in the UK, supermarkets using leverage to obtain planning permission that would be denied to others, whilst 69.4 per cent (presciently) indicated as a possible risk that large organizations would use offshore tax arrangements to arrange their financial affairs.[186] As this last example illustrates, public perceptions of the extent of 'corruption' are not excessively influenced by whether or not a particular example of corruption does or does not offend against the law.[187] Overall, however, whilst 65.5 per cent thought political parties to be corrupt, and 55.7 per cent considered Parliament to be corrupt, only 43.8 per cent

[181] Transparency International (2013). [182] Transparency International (2011), at 1.
[183] Transparency International, *Corruption in the UK Part 1: National Opinion Survey* (n 175) 4.
[184] ibid 6. [185] Alina Mungiu-Pippidi (n 177) 4.
[186] https://www.theguardian.com/business/2016/aug/17/firms-giving-advice-on-aggressive-tax-avoidance-could-face-large-fines.
[187] See D Kaufmann and P C Vincente (2011).

considered business to be corrupt.[188] Unsurprisingly, thus, 48.1 per cent considered government efforts to tackle corruption to be either ineffective or very ineffective, with only 24.5 per cent indicating that they thought government efforts had been 'somewhat effective'.[189]

Parliament's strategy for tackling business corruption nationally and internationally has been criminal law-led, even though research indicates that the prospects for national jurisdictions obtaining convictions relating to bribery overseas are minimal.[190] By contrast, the main focus where risks of corruption in the political sphere are concerned has been on regulation and guidance, rather than on criminalization. Prominent examples include the guidance on and procedures for the making of public appointments by ministers,[191] and the work of the IPSA.[192] Of course, few doubt the need for such regulation and guidance. However, the focus on them has been maintained in the political sphere, even though in domestic cases the prospects for obtaining convictions in cases of serious wrongdoing appear to be good, were prosecutors only willing to bring cases. In part, then, it is a question of balance, a balance that has been struck in a way too favourable to politicians, when it comes to the need for the criminal law to lead the way in tackling corruption.

Transparency International's National Integrity System, designed to assess national institutions in terms of their ability to act effectively as a bulwark against corruption, rates the UK business sector as 'strong' (in the light of the Bribery Act 2010), but the legislature and political parties as only 'moderate'.[193] There is, then, at least a case to be made for greater use of the criminal law in tackling corruption in politics. Using nepotism as an example, whereas this practice may have a perfectly sound justification in the marketplace, it seems clear that when it reflects the conduct of officials it may warrant criminal prohibition (although the issue is a complex one). In the UN's view:

> Conflicts between official duty and private self-interest should be properly dealt with, although defining what conflicts should be made criminal is very culture-bound... It is only at the point where the self-interest of an official is so strong or expressed in a way so indicative of a wrongful purpose, in a manner to be presumed to threaten the public good, that criminalization should be considered.[194]

In contrast, however, to the position where corporate corruption is concerned, Parliament has been slow to recognize the potential of exposure to a greater risk of criminal conviction as a means of reducing instances of nepotism and improper use of the revolving door in the public sector, and in Parliament in particular. This has been because, in many instances of corruption identified by the public (lobbying; exploitation of 'revolving door' situations; employment of family members),

188 Transparency International (n 175) 7.
189 ibid.
190 See Nicholas Lord (2014).
191 See Gerry Grimstone (2016). Over 1,800 public appointments were made in 2014–15.
192 http://parliamentarystandards.org.uk/Pages/default.aspx.
193 Transparency International, 'Corruption in the UK; Overview and Policy Recommendations' (n 182) 16.
194 United Nations (n 172) 12–13.

politicians have simply failed to recognize that they are doing anything wrong, or if they do, they do not care. 'Wrongful-purpose' nepotism, of a kind appropriate for criminalization, ought clearly to include instances in which officials exercise their discretion to employ relatives other than through an open job search based on merit; but that has not been the case in the UK. Although it is no longer regarded as acceptable for MPs to augment family income through the employment of relatives irrespective of merit,[195] that is regarded as a purely regulatory matter, and not a proper subject for criminal prosecution.

4.7 Before *R v Chaytor*: The 2009 Expenses 'Scandal'

> If men should not be called to account for possessing the people with an ill opinion of the Government, no Government can subsist; for it is very necessary for every Government that the people should have a good opinion of it . . . This [the publishing of an ill opinion] has been always look'd upon as a crime, and no government can be safe unless it be punished.[196]

It is no longer an offence to speak ill of the government.[197] However, during the period of the so-called 'rotten' Parliament of 2005–2010,[198] MPs made strenuous efforts to prevent the release of information about their own conduct, in claiming allowances, that could lead to the formation of such an ill opinion.[199] When that information finally entered the public domain, it was to lead, amongst other things, to the most serious allegations in living memory of widespread corruption in the UK Parliament.[200] In consequence, no less than 52 per cent of MPs were recommended by a formal enquiry to repay money claimed in the form of an allowance (a total of £1.12 million),[201] a (small) number of MPs were prosecuted for false accounting,[202] quasi-independent regulation of expense and allowance claims was introduced,[203]

[195] Independent Parliamentary Standards Authority, *The Scheme of MPs' Business Costs and Expenses 2017–18* (n 47) 3.22.

[196] *R v Tutchin* (1704) 90 Eng Rep 1133, at 1133–34 (Holt CJ).

[197] For example, the crimes of sedition and seditious libel were abolished by the Coroners and Justice Act 2009, s 73.

[198] http://www.telegraph.co.uk/news/election-2010/7573025/General-Election-2010-Good-riddance-to-the-Rotten-Parliament.html.

[199] http://www.telegraph.co.uk/news/newstopics/mps-expenses/6360729/Jack-Straw-tried-to-conceal-MPs-expenses.html. A brief timeline of Parliament's efforts to keep the information secret is to be found at http://www.telegraph.co.uk/news/newstopics/mps-expenses/6499657/MPs-expenses-scandal-a-timeline.html.

[200] From 8 May 2009 onwards, the *Daily Telegraph* began to publish full details of MP's expense claims, and this can be regarded as the time when the issue of MPs' expenses came to be regarded as a 'scandal' in the making. See Robert Winnett and Gordon Rayner (2009).

[201] House of Commons Members Estimate Committee (2010).

[202] http://www.telegraph.co.uk/news/politics/conservative/8220171/MPs-expenses-10th-file-handed-over-to-Crown-Prosecution-Service.html.

[203] See Parliamentary Commissioner for Standards Office http://www.parliament.uk/mps-lords-and-offices/standards-and-financial-interests/parliamentary-commissioner-for-standards/parliamentary-commissioner-for-standards/; Independent Parliamentary Standards Authority http://www.theipsa.org.uk/mp-costs/.

scandal-hit MPs had their vote shares reduced, and they were more likely to retire from politics before the next election.[204]

It is, of course, important not to overplay the sense in which these developments, although they certainly involved a genuine 'scandal',[205] involved grand corruption on a significant scale. For example, the £1.2 million that it was recommended that MPs repay pales into insignificance compared to the £35 billion allegedly taken for his private use out of Indonesia's economy by President Suharto.[206] More broadly, there is strong evidence to suggest that, in general, MPs in the UK do not flagrantly abuse their expenses.[207] However, what is significant about the UK scandal was—and continues to be—the immunity of MPs respecting the systems they put in place, or allow to develop, that give rise to the *widespread* nature of abuses, even if in individual cases the sums involved are small. One important illustration is provided by the assisted costs allowance (ACA).[208]

It is obviously a basic requirement of fairness that MPs who can only attend Parliament by travelling long distances should be entitled to support to ensure that they can do so without disadvantage, in financial or personal terms (where the latter includes the prospects for a family life). To that end, the ACA was first put in place in 1971, to cover the costs of staying in London, or (where an MP did not live in his or her constituency) of staying in the constituency. The independent Senior Salaries Review Body had recommended that, on the financial side, this allowance should take the form of a daily subsistence rate.[209] However, the government opted for a more opaque system, in which an MP could have expenses reimbursed up to an annual limit. Having started at £750 in 1972, that limit was raised consistently, even in the absence of a recommendation to that effect from the Senior Salaries Review Body. For example, between 2004 and 2008 (during the 'rotten' Parliament), it went up as follows:

2004/05–£20,902
2005/06–£21,634
2006/07–£22,110
2007/08–£23,086
2008/09–£24,006.[210]

Moreover, the allowance was made more generous in a number of ways over ensuing years, through 'resolutions' approved by the House of Commons and beyond the scrutiny of the Courts, rather than through legislation.[211] In 1983, the allowance was exempted from income tax. Only two years later, in 1985, parliamentarians decided there was no reason why they should not use the allowance to purchase a

[204] Valentino Larcinese and Indraneel Sircar (2012).
[205] OED: 'An action or event regarded as morally or legally wrong and causing general public outrage'.
[206] https://www.theguardian.com/world/2004/mar/26/indonesia.philippines.
[207] Timothy Besley and Valentino Larcinese (2011). See also Raphael Heuwiser (2015).
[208] The following account is taken largely from Legg (n 59).
[209] See Legg (n 59) para 13. [210] ibid para 14.
[211] House of Commons (2009), at 5.

second home, rather than staying in a hotel (there was no substantive debate about the issue). Mortgage interest payments could then be claimed. In due course, claims were permitted when a mortgage had been increased to fund improvements to take advantage of new mortgage products.[212] These developments led to the widespread practice, a practice that was to attain great notoriety in the media, of 'flipping'.[213] In broad terms, first, this practice involved MPs claiming mortgage interest payments relating to the refurbishing of a second home (ostensibly, a home owned to make it easier to stay near Westminster, or near to the relevant constituency). Secondly, MPs would then artificially reverse or 'flip' the arrangement, by declaring their hitherto first home to be their 'second home' (with their hitherto second home now becoming the 'first home'). That permitted them to go through the process of claiming mortgage interest payments yet again in relation to the new 'second home'—frequently, the MP's original private residence—perhaps to refurbish it at the taxpayers' expense. During the rotten Parliament 2005–2010, some fifty MPs did this in the year 2009 alone.[214] Nowhere in the applicable sections of the Green Book (the guide for MPs when they incur costs), valid at that time, was the practice of 'flipping' mentioned, let alone approved, even though it is of course anticipated that the address of an MP may change from time to time.[215]

In his review of the ACA, Sir Thomas Legg was highly critical of the way in which MPs had allowed the system to develop. He said:

> The ACA system was deeply flawed. In particular, the rules were vague, and MPs were themselves self-certifying as to the propriety of their use of the allowance. Taken with the prevailing lack of transparency and the 'culture of deference', this meant that the Fees Office's decisions lacked legitimacy; and many of them were in fact mistaken.[216]

Legg's point about self-certification should not be overlooked. Until April 2008, self-certification (non-vouchable expenditure) by MPs applied to expenses up to £250, before being reduced to £25 thereafter; until that time it had amounted to a not insubstantial 4.3 per cent of the total cost to the taxpayer.[217] Inexcusably, receipts for expenditure on mortgages were commonly not kept by MPs, even when the rules of the House required that they be retained,[218] meaning that compliance with the rules could not be checked: surely, an example of misconduct in itself. Prosecutors seem to have forgotten that, as we saw in Chapter 3, at common law such an 'undue razure' of an important record 'was a great offence, for which even a judge himself was punishable by fine and imprisonment'.[219]

As a result of Legg's recommendations, putting aside those asked to repay trivial sums, 238 MPs were requested to pay back sums between £1,000 and £40,000

[212] Legg (n 59) para 16.
[213] http://www.theguardian.com/politics/2009/dec/10/mps-expenses-50-flipped-homes.
[214] ibid. [215] House of Commons (2009), at 18. [216] Legg (n 59) para 2.
[217] Office of the Leader of the House of Commons (2008), at foreword.
[218] Legg (n 59) para 9: 'a particular challenge has proved to be the widespread lack of proper evidence on the record from MPs to support substantial payments, especially of mortgage interest, even though this was expressly required by the rules'.
[219] Sir Matthew Hale (1736), at 646.

(although only three were asked to pay back more than £40,000). This reaffirms the point made earlier that it is not so much the total sums involved that should concern us, but how widespread self-preferential financial (mal)practice had become. In that respect, parliamentarians have always themselves been in denial, clinging to the view that misconduct—if engaged in at all—is confined to a few individuals. As recently as 2013, the then Leader of the House of Lords, Lord Hill, discouraged too much intervention in MPs' practices in relation to the expenditure of public money, suggesting that:

> Most people [MPs] behave properly ... Most are good and there are a small number in any walk of life who are not. I prefer an approach that comes down hard on the small number of people rather than an overly prescriptive approach that ties everyone up in knots.[220]

So far as Lord Hill was concerned, any evidence of systematic impropriety was best understood as a forgivable and forgettable instance where 'boys will be boys' ('nod, wink', he might have added).[221] A rather different analysis of the same issue is provided by Kelso:

> There emerged in the House of Commons, as a collective entity, the idea that the ACA expenses could be treated as part of the salary of an MP. There emerged, in other words, a culture of entitlement.[222]

Sir Thomas Legg was not alone in regarding the ACA system as dysfunctional and open to corrupt abuse (although he did not expressly use the latter term). By 2008, the Senior Salaries Review Body had already expressed the view that:

> Although ... we have received no substantive evidence of abuse, we are concerned that it is in the area of ACA that the greatest scope for abuse is thought to exist ... this element of the expenses regime gives rise to more problems and misunderstandings, both within and outside the House, than any other and a fuller review of the ACA might be appropriate.[223]

Unlike Legg, of course, the Senior Salaries Review Body had not conducted a comprehensive investigation into ACA practices, and so was not in a position to consider whether or not 'substantive evidence of abuse' existed. It is also important to point out that the development and use of the ACA system from the 1990s onwards took place against a backdrop of ever-greater expectations respecting the integrity of MPs in their professional conduct.

The Nolan Committee and Report of 1995, the principles of which applied to parliamentarians,[224] had set down seven principles of public life that included 'Selflessness: Holders of public office should act solely in terms of the public interest', and 'Accountability: Holders of public office are accountable to the public for their decisions and actions and must submit themselves to the scrutiny

[220] *Evening Standard* (15 November 2013). [221] ibid.

[222] Alexandra Kelso (2009), at 332. [223] Cited by Legg (n 59) para 17.

[224] In July 1995, the House of Commons agreed to adopt the Nolan principles as part of its Code of Conduct for Members of Parliament.

necessary to ensure this'.[225] In that regard, the MPs' Code of Conduct makes plain that MPs must:

> act on all occasions in accordance with the public trust placed in them. They should always behave with probity and integrity, including in their use of public resources.[226]

Evidence suggests that MPs themselves take very little interest in the Nolan principles.[227] Even so, the version of the so-called 'Green Book' (the official guide to MPs on their allowances) that was published in March 2009 had made crystal clear the following principles for claiming allowances:

> 1. Claims should be above reproach and must reflect actual usage of the resources being claimed …
> 2. Claims must only be made for expenditure that it was *necessary* for a Member to incur to ensure that he or she could properly perform his or her parliamentary duties …
> 3. Members must ensure that claims do not give rise to, or give the appearance of giving rise to, an improper personal financial benefit to themselves or anyone else.[228]

In some respects, this guidance had been watered down, in terms of its insistence on the absolute propriety in the use of allowances. Whereas, in 2 above, it is said that claims may only be made for 'necessary' expenditure, the 1985 version of the Green book had insisted that expenses must be '*wholly, exclusively and necessarily* incurred when staying away from their main UK residence for the purpose of performing Parliamentary duties'.[229] Tellingly, in that regard, one of the first steps taken by the IPSA, set up in the wake of the expenses scandal, was to end the practice of using public money to engage in second home purchase by MPs.[230] Predictably, orders made requiring MPs to repay the profits they had made from this scam were fiercely resisted.[231]

I now turn to a second example of MPs seeking immunity from prosecution, for establishing or permitting systems of expenditure that involve or are open to corrupt abuse through self-preference. This concerns the employment by MPs of family members as part of their political 'team'. As we saw in section 4.3, this practice revived in a new form the nepotism prevalent in Parliament during the eighteenth century.[232] In 2014–15, MPs' expenditure on staffing was about £83 million, amounting to no less than 80 per cent of their spending on their business costs and expenses.[233] This is attributable to the fact that, by 2008, the House of Commons

[225] See Committee on Standards in Public Life (1995).

[226] House of Commons (2015), at para iii(7), my emphasis.

[227] http://www.theguardian.com/politics/2014/jul/14/mps-course-seven-principles-public-life-report.

[228] House of Commons (2009) at 7.

[229] Cited by Legg (n 59) para 56.

[230] Independent Parliamentary Standards Authority (2016a), at para 30. http://news.bbc.co.uk/1/hi/uk_politics/8592174.stm (29 March 2010).

[231] http://www.telegraph.co.uk/news/politics/9728247/MPs-expenses-MPs-hire-lawyer-to-fight-watchdog-order-to-repay-second-home-profits.html.

[232] http://www.theguardian.com/politics/2015/jun/29/mps-continue-hire-relatives-as-staff; Horder, '*R v Bembridge* (1783)' (n 55).

[233] Independent Parliamentary Standards Authority (2017a), at para 73.

had extended the scheme to cover the employment of up to 3.5 members of staff per MP.[234] Immediately *after* the so-called 'expenses scandal' that revealed these practices, and the ushering in of a new regulatory regime, spending by each MP on their own staff costs did not fall, but actually rose from £54,059,00, in 2010–11, to £82,975,00 in 2014–15.[235] It is, of course, necessary for MPs to have administrative support, but the system for providing it has been justly described by the IPSA as 'the least regulated area of spending'.[236] The political case for the scheme—in theory, a strong one—continues to be undermined by the involvement of MPs in the widespread use of it to engage in nepotism and personal favouritism.

In 2009, the Committee on Standards in Public Life remarked that 'MPs offices are not family businesses. They are supported by public funds',[237] and in Recommendation 15 the Committee said:

> MPs should no longer be able to appoint members of their own families to their staff and pay them with public funds. Those currently employing family members should be able to continue to do so for the life of one further Parliament or five years, whichever is the longer.[238]

Nothing came of this recommendation within the ensuing five years. That is because there is a yawning gulf between what MPs themselves, from the top down, regard as corrupt in relation to the use of expenses to employ relatives, and what, from the bottom up, the public regards as corrupt conduct in this respect.

A study of perceptions of corruption in public life, bringing together data from 2005 and from a decade later, showed that whereas only 15 per cent of MPs regarded hiring a relative as a corrupt practice, over 54 per cent of the public considered it to be corrupt.[239] The involvement in constituency or parliamentary work (but not on a salaried basis) of a spouse or partner could perhaps be justified, even to the exclusion of a better-qualified 3rd party, in the general interests of supporting what will otherwise prove difficult for MPs: the maintenance of a shared life with a spouse or partner. However, such a justification cannot possibly apply to other family members or 'connected parties' (as they are known). Even before Nolan, the Office of the Leader of the House of Commons had suggested in 2008 that:

> Recent instances of MPs employing their children have raised public concern and dented public confidence. We are therefore consulting on whether MPs' children should be barred from paid employment in their parent's constituency or Parliamentary offices, or in any other role relating to the parent's work as an MP.[240]

[234] In itself, that extension should not be regarded as unwarranted, given increasing expectations and demands made of MPs. See the analysis by the Independent Parliamentary Standards Authority, *IPSA's First Parliament 2010-2015: Regulation, Support and Remuneration* (n 230) paras 38–41.

[235] Independent Parliamentary Standards Authority, *IPSA's First Parliament 2010-2015: Regulation, Support and Remuneration* (n 230) Annex C, table 3. That is not to suggest that this increase was tainted by corruption.

[236] Independent Parliamentary Standards Authority, *Review of the Scheme of MPs' Business Costs and Expenses and IPSA's Publication Policy: Consultation Report and Equality Impact Assessment* (n 233) para 73.

[237] Committee on Standards in Public Life (2009), at para 6.20.

[238] ibid para 14. [239] Nicholas Allen and Sarah Birch (2015), at 84.

[240] Office of the Leader of the House of Commons (2008), at para 10. The 'recent instances' referred to here included the case of Derek Conway, respecting the undocumented employment of his two sons: Standards and Privileges Committee (2009).

Such concerns were largely ignored, until relatively recently.

MPs have certainly filled their boots—and their family incomes in particular—through the use of this quite extraordinary privilege that they have granted themselves. In 2015, over 135 MPs employed a wife, husband, or other close family member, costing in the region of £4.5 million to cover between 130 and 160 employees (5.7% of total expenditure on staff).[241] The average salary paid to a family member is £25,000, £5,600 higher on average than the salaries offered to non-family members, in virtue of the fact that family members are commonly allotted more senior roles.[242] That simply reinforces the case for the (cynical) view that, as Nolan indicated,[243] the practice has more to do with boosting family income—treating the expense system as a way to establish a business for the family—than with ensuring that the best person is employed to do the job. In that regard, the practice has always conformed rigidly to gender stereotypes. In 2012–13, whereas 26.6 per cent of male MPs employed a 'connected' party, only 12.9 per cent of female MPs did so, with male MPs far more likely to have their spouse as the connected party employed.[244]

The IPSA has flip-flopped on the issue. Having initially been inclined to support the Nolan view that nepotistic practices at public expense should end, IPSA was persuaded in 2010 that:

> [T]here were no significant grounds for concern that public funds were being misused ... ... We also received evidence of the valuable role that connected parties play in running MPs' offices and maintaining contact with the local community when MPs are in Westminster. We decided, therefore, to allow the practice to continue, with safeguards, including the restriction to one connected party per MP and the annual publication of all employed connected parties' names and salaries ...[245]

This analysis simply misses the point. The most important issue is the fact that the employment of relatives at the taxpayers' expense is *itself* a corrupt misuse of the staffing budget. Restricting engagement in such nepotism to only one member of the family is a 'checkerboard' solution, lacking in any kind of principled basis.[246] It is a lesser, although still important, concern whether the way in which relatives are employed gives rise to further misuse, although the higher salaries paid to family members show that just such further misuse does occur. Yet, in 2016, this analysis was repeated, with the IPSA saying that:

[241] Independent Parliamentary Standards Authority, *IPSA's First Parliament 2010–2015: Regulation, Support and Remuneration* (n 230) table 3, Annex C; http://www.telegraph.co.uk/news/newstopics/mps-expenses/11706561/One-in-four-MPs-employs-a-family-member-the-full-list-revealed.html.

[242] Independent Parliamentary Standards Authority, *IPSA's First Parliament 2010–2015: Regulation, Support and Remuneration* (n 230) table 3, Annex C; http://www.bbc.co.uk/news/uk-politics-36260573 (11 May 2016).

[243] Committee on Standards in Public Life (n 237) para 6.20.

[244] Independent Parliamentary Standards Authority, *Review of the Scheme of MPs' Business Costs and Expenses and IPSA's Publication Policy: Consultation Report and Equality Impact Assessment* (n 233) para 127. For a helpful bar chart illustrating the extent to which the system has been used to provide employment for wives right up to 2017 see http://www.bbc.co.uk/news/uk-england-40709220.

[245] Independent Parliamentary Standards Authority (2016b), at para 56.

[246] On the absurdity of checkerboard solutions to matters of principle see Ronald Dworkin (1986), at 178.

> We found no ground for concerns for the majority of connected parties … but given that there remains a perception of risk to taxpayers' money, we are obliged to address it. Therefore we are consulting again on the practice, but only in respect of the employment by MPs of any new staff. Connected parties who are already in employment by MPs will have their contracts honoured … To do otherwise would be unfair to those concerned, and legally challengeable.[247]

Surprisingly, the fact that, as the IPSA itself noted,[248] the salaries of connected parties were found to have risen at twice the rate of other staff was not thought to amount to a 'ground for concern'.[249] More importantly, the sense—quite plain in the Nolan Committee Report[250]—that nepotism in the use of staff allowances is wrong per se is not evident here. The concern of the IPSA is now seemingly only with the financial risks, rather than with the wrongfulness, of MPs' practices.

However, IPSA has at least delivered on its promise to curtail the long-term practice of nepotism amongst MPs. In its 2017–18 guidance, the IPSA declared that it would no longer meet the cost of the employment of 'connected parties' by MPs,[251] after the general election following 1 April 2017.[252] However, that restriction applies only to new employees. So far as existing family member employees are concerned, IPSA explicitly contemplates that such arrangements may continue indefinitely into the future.[253] Moreover, even after the general election following 1 April 2017, if an MP's employee becomes a connected party—as by marriage—the MP will have a full two years to continue to employ that person, before having to end the arrangement.[254] That is a period so long it would be sufficient in law for the marriage to be then ended through mutual agreement, had the parties commenced their separation immediately upon marriage.

4.8 Before *R v Chaytor*: The Immunity of MPs from Criminal Liability

> If an arrangement could be made to stop men from using office as a means of private gain, it would provide a way – the only possible way – for combining democracy with aristocracy.[255]

In a very important sense, MPs are, for the purposes of the criminal law, to be treated as ordinary citizens. If an MP engages in domestic violence, conspires to defraud, commits a sexual assault, or engages in some other criminal activity, he or she has no claim to special treatment in the form of an exemption from the courts'

[247] Independent Parliamentary Standards Authority, *Review of the MPs' Scheme of Business Costs and Expenses and IPSA's Publication Policy: A Consultation* (n 245) para 58.

[248] ibid para 57.

[249] The salaries rose 50 per cent in the four years following the general election of 2010: http://www.thesundaytimes.co.uk/sto/news/Politics/article1492865.ece.

[250] Committee on Standards in Public Life (n 237) para 14.

[251] On the definition of connected parties see Independent Parliamentary Standards Authority, *The Scheme of MPs' Business Costs and Expenses 2017–18* (n 47) para 3.19, and section 4.2.

[252] ibid paras 3.22–3.23. [253] ibid para 7.8. [254] ibid para 7.8.

[255] Aristotle, *The Politics*, Bk V, Ch viii, 17.

jurisdiction.[256] Further, it should not matter, in this respect, that such an offence takes place within the curtilage of the palace of Westminster, or even on the floor of the House. The courts have jurisdiction to try MPs in the criminal courts in such cases, cases of what are referred to as 'ordinary' crimes.[257] However, in some circumstances, the courts' jurisdiction is ousted, in respect of alleged criminality on the part of MPs, conferring on MPs a kind of immunity from prosecution.

There is no single justification for the ousting of the courts' criminal (and civil) jurisdiction. As we will see, the most important and compelling justification is where the taking of jurisdiction by the courts, in respect of some piece of conduct, would impinge on parliamentarians' freedom of speech or expression. It would be helpful to think of the freedom-of-expression function of parliamentarians as protected from scrutiny in the courts, because the possibility of such scrutiny threatens the intrinsic political value of this crucial function as an autonomous function. A democratic political system will not flourish as it should if politicians must be guarded in what they say in Parliament, or in a committee of the House, for fear of legal consequences.[258] The freedom-of-expression function is clearly not the only parliamentary function with intrinsic political value. MPs' representative function—their function as representatives of their constituents—also has great intrinsic political value. However, actions performed in the discharge of that function are not protected from civil or criminal liability in the same way, or to the same extent. Depending on their nature, such actions may fall instead to be protected by so-called 'qualified' privilege, which is concerned with communication and its vulnerability to actions for libel.[259] Communications between a constituent and an MP, or between an MP and a minister, may be protected from legal action, because they fall within a broader category of actions protected in this respect by the common law:

> A privileged occasion is an occasion where the person who makes a communication has an interest, or a duty, legal, social or moral, to make it to the person to whom it is made, and the person to whom it is made has a corresponding interest or duty to receive it.[260]

Qualified privilege is not of further relevance to this discussion, except in relation to one point. Qualified privilege is lost in any instance where the statement in question is not made in good faith, or through malice or the like. As Lord Bingham has put it: 'the protection . . . would be lost if the member were shown to have made the statement in question without believing it to be true or from some ulterior or wrongful motive'.[261] As explained in Chapter 3, the loss of legal protection from action when a public official acts maliciously or corruptly, and so on, is an important constitutional principle.

Alongside this 'intrinsic value' justification for immunity from suit, there is also a different (albeit related) justification for excluding the jurisdiction of the courts

[256] See now *R v Chaytor* (n 9) para 18 (Lord Phillips).
[257] ibid.
[258] On the prevention of private law actions in relation to words spoken in Parliament see *A v UK* (2003) 36 EHHR 51.
[259] See Oonagh Gay and Hugh Tomlinson (2013), at 62–64.
[260] *Adam v Ward* [1917] AC 309 (HL), at 334 (Lord Atkinson).
[261] Lord Bingham (1999), at 109.

in criminal cases. This justification applies to the freedom-of-expression function of Parliament, but covers a much broader range of parliamentarians' activities. This we can call the 'balance-of-powers' justification. It is capable of application to parliamentary activity whether or not that activity has intrinsic (democratic) value. By way of contrast with the intrinsic value justification, the balance-of-powers justification for excluding the courts' jurisdiction is not that the activities of the parliamentarians in question would be stripped of their (intrinsic) value, as such, if they were liable to judicial scrutiny. The balance-of-powers justification has different sides to it. On the MPs' side, it stands for the view that matters relating to parliamentary activity (howsoever defined) are best left beyond court scrutiny to elected parliamentarians, as the latter are accountable to the electorate for their activities in a way that the courts and the executive are not. On the judges' side, it stands for the view that, in the discussion of some issues, there is an inherent risk of (party) politicization that makes these issues unsuited to justiciability in the courts. To turn such issues into justiciable issues risks compromising the perceived, if not the actual, impartiality of the judges pronouncing on them. Of these two sides to the justification, the MPs' side is, today, perhaps the stronger of the two. Judges are frequently called on to resolve disputes of a highly controversial political nature, without any suggestion that they must inevitably draw on their own party political beliefs (or otherwise act in a partisan way) in order to reach a conclusion.

Suppose that the House of Commons decides to spend £100,000 on Christmas decorations for the House, even though (let us say) all parties had given election manifesto commitments to reduce non-essential expenditure on the parliamentary estate. The balance-of-powers justification holds that the legitimacy of the decision to incur such expenditure should not be a justiciable issue. It would be a different matter if, for example, having received the decorations from a manufacturer, the House refused to pay the bill. Non-payment of the bill would be a justiciable issue, in the form of a normal private law action against the House as a corporate body.[262] Such an action is permissible, because it does not challenge the legitimacy of the decision to put up the decorations in the first place. The action is only concerned with the way in which the House carried out, or rather failed to carry out, the contract. By contrast, suppose someone sought judicial review of the decision to spend the £100,000, on the grounds that it was irrational, or failed to take into account the manifesto commitments on expenditure in relation to the parliamentary estate. This is a challenge to the legitimacy of the decision, and for that reason it is not justiciable, under the balance-of-powers justification. As Lord Phillips has put it:

> Different considerations apply to claims for judicial review in relation to the conduct by each house of its internal affairs. The courts will respect the right of each house to reach its own decision in relation to the conduct of its affairs.[263]

[262] See now the discussion in *R v Chaytor* (n 9) paras 67–75.

[263] *R v Chaytor* (n 9) para 76, citing *R v Parliamentary Commissioner for Standards ex parte Fayed* [1998] 1 WLR 669.

For similar reasons, such decisions cannot be impugned through prosecutions for misconduct in a public office. The balance-of-powers justification holds that it should not be for the courts to superintend such conduct and pass formal judgment on it, through the medium of criminal prosecution. Better to have no supervision at all than the supervision undertaken and judgment passed by the wrong kind of body, an unelected body; or so the argument runs. With these justifications for ousting the courts' jurisdiction in mind, let us turn to ways in which the justifications are embedded in current practice.

We need to understand something about what is generally and aptly known as parliamentary 'privilege', the immunity of parliamentarians from accountability to the courts. There are two related aspects to privilege: (a) privilege in relation to free expression, and (b) what is called Parliament's 'exclusive cognisance', its sole control over the handling of Parliament's business (howsoever defined).[264] So far as (a) is concerned, as is well known, Article 9 of the Bill of Rights declares that: 'the freedom of speech and debates or proceedings in Parliament ought not to be impeached or questioned in any court or place out of Parliament'. On the face of it, Article 9 appears to be concerned with the intrinsic value justification, described above. That is to say, it appears to be concerned with protecting parliamentarians' freedom of expression when they are engaged in proceedings in Parliament. Constitutionally, the explanation for (a) is clearly the centrality of free parliamentary speech and representation to the health of democracy:

> A primary function of Parliament is to debate and pass resolutions freely on subjects of its own choosing. This is a cornerstone of parliamentary democracy. The performance of this function is secured by the members of each House having the right to say what they will (freedom of speech) and discuss what they will (freedom of debate). These freedoms, the single most important parliamentary privilege, are enshrined in article 9 of the Bill of Rights 1689.[265]

Clearly, if the value is to be maintained of Parliament being free to make or unmake whatever policies and laws it chooses, its members should be free to speak on such matters, without the imposition of external constraints, superintendence, or the fear of legal consequences. Accordingly, the parliamentary privilege at issue in (a) is regarded as an absolute privilege that cannot be waived or relinquished by Parliament.[266]

The absolute nature of the privilege explains why the government-led review of parliamentary privilege concluded that, when certain forms of speech took place in the course of debates or proceedings in Parliament, it should not be possible to adduce evidence of them in any criminal prosecution.[267] These acts were as follows:

[264] Oonagh Gay (2013), at 4.

[265] Joint Select Committee on Parliamentary Privilege (1998–99), at para 36.

[266] See *R v Chaytor* (n 9) paras 47–48 (Lord Phillips).

[267] Office of the Leader of the House of Commons (2012), at para 123.

(a) Use of threatening words or behaviour intended to stir up racial or religious hatred, under the Public Order Act 1986 as amended by the Racial and Religious Hatred Act 2006;
(b) Use of threatening words or behaviour intended to stir up hatred on the grounds of sexual orientation, under the Public Order Act 1986 as amended by the Criminal Justice and Immigration Act 2008;
(c) Threatening or abusive behaviour under Criminal Justice and Licensing (Scotland) Act 2010;
(d) Encouragement of terrorism, under the Terrorism Act 2006;
(e) Criminal contempt of court under the Contempt of Court Act 1981 (which makes it a strict liability offence to publish material which creates a substantial risk of prejudice or impediment to active court proceedings. 'Publication' includes communication by speech);
(f) Breach of the Official Secrets Act 1989.[268]

In addition, the review took the view that the ban on evidence being adduced from speeches or proceedings in Parliament should extend to criminal proceedings for misconduct in a public office, as it should not be possible to circumvent the ban in relation to the specific offences just mentioned, through the simple expedient of charging misconduct. In itself, that view is unexceptionable. As indicated above, it also applies with equal force to parliamentarians' representative functions (such as their investigation of matters raised by constituents) irrespective of whether those functions involve freedom of speech or expression as such.

At this point, however, we should take note of an important limitation on or qualification to MPs' privilege, even in its absolute form. This could be called the 'poisonous tree' limitation.[269] Criminal evidence lawyers are familiar with the problem expressed in the metaphor of the 'fruits of the poisonous tree'.[270] Suppose a man is coerced into confessing to a theft, and indicates under duress where the stolen goods are to be found. Even if the confession is inadmissible as evidence of guilt because it was coerced (the poisonous tree), does that automatically entail that the man's ability to locate the stolen goods—the (evidential) fruit of the poisonous tree—is also inadmissible as evidence of guilt? It does not.[271] In relation to parliamentarians' potential criminal liability, a similar issue arises.

Let us start with a simple example. Suppose that a company invites an MP to its offices and pays him or her (bribe 1) to offer another MP a bribe (bribe 2) during the course of a parliamentary committee meeting, which the first MP does. In this example, it is arguable that bribe 2 cannot be the subject of a prosecution in the courts

[268] Added to this list were some offences relating to the passing on of information: Office of the Leader of the House of Commons (2012), at para 127.
[269] See the discussion in Robert M Pitler (1968).
[270] *HM Advocate v P (Scotland)* [2011] UKSC 44.
[271] Police and Criminal Evidence Act 1984, s 76(4).

under the Bribery Act 2010, because it is protected by Article 9.[272] That is because the conduct at issue in bribe 2 is part and parcel of a proceeding in Parliament, and so cannot be called into question in a court of law. However, the conduct involved in bribe 1, can be prosecuted under the 2010 Act, because it did not take place during the course of any speech, debate, or proceeding in Parliament.[273] The same analysis applies when we are concerned with the 'fruits of the poisonous tree'.[274]

Suppose an MP makes a speech in Parliament favouring public investment in a town. She does this mainly because she secretly hopes and expects that the local town councillors—hearing of the speech—will reward her for having made it. When she meets the councillors later on a visit to the town, they offer her a financial reward for having made the speech and she accepts. In this example, the making of the speech in Parliament—the poisonous tree—cannot be made subject to criminal prosecution (as, say, an attempt to commit bribery, through taking a more than merely preparatory step), because that is barred by Article 9. By contrast, the 'fruit' of this poisonous tree, the acceptance of the offered reward, can be made the subject of a prosecution for bribery. As Buckley J put it:

> [C]orruption is complete when the bribe is offered or given, solicited or taken. If . . . a bribe is given or taken by a member of Parliament, to use his position dishonestly, that is to favour the briber as opposed to acting independently and on the merits, the crime is complete. It owes nothing to any speech, debate or proceedings in Parliament. Proof of the element of corruption in the transaction is another and quite separate consideration.[275]

These distinctions are important ones for our purposes. If MPs, using the scope of privilege, agree on a corrupt policy or arrangement, that agreement cannot in itself be subjected to legal action. By contrast, extra-parliamentary action in accordance with that corrupt policy should in principle be so subject. It ought to follow that it should not necessarily be a defence to legal proceedings that an MP correctly believed his or her (corrupt) extra-parliamentary action to be in accordance with a policy or arrangement agreed on in the course of parliamentary proceedings. What should matter is whether or not, judged from the bottom up by reference to the standards of ordinary people, his or her conduct is to be regarded as corrupt (or, more broadly, as misconduct). However, as we will see, that is not the law's position.

The law's understanding of the reach of exclusive cognizance is controversial, because it confers immunity on parliamentarians in relation to kinds of parliamentary business going beyond those activities of parliamentarians that have intrinsic value when engaged in autonomously (the free expression activities).[276] Although exclusive cognizance is a doctrine that is broader in scope than Article 9, Article 9 does

[272] The giving and acceptance of bribe 2 would, however, be conduct contrary to the House of Commons Code of Conduct (2015), at para 5 (11 and 12).

[273] See *R v Greenway* [1998] PL 356, approved by the Supreme Court in *R v Chaytor* (n 9) paras 42–44 (Lord Phillips).

[274] For the same analysis in civil law see *Buchanan v Jennings (Attorney General of New Zealand intervening)* [2005] 1 AC 115.

[275] *R v Greenway* (n 273) 361–62.

[276] See further, on this point, John Saunders (2017).

a good deal of the exclusionary work. That is because Article 9 is not confined to parliamentarians' free expression functions. It covers 'proceedings in Parliament' in a wider sense. In understanding the doctrine of exclusive cognizance, as the Joint Committee on privilege noted, we start with Blackstone's understanding of the law and custom of Parliament:

> [W]hatever matter arises concerning either house of Parliament, ought to be examined, discussed, and adjudged in that house to which it relates, and not elsewhere.[277]

Exclusive cognizance is founded in the balance-of-powers justification, given above. It operates as a broader guarantee of parliamentary independence from judicial or executive interference ('back seat driving') in the way that parliamentarians go about the tasks which—as they see it—it is their role to perform.

Erskine May's *Parliamentary Practice* has defined the kinds of activities covered by 'proceedings in Parliament' in this way:

> The primary meaning of proceedings, as a technical parliamentary term ... is some formal action, usually a decision taken by the House in its collective capacity. This is naturally extended to the forms of business in which the House takes action, and the whole process, the principal part of which is debate, by which it reaches a decision.[278]

The reference at the end here to debates (covered in the freedom-of-expression discussion, above) is not what is at issue in relation to the wider reach of exclusive cognizance. More significant are the business decisions taken as part of the running of Parliament, illustrated earlier by the Christmas decorations example.

Here are some further examples. In 2014–15, the House of Commons had custodial responsibility for assets worth £1002.4 million, incurred £30 million worth of capital expenditure, and had a resource budget of £210 million.[279] Recent parliamentary spending has included around £20,000 annually on cut flowers for the House of Commons,[280] over £1 million on renovating the House of Commons' gym,[281] and over £265,770 in four years on champagne for the House of Lords (an average of five bottles for each peer, every year).[282] The reach of exclusive cognizance means that spending decisions of this kind cannot be challenged or otherwise brought into question in the courts, whether through proceedings for judicial review or through criminal proceedings. This is so, even though such decisions have little or nothing to do with the freedom to speak in Parliament, or with (say) the role of parliamentarians as representatives of the people: the intrinsic value considerations, as explained above. Even so, it is well understood that the doctrine of exclusive

[277] Sir William Blackstone (n 75) bk 1 58–59, cited in the Joint Select Committee on Parliamentary Privilege (2013–14), at para 15.

[278] Erskine May (2004), cited by Lord Phillips in *R v Chaytor* (n 9) para 28.

[279] The House of Commons (2014–15).

[280] http://www.parliament.uk/site-information/foi/foi-and-eir/commons-foi-disclosures/other-house-matters/costs-of-cut-flowers-for-the-house-of-commons/.

[281] http://metro.co.uk/2013/10/27/taxpayers-to-pick-up-250000-bill-for-mps-gym-refurbishment-4162726/.

[282] https://www.theguardian.com/politics/2014/dec/07/champagne-house-of-lords-reform-taxpayer.

cognizance is less well protected constitutionally than the free expression and representative functions of Parliament (the functions whose autonomous flourishing have intrinsic political value). This is the understanding, even though—as indicated above—it is complicated by the fact that the wording of Article 9 covers a wide range of parliamentary activity in virtue of its reference to parliamentary 'proceedings'. Exclusive cognizance may be waived or relinquished by Parliament, unlike the absolute privilege involved when the free speech is at stake.[283]

It is worth noting at this point that Parliament's powers to discipline its members are covered by the exclusive cognizance doctrine: 'The jurisdiction of the Houses over their own members, their right to impose discipline within their walls, is absolute and exclusive'.[284] In the seventeenth century, this power was also linked to the protection of free speech in Parliament:

> To the end that all the Debates in this House should be grave and orderly, as becomes so great an Assembly; and that all Interruptions should be prevented; Be it Ordered and Declared, That no Member of this House do presume to make any Noise or Disturbance, whilst any Member shall be orderly debating, or whilst any Bill, Order or other Matter, shall be in reading or opening: And, in case of such Noise or Disturbance, that Mr Speaker do call upon the Member, by Name, making such Disturbance: And that every such Person shall incur the Displeasure and Censure of the House.[285]

The importance of exclusive cognizance in this instance is that courts have no jurisdiction to say whether, and if so to what extent, an MP should be disciplined for misconduct by Parliament itself. Parliament has decided that, set against the new regulatory background governing such matters, there can now be an investigation into an MP's misconduct by the Parliamentary Commissioner for Standards.[286] Where the misconduct is so serious that mere rectification is an insufficient remedy, the Commissioner can refer the issue to the Committee on Standards, which can apply its own sanctions.[287]

In that regard, the Houses of Parliament have granted themselves the right to decide on censure and sanction for forms of misconduct engaged in by MPs when the misconduct extends well beyond anything connected to free speech. Two prominent examples are the misuse of expenses, and the failure to declare conflicts of interest. The nature of these sanctions is linked to the nature of parliamentary processes. So, the most severe sanctions are suspension or expulsion from Parliament. These will be the remedies even in cases where the MP in question has been engaged in conduct tantamount to fraud or bribery. For example, in the case of Patrick Mercer MP, Mercer was found to have allowed payments by third parties to influence his parliamentary actions, and deliberately to have failed to

[283] *R v Chaytor* (n 9) 89–93.

[284] *Bradlaugh v Gossett* (1884) 12 QBD 271, at 275 (Coleridge CJ).

[285] *HC Journal* (22 January 1693).

[286] http://www.parliament.uk/mps-lords-and-offices/standards-and-financial-interests/parliamentary-commissioner-for-standards/.

[287] See generally Parliamentary Commissioner for Standards (2015).

declare crucial financial interests.[288] The Standards Committee went so far as to say of his conduct:

> We are not aware of a case relating to a sitting MP which has involved such a sustained and pervasive breach of the House's rules on registration, declaration and paid advocacy.[289]

The sanction applied to Mercer was six months' suspension from Parliament (including loss of salary and pension contributions).

Parliament's exclusive cognizance in such cases means, of course, that there can be no independent review of the penalty. However, we must keep in mind that the taking place of such an in-house investigation does not preclude subsequent police investigation and prosecution in a criminal court; but for no discernible reason criminal proceedings against Mercer in respect of his misconduct did not follow, notwithstanding its gravity. By contrast, in the case of Denis MacShane MP, the Standards Committee agreed that the Parliamentary Commissioner for Standards should suspend an enquiry into his misconduct, pending the instigation of criminal proceedings.[290] MacShane was eventually suspended by Parliament for one year, and also convicted in the courts of false accounting in respect of fake invoices amounting to nearly £13,000, receiving a sentence of six months' imprisonment.[291] In principle, of course, there is nothing to object to—and indeed, much to commend—in institutions (parliaments, schools, employers) having their own disciplinary systems and procedures. Such systems and procedures must frequently be applied even when the conduct at issue is or may also be subject to criminal proceedings. After all, if, say, a bank employee commits a serious theft, it would be normal and expected that he or she would be subject to an internal process that may lead to dismissal, even if he or she is also subject to criminal sanctions. The same is true of a parliamentarian. The fact that exclusive cognizance attaches to the nature and application of Parliament's disciplinary procedures simply indicates that there is an unacceptable risk—given the likely nature of the issues—of politicization of those procedures in court proceedings, when MPs' conduct is the focus.

We should note, however, that what started as a disciplinary jurisdiction in relation to the preservation of the value of free speech in Parliament, has broadened into a disciplinary jurisdiction relevant to attempts to preserve the reputation of parliamentarians, in the eyes of the public. Parliament uses its exclusive cognizance, in relation to the disciplining of MPs, in order to ensure that MPs uphold high ethical standards of conduct in the course of their parliamentary business. The acceptance by Parliament that its members must not merely remain free to speak and to represent their constituents, but must also adhere to high ethical standards in the course of parliamentary business, raises important issues. It is one thing to say that, *qua* parliamentarians, MPs must be free to exercise important but limited *rights* (of

[288] See the discussion in House of Commons Committee on Standards (2013–14). Amongst other things, Mercer set up an All Parliamentary Group to further his own commercial interests.

[289] ibid para 27.

[290] House of Commons Standards and Privileges Committee (2010–11).

[291] http://www.theguardian.com/politics/2013/dec/23/denis-macshane-jailed-bogus-expenses.

debate, speech, and representation), and must hence be free from supervisory jurisdiction in respect of the exercise of those rights. It is another to say that, as regards an ever-widening wide range of *duties*, parliamentarians can be the sole judges of what those duties are and when they have been broken.

For Blackstone, it was undesirable to set down—by statute or otherwise—the precise limits of exclusive cognizance:

> If therefore all the privileges of parliament were once to be set down and ascertained, and no privilege to be allowed but what was so defined and determined, it were easy for the executive power to devise some new case, not within the line of privilege, and under pretence thereof to harass any refractory member and violate the freedom of Parliament. The dignity and independence of the two houses are therefore in great measure preserved by keeping their privileges indefinite.[292]

This is a version of what I described as the balance-of-powers justification for the ousting of the courts' (or the executive's) jurisdiction. One might question whether the risk of harassment of members by the executive, or violation of parliamentary freedoms, is still today such that no limit or check should ever be placed on Parliament's privileges and hence on the reach of exclusive cognizance; and, indeed, the courts reserve the right to police the boundaries of exclusive cognizance. As a result of the decision of the Supreme Court in *R v Chaytor*,[293] it is now clear that the courts are the ultimate arbiters of the legal scope of exclusive cognizance, even though they will accord great weight to the views of Parliament itself on the scope of this privilege.

I will consider *Chaytor* in the next section. There is, however, a question left unaddressed by Blackstone in this passage. Put aside the question whether exclusive cognizance should remain an open-ended concept, as Blackstone supposed. Are there some kinds of parliamentary activities, in particular the discharge of certain ethical obligations bearing on financial responsibilities, which the courts are in fact well placed to and should superintend? I believe that there are and that Blackstone himself provided us with the reason for so thinking. As we saw in Chapter 3, Blackstone rightly identified self-preferential (corrupt) actions by public officials as a unique kind of betrayal of ordinary people, in whose interests officials are meant to be acting, a betrayal fit for severe punishment. The courts should be willing to follow this lead, in restricting the scope of exclusive cognizance through the application of the misconduct offence. What is more, in so doing they should not shrink from using the offence creatively to attack systematic corruption that has been given the cloak of legitimacy by common practice or the tolerance of regulators. As Buckley J robustly put the point in *Greenway*:

> That a member of Parliament against whom there is a prima facie case of corruption should be immune from prosecution in the courts of law is to my mind an unacceptable proposition at the present time. I do not believe it to be the law.[294]

[292] Sir William Blackstone (n 75) bk 1 164. However, no new privileges can be created: see the discussion in Liam Lawrence Smyth (2013), at 3–33.

[293] *R v Chaytor* (n 9).

[294] *R v Greenway* (n 273) 363.

Key examples, considered earlier, are MPs' abuse of the ACA and their employment of family members at public expense.

4.9 *R v Chaytor*: The Approach of the Court of Appeal

In *Chaytor*,[295] three MPs were charged with false accounting, contrary to section 17 of the Theft Act 1968. The charges were based on allegations that they had dishonestly claimed for expenses relating to the conduct of parliamentary business that were not in fact incurred. In two out of the three cases, the claims related to the ACA, discussed above. In one of these two cases (Elliot Morley), it was alleged that there had been claims for the repayment of mortgage interest when the mortgage had already been paid off. In the second of these two cases (James Devine), it was alleged that there had been claims for the costs of cleaning and property maintenance services that had in fact never been supplied. In the third case (David Chaytor), the defendant had claimed for the costs of IT services provision when the services had never been provided. All three defendants sought to meet the Prosecution's case, not by denying that they had been dishonest or had acted with a view to making a gain, but simply by asserting that the courts had no jurisdiction to try them, because a trial would infringe parliamentary privilege. This argument failed at every level from the Crown Court upwards. The defendants were ultimately convicted under section 17 of the 1968 Act, and sentenced to terms of imprisonment.

For our purposes, what is important about the case is what the Court had to say about parliamentary privilege, and hence about the reach of the criminal law. In the Court of Appeal, a very strong Court (Lord Judge CJ, Lord Neuberger MR, and Sir Anthony May) rejected the MPs' contentions in relation to privilege on the grounds that it was the dishonesty of the expense claims that stripped those claims of the protection of privilege:

> In truth, it is impossible to see how subjecting dishonest claims for expenses to criminal investigation would offend against the rationale for parliamentary privilege ... [O]n the basis that the implementation of the scheme might constitute a proceeding in Parliament, it does not follow as a matter of logic, convenience or principle, that the dishonest actions of a member when making his claim should be immune from criminal prosecution.[296]

This analysis is consistent with the Blackstonian 'republican' view that, when considering the criminality of public officials, what matters is whether those officials have betrayed the public interest principles that underpin their position as officials.[297] Clearly, the dishonest submission of a false expense claim meets that criterion.

However, the Court of Appeal narrowed the application of this approach to claims that were, in themselves, a betrayal of the scheme set up for claiming expenses. The court declared that:

[295] *R v Chaytor* (n 9).
[296] [2010] EWCA Crim 1910, at 76 and 78.
[297] See ch 3.

> [T]he decision to set up [the system], and the terms of the system could not be subject to the court's jurisdiction. Be that as it may, it does not then follow that the dishonest operation of this system by individual members is excluded from it.[298]

Further, the Court of Appeal was unwilling to consider (regarding it as irrelevant), 'whether the action of officials in allowing the defendants' claims is or may be privileged . . .'.[299]

In effect, what the Court of Appeal is saying is that:

(a) a dishonest, and for that reason unauthorized, use of a scheme set up by Parliament falls outside the scope of privilege, and may be subject to prosecution; but

(b) an authorized use of a dishonest and corrupt scheme set up by Parliament will fall within the scope of privilege, and cannot be subject to prosecution.

Whilst (b) is not explicitly set down by the Court of Appeal, it is implied by the passage cited above. If that is right, then the Court of Appeal has run together two issues that should be kept separate.

The first issue is whether, if an expenses scheme shot through with corruption is drawn up by Parliament during the course of a parliamentary proceeding, it is (and should be) subject to parliamentary privilege. The answer to that is 'yes', if Article 9 and the intrinsic value of Parliament's free expression function is to be regarded as a constitutional fundamental. If they are to be truly free from external interference, parliamentarians cannot be free only to say or do things that are morally right or permissible. What that should mean, however, is merely that the conduct of those party to the drawing up of the scheme, in the course of the relevant parliamentary proceedings, cannot be called into question in any court. By contrast, following the logic of *Greenway*,[300] when parliamentarians help themselves to benefits flowing from the corrupt nature of such a scheme (the fruits of the poisonous tree), other than in the course of parliamentary proceedings, they *should* be exposed to possible criminal prosecution. So, (b) above ought to be rejected. However, we must carefully consider the following argument against the following line of reasoning.

It might be said that the *Greenway* case is different in a crucial respect. In that case, the bribery offence—including, crucially, the fault element—was completed outside the scope of a parliamentary proceeding. So, there was no need to call into question a proceeding in Parliament in order to sustain the charge. By contrast, suppose that an MP benefits him or herself through simple compliance with a corrupt scheme devised in the course of a parliamentary proceeding. Then, the relevant fault element will be lacking unless the scheme itself is called into question as corrupt, and the MP's conduct hence condemned as a conniving exemplification of it. The answer to this objection takes us back to the discussion in Chapter 3 of different kinds of accountability for public sector wrongdoing: 'top-down' forms of accountability,

[298] [2010] EWCA Crim 1910, para 78.
[299] ibid para 69.
[300] *R v Greenway* (n 273).

and 'bottom-up' forms of accountability. In other words, the answer raises a fundamental question concerning the standards by which, and the people to whom, MPs should be accountable. The assumption made by the Court of Appeal in *Chaytor* is that what matters is whether an MP has acted dishonestly, when 'dishonesty' is judged by the standards set by his or her parliamentary colleagues, taking decisions behind the shield of exclusive cognizance (top-down accountability). The Court of Appeal's decision thus endorses a kind of democratic authoritarianism inimical to the 'bottom-up' forms of accountability favoured by a republican approach to the role of MPs. I will return to this issue when we have considered the decision of the Supreme Court.

4.10 *R v Chaytor*: The Supreme Court Decision

The Supreme Court (through the judgment of Lord Phillips) began by exploring the basic constitutional relationship between the courts and Parliament, on the question of the scope of privilege. In Lord Phillips' opinion (contra Blackstone[301]), the scope of privilege is ultimately a legal matter for the courts, although the courts will naturally 'pay careful regard to any views expressed in Parliament by either House or by bodies or individuals in a position to speak on the matter with authority'.[302] That is an illustration of what has been called the attitude of 'respectful deference' towards parliamentary authority.[303] In that regard, Lord Phillips himself relied, in part, on a letter written by the Clerk of the Parliaments to one of the defendants. The letter indicated the clerk's view that a decision on what evidence is admissible in court is 'ultimately a matter for the court, not the House', because it falls outside the scope of a proceeding in Parliament.[304] Lord Phillips' approach gives the courts a broad basis on which to form a view on the scope of privilege. His approach includes the possibility that the view of (say) a parliamentary clerk might be preferred to the collective view of one or other House.

Beyond relying on precedent, Lord Phillips does not give any substantive justification for regarding the courts as the ultimate legal authority on the scope of privilege. An alternative approach would be to allow a stay of proceedings in any case, pending a ruling by a designated parliamentary authority on whether or not privilege applied to relevant evidence in the case. Such a ruling would then be regarded by a court as final and dispositive.[305] Yet, that is not the approach in English law. Whether what is in issue is the intrinsic value justification for privilege, or the balance-of-powers justification for privilege, the courts will not allow Parliament to have the final say over the legal scope of parliamentary privilege. In so far as it is not obvious, one reason for preferring such an approach is clearly so that the scope of privilege (in so far as it is not defined by statute) can be subjected to the demands of the rule of law. Another

301 See text at n 268 above.
302 *R v Chaytor* (n 9) para 16, citing *Stockdale v Hansard* (1839) 9 Ad & El 1 para 157.
303 See the discussion in David Dyzenhaus (1997).
304 *R v Chaytor* (n 9) para 15.
305 For the use of such an approach see section 4.12.

reason, albeit one not articulated as such in *R v Chaytor*, should be the prevention of corruption.

Turning his attention to the expense claims, Lord Phillips draws a distinction between what he calls 'Parliamentary business', and what he regards as 'Parliamentary proceedings' (the broader wording of Article 9).[306] For Lord Phillips, only conduct falling under the description of 'Parliamentary proceedings' is covered by privilege. For him, the making of expense claims—whether or not dishonest[307]—may well form part of a broad notion of parliamentary business. Accordingly, the submission of a dishonest claim is no 'ordinary crime' (like assault or criminal damage).[308] However, in his view, such claims are not part of 'Parliamentary proceedings'.[309] He understands the latter in terms of the intrinsic value justification for privilege, relating to the free expression and debating function of Parliament:

> [T]he principal matter to which art 9 is directed is freedom of speech and debate in the Houses of Parliament and in parliamentary committees. This is where the core or essential business of Parliament takes place.[310]

Conduct that takes place outside one of the Houses, or outside one of its committees, may still fall within the scope of Article 9 privilege. Whether it does will depend on whether the disapplication of privilege would be 'likely' adversely to affect the 'core or essential' business of Parliament, namely its free speech and debate function.[311] For Lord Phillips, the making of expense claims—whether or not they are dishonest—simply does not meet this test for the application of privilege:

> Scrutiny of claims by the courts will have no adverse impact on the core or essential business of Parliament, it will not inhibit debate or freedom of speech. Indeed, it will not inhibit any of the varied activities in which Members of Parliament indulge that bear in one way or another on their parliamentary duties. The only thing that it will inhibit is the making of dishonest claims.[312]

What about the question of whether the making of expense claims falls within the broader scope of exclusive cognizance 'the exclusive right of each House to manage its own affairs without interference from the other or from outside Parliament'?[313] It might be argued that the making of an expense claim ought to be regarded as a privileged activity because it is a necessary incident of performing an intrinsically valuable political function, namely a representative function. So, the argument might run, it should be for Parliament alone to supervise and discipline claimants in

306 *R v Chaytor* (n 9)para 25.

307 On this point, the Supreme Court disagreed with the Court of Appeal, which, as we have seen, saw special significance, from the point of view of whether privilege applied, in the fact that an expense claim was dishonest.

308 *R v Chaytor* (n 9) para 25. On this point, Lord Phillips differs from Lord Rodger, with the latter taking the view that an offence against s 17 of the Theft Act 1968 is an ordinary crime: see para 122. For the purposes of the present discussion, the difference of opinion is not important.

309 See *R v Chaytor* (n 9) para 44. 310 ibid para 47. 311 ibid.

312 ibid para 48. 313 ibid para 63 (Lord Phillips).

relation to the discharge of that function. Whilst this line of argument is not specifically rejected by the Supreme Court, it falls victim to the Court's restriction of the scope of exclusive cognizance to 'collective'—policy—decisions made by the House or by its committees, as opposed to individual acts on the part of MPs related to those decisions.[314] So, for Lord Rodger:

> In short, there is nothing in the allegations against the appellants which relates in any way to the legislative or *deliberative processes* of the House of Commons or of its Members, however widely construed.[315]

Drawing on the 1999 Joint Committee Report on Privilege,[316] speaking of decisions taken by the Houses or their committees, Lord Phillips says:

> The 1999 Report distinguishes, however, between such decisions and their implementation, expressing the view that the latter is not subject to privilege. I consider that view to be correct.[317]

As indicated earlier, in essence, this approach is much the same as that adopted by the Court of Appeal, subject to the Supreme Court's point that whether or not an action purporting to be an 'implementation' of a decision is covered by privilege does not depend on its honesty or dishonesty. The approach implies, thus, that it is only where an act (other than an act itself forming part of a proceeding in Parliament) is corrupt or dishonest independently of the scheme to which it relates that the act can amount to criminal misconduct or a dishonesty offence.[318] Suppose, by contrast, that an extra-parliamentary act, such as the submission of an expense claim or the employment of a relative, simply reflects the (corrupt) terms of a scheme set up by a committee of one of the Houses, rather than contravening that scheme. In such a case, the act cannot be impugned as dishonest or corrupt, simply in virtue of the scheme itself being corrupt or dishonest. For, the scheme was drawn up as part of a proceeding in Parliament—or was otherwise part of the Houses' deliberative processes—that it is no function of the courts to call into question.

The implications of this can be appreciated by looking at the facts underlying the prosecution of David Chaytor himself. According to the Supreme Court:

> Mr Chaytor [wa]s charged with making use of an expenses claim form for incidental expenses provision in relation to two invoices relating to the supply of IT services when no such services had been supplied. He [wa]s further charged with making use of expenses claim forms for additional costs allowance in respect of payments of monthly rent when such payments had never been made.[319]

On the Supreme Court's reasoning, this charge would have had no legal foundation had MPs previously agreed amongst themselves, as a matter of policy, that (let us say, for the sake of argument) up to a certain amount, such claims should be allowed even

314 See Sally Lipscombe and Alexander Horne (2013), at 83.
315 *R v Chaytor* (n 9) para 122 (my emphasis).
316 Joint Committee on Parliamentary Privilege (1998–99).
317 See *R v Chaytor* (n 9) para 89. 318 ibid para 90. 319 ibid para 6.

when known to be false. Chaytor was thus, in a way, simply unlucky. Unfortunately for him, the MPs' scheme of allowances, corrupt in many ways, was in a crucial respect ethically respectable: it required expenses of the exact kind he claimed to match actual expenditure. At that time, in relation to other kinds of expenses, MPs were entitled to self-certify that they were incurred properly:[320] *carte blanche* to commit the very kind of false accounting of which Chaytor was convicted.

Parliament applied a sticking plaster to the problem, in the form of a new offence of providing false or misleading information relating to a claim under the MPs' allowances scheme, by virtue of section 10 of the Parliamentary Standards Act 2009. We should note, however, that the offence carries a maximum sentence of one year's imprisonment, whereas if the identical conduct were to be prosecuted under the Fraud Act 2006, the maximum sentence would be ten years' imprisonment. It seems that there is one (lenient) rule for expense-fiddling MPs, and another (much harsher) rule for ordinary citizens who fiddle their expenses.[321] There could, thus, be few better examples of the need for prosecutors and the courts to take the initiative, and vigorously to pursue corruption amongst MPs through the use of the misconduct offence (and nothing less). In expense abuse cases, the justification would be the constitutional appropriateness of this offence. It is the offence best suited (unlike the section 10 offence) to capture the element of public betrayal involved when MPs act corruptly or fraudulently. Morally speaking, the offence under the 2009 Act is not worth the paper it is written on.

To return to the main theme, the Supreme Court's position is open to the same criticism made above of the decision of the Court of Appeal. Those who have been party to a resolution of the House (or to some other collective decision made on its behalf) are and should be protected by privilege from challenge in court respecting that decision *as such*. The 'intrinsic value' justification for Article 9 demands no less. Even so, that need be no bar to criminal prosecutions of individual action taken in pursuance of those decisions, if the courts are prepared to take a 'bottom-up' view of the locus of accountability. Even during the period of the rotten Parliament 2005–2010, there were MPs who took care to ensure that they did not exploit the opportunities made available to them to use public money to renovate their private homes, or turn their staffing allowance into a subsidy for a family business, even though they were not people with independent wealth.[322] From a bottom-up perspective, the issue is whether, when incurring expenditure—*ex hypothesi*, in accordance with a scheme agreed by Parliament—an MP is aware that the expenditure would be regarded as corrupt by ordinary honest people: the test for dishonesty applied generally in theft.[323] In that regard, the fact the expenditure was authorized by a scheme agreed on from the top down by Parliament may be some mitigation,

[320] See Legg (n 59) para 26.

[321] I say one 'rule' has been created for MPs and another for ordinary citizens, because now that the offence under s 10 has been created to deal with expenses fraud, it would be hard to justify a prosecution of an MP under the Fraud Act 2006 for such conduct.

[322] http://www.telegraph.co.uk/news/newstopics/mps-expenses/5342811/MPs-expenses-The-saints-Part-i.html.

[323] *R v Ghosh* (n 157).

or even in some cases a reason not to prosecute; but it should not be a bar to the courts' criminal jurisdiction. To acknowledge the existence of such a bar is to prefer democratic authoritarian to republican forms of accountability. It is, hence, to treat as matters of absolute trust issues on which we should place only conditional trust in elected representatives.[324]

4.11 A More Republican Approach to Misconduct in Cases of Expenses Abuse

Take the case of an MP who has employed a son or daughter, or who has used the ACA to increase the value of his or her homes, by switching to and fro their designation as primary and secondary residences for the purposes of claiming mortgage interest relief or the costs of home improvements.[325] It should be possible to charge such an MP with misconduct in a public office, on the grounds that such conduct is an abuse of the public's trust. As I indicated at the end of the last section, it should be no defence to that charge, although it may be some mitigation, that what was done was in accordance with a scheme set down by resolution or in committee for the employment of relatives or friends, or for the use of the ACA (the top-down view). In the case of misconduct, the test should be a bottom-up test: did the MP wilfully misconduct him or herself in such a way as to amount to an abuse of the public's trust, by acting to benefit him or herself or his or her relatives, in the light of the standards that he or she realized that an ordinary honest person of integrity would apply? The introduction of such a test would provide a healthy dose of positive encouragement to all individual MPs, to ensure that their colleagues do not agree behind the shield of immunity from suit to corrupt schemes of remuneration.

In the case of the use of public money to employ family members, there can be no principled objection to prosecution simply on the grounds that the practice has hitherto grown up unopposed. For example, to provide some analogies, that there is a culture of small-scale fraud or theft at work,[326] of ignoring workplace safety requirements,[327] or of offering bribes when in particular countries,[328] need not itself prevent prosecution for the relevant offence being perfectly proper. Indeed, that such practices have grown up may in itself provide a positive reason to prosecute, in order to mark the law's disapproval. Further, that individuals have been given some kind of official encouragement or even authorization to engage in a practice will not necessarily be a bar to prosecution.[329] Assuming that there would be no evidentiary difficulties in bringing a prosecution, two initial questions arise. First, there is the question of whether the legal test for misconduct in office would be satisfied, the test of whether an MP who employed a relative has, in so doing, wilfully misconducted

[324] See the discussion of absolute and conditional trust in ch 1.

[325] See the discussion in section 4.7.

[326] *R v Feely* [1973] QB 530.

[327] http://www.hse.gov.uk/pubns/hse41.pdf.

[328] Bribery Act 2010, s 5(2).

[329] *South Tyneside Borough Council v Jackson* [1988] EHLR 249. See generally the discussion in Andrew Ashworth, 'Testing Fidelity to Legal Values' (2002).

him or herself to such a degree as to amount to an abuse of the public's trust in the office holder (without reasonable excuse or justification). Secondly, there is the question of whether there is a public interest in pursuing a prosecution for this offence, in these circumstances.

Considering the legal test first, it is clear without the need for further argument that, in employing relatives, MPs are acting in their capacity as public office-holders. A key question, thus, is whether, in so acting, they are 'wilfully' misconducting themselves. In the leading case of *Attorney-General's Reference No 3 of 2003*,[330] the court approved the definition of wilful as 'deliberately doing something which is wrong knowing it to be wrong or with reckless indifference as to whether it is wrong or not'.[331] This element of the offence is closely analogous to the *Ghosh* requirement for dishonesty in theft, where the defendant must be found to have known or been aware that ordinary people would regard his or her conduct as dishonest.[332] It is strongly arguable that a jury would find this element of the offence to be satisfied in many instances, perhaps particularly in those cases where MPs have employed more than one family member, thus using their allowances to create, in effect, a family business.[333] So, is the misconduct of such a nature or degree as to amount to an 'abuse' of the public's trust? Again, it is strongly arguable that for an MP to use public money to engage in nepotism is, in and of itself, such an abuse.

In *R v Chapman*,[334] the Court of Appeal indicated that there were two ways to assist the jury to understand the 'nature or degree' test:

> The first is to refer the jury to the need for them to reach a judgment that the misconduct is worthy of condemnation and punishment. The second is to refer them to the requirement that the misconduct must be judged by them as having the effect of harming the public interest.[335]

Although presented as independent of one another, the second of these is clearly capable of amounting to evidence of the first. Nepotism perverts or damages a valued culture of commitment to impartiality in public appointments, and tends to contribute to the entrenchment of any existing inequalities in terms of access to opportunities. To engage in nepotism is, then, to damage the public interest, and not simply to manifest a more or less forgivable personal moral failing, furbishing the case for regarding it as criminal.[336]

Turning now from the formal elements of the offence to the public interest in prosecution, it is an irony that the very chaotic lack of integrity in the way that

330 [2004] EWCA Crim 868.   331 ibid para 28.

332 *R v Ghosh* (n 157). In this context, the *Ghosh* test is more appropriate than the test for dishonesty suggested in *Ivy v Genting Casinos UK Limited* [2017] UKSC 67.

333 See the discussion in section 4.7.   334 [2015] EWCA Crim 539.

335 ibid para 34 (Cranston J).

336 It is a defence to misconduct in a public office that there was a justification or excuse for one's conduct, although the Law Commission has – rightly – suggested that the defence should be abolished: Law Commission, *Reforming Misconduct in Public Office* (n 28) para 5.210. The claim that MPs were only following existing practice may re-emerge as a potential basis for excuse (if not justification) in relation to the employment of relatives. Even so, without some redeeming moral feature, such claims should be rejected as a basis for complete acquittal (although they may still be relevant at the point of sentence).

MPs organized the expenditure of public money, during the rotten Parliament 2005–2010, was treated by the CPS as a reason *not* to take out criminal proceedings against corrupt MPs.[337] This approach was too timorous and too narrow. It was too timorous in that, even in the absence of precise guidance on the use of expenses, there was—as we have seen—plenty of official guidance available to MPs that they should never use public money in a way that could give the appearance of an improper personal financial benefit to themselves, let alone actually involve such impropriety.[338] The CPS approach was additionally too narrow, in that it was focused only on the absence of formal procedures as a basis for guidance to MPs; but misconduct in public office cannot be confined only to knowing or reckless departures from established procedures. It must be, and has always been, capable of application to knowing or reckless engagement in substantive wrongdoing, irrespective of whether such wrongdoing also involves a formal departure from an established procedure (the 'substantive' principle). Were it otherwise, behaviour so unthinkable that no one had ever thought to try to prevent it, through establishing a procedure to be followed that ruled it out, would not be caught by the offence. Even if public services are now so subject to detailed regulation and guidance that this possibility is unlikely, the 'substantive' principle should remain.

More broadly, there is some legitimate scope for the application of the misconduct offence to overarching or systematic failures, such as toleration of abuses, even though the offence has never been used in that way. An example might be the well-publicized toleration by the House of Lords authorities of abuse of the system of daily allowances (to which I return in section 4.12).[339] It is a sad indictment of the culture surrounding our system of criminal law and criminal prosecution that it would never occur to a prosecutor or judge to use the offence in that way against senior parliamentarians or their officials. By contrast, were a local government official (say) knowingly to fail to report the expenditure of public money allocated for housing repairs on an official's private house, that would be seen as, and prosecuted as, misconduct.[340] There can be little doubt that, where the deterrence and punishment of personal corruption is concerned, there is one (lenient) standard for members of the legislature, and another (harsh) standard for other public officials.

4.12 The Hanningfield Prosecution: A Test Case

Lord Hanningfield is a convicted expenses abuser, who served a term of imprisonment for false accounting in 2011. In September 2015, he was again charged with

[337] See the decision in the Derek Conway case http://www.politics.co.uk/news/2009/1/29/derek-conway-guilty-of-breaching-standards.

[338] See the discussion in section 4.7.

[339] http://www.telegraph.co.uk/news/2017/03/13/inquiry-finds-peers-claiming-300-day-no-work-axed-avoid-press/.

[340] This example is based on an analogy with the facts in *R v Bowden* [1996] 1 WLR 98.

false accounting, contrary to section 17 of the Theft Act 1968.[341] On the second occasion, the allegation was that he had dishonestly claimed a daily allowance or travelling expenses for attending Parliament, on a series of eleven days in July 2013, when he was not entitled to do so.[342] It was alleged that the total amount in question wrongfully claimed was around £3,300. In 2014, Hanningfield had been temporarily suspended by the House of Lords, for claiming the £300 daily allowance on the eleven days in question when he had not in fact undertaken any parliamentary work. In reaching its decision to suspend Hanningfield, the Privileges Committee of the House of Lords observed:

> The Commissioner for Standards undertook an investigation which focused on eleven sitting days in July 2013 when Lord Hanningfield was on the parliamentary estate for fewer than 40 minutes and claimed £300 for each day. The Commissioner found that Lord Hanningfield did not undertake parliamentary work on the days in question and so breached paragraph 10(c) of the Code of Conduct. The Commissioner found that Lord Hanningfield wrongly claimed £3,300 in daily allowance. In making incorrect claims the Commissioner found Lord Hanningfield failed to act on his personal honour.[343]

The prosecution subsequently undertaken by the CPS focused on the same incidents. However, following a submission from Jeremy Johnson QC on behalf of the House of Lords authorities concerning the scope of exclusive cognizance,[344] the prosecution was abandoned.[345] The trial judge, His Honour Judge Alistair McCreath, is reported as saying that exclusive cognizance extends to the definition of 'Parliamentary work'.[346] So, if Hanningfield had attended Parliament on the days in question to engage in parliamentary work, even for forty minutes or less, a charge of false accounting in respect of a claim for the daily allowance could not be sustained. For, such a charge would involve challenging the view that such a short period of attendance was a day's 'Parliamentary work', and whether it was a day's parliamentary work was a matter for Parliament alone.[347] In fact, as the submission on behalf of the House of Lords authorities itself indicates, this puts the issue in a misleading way.

The submission claims (rightly) that any decision by the House of Lords setting up the rules of the scheme for financial support of members is covered by the doctrine of exclusive cognizance.[348] Less plausibly, the submission goes on to suggest that, in this respect, any advice given by the clerk (the head of the House administration and the accounting officer) on what amounts to 'Parliamentary work' is also covered by the doctrine. That is less plausible, because it would mean that a corrupt decision by the clerk to rule in favour of a member, so far as the extent of 'Parliamentary work'

[341] http://www.bbc.co.uk/news/uk-england-essex-34668301.

[342] ibid.

[343] House of Lords' Committee for Privileges and Conduct (2013–14), *14th Report: The Conduct of Lord Hanningfield* (2013–14) para 4.

[344] Jeremy Johnson QC (2016); see also http://www.parliament.uk/business/news/2016/july/hanningfield-statement/.

[345] http://www.theguardian.com/politics/2016/jul/18/hanningfield-acquitted-of-expenses-after-parliament-intervenes-with-court.

[346] For the official understanding of 'Parliamentary work' see House of Lords (2013) para 3.1.

[347] ibid.

[348] Johnson QC (n 344) para 16.

was concerned, could not be the subject of prosecution, even if it was a perversion of the rules of the scheme set down by the House. I will come back to this point in a moment. What seems to have been downplayed or overlooked by the prosecution and the judge in the case is the clear view set out at the end of the submission that:

> The Clerk's views as to what does or does not amount to Parliamentary work are not probative of the question of whether the Defendant honestly believed that he was entitled to make the claims that form the substance of these proceedings. The position might be different if there was some evidence that the Clerk (or somebody else) had explained to the Defendant what the Clerk did and did not believe amounted to Parliamentary work and if the Defendant had purported to rely on that explanation. However, that is not this case.[349]

Two points arise from this important passage. First, arising from the first part of the passage, suppose that the court could not in law adjudge whether or not Hanningfield was in fact engaged in 'Parliamentary work'. Even so, if Hanningfield did not honestly believe that he was so engaged, then his submission of a claim amounts to an *attempt* to commit an offence contrary to section 17 of the 1968 Act. Having received the House of Lords authority submission, the prosecution should have sought to amend the indictment accordingly. Secondly, pursuing the point made above, we should reject the suggestion in the latter part of the passage: that Hanningfield would have been able to shelter behind a claim of exclusive cognizance, merely if he had relied on a statement by the clerk concerning what he (the clerk) believed to be included within the scope of 'Parliamentary work'. Even if Hanningfield relied on such a statement, it is doubtful whether in law he could argue that a prosecution would be an abuse of process simply because he relied on an (erroneous) official statement.[350] In any event, that is clearly not the same as suggesting that the doctrine of exclusive cognizance covers a parliamentary official's view—rather than Parliament's own view—about the scope of an expenses scheme. It should always be open to a court to decide that an official's view of the scope of a scheme is wrong, as when, for example, pressure has been brought to bear by members of the House on officials to broaden the scope of the scheme so that they (the members) may more easily act in a self-serving way.[351]

The decision in the second Hanningfield case is thus pusillanimous and overcautious.[352] There was clearly evidence that the defendant might have been abusing the daily allowance privilege, as indeed the Commissioner for Standards had found.[353] So, in order to sustain the prosecution, it would not even have been necessary to cast doubt over Parliament's understanding of the scope of 'Parliamentary work'. It is right to regard decisions of the Houses of Parliament as in themselves covered by the doctrine of exclusive cognizance. However, that should not protect

[349] ibid para 17. [350] See Ashworth, 'Testing Fidelity to Legal Values' (n 329).

[351] In that regard, Sir Thomas Legg had spoken euphemistically of the 'culture of deference' shown by the Fees Office towards MPs making demands for expenses reimbursements: see Legg (n 59) paras 26–27.

[352] For more detailed criticism see Saunders (n 276).

[353] House of Lords Committee for Privileges and Conduct, (2013–14) para 4: 'The Commissioner found that Lord Hanningfield wrongly claimed £3,300 in daily allowance. In making incorrect claims the Commissioner found Lord Hanningfield failed to act on his personal honour'.

an individual parliamentarian from prosecution in respect of what is (in the eyes of ordinary people) corrupt or dishonest conduct, even when that conduct is a *bona fide* reflection of a parliamentary decision. Suppose Hanningfield had thought—and been right to think—that Parliament took the view that he was entitled to define 'Parliamentary work' in any way he chose, including the 'work' involved in simply registering his presence in Parliament. On my account, it should still be possible to prosecute him for misconduct in public office, albeit not in such a case for 'false' accounting.[354] The question for the court in such a case should be: 'If his conduct was to benefit himself, then by the standards expected by the general public of a member of Parliament, did he wilfully misconduct himself to such an extent as to amount to an abuse of the public's trust'?

4.13 Political Party Liability and Negotiated Justice

In a republican state, it can and should be part of the responsibility of prosecution services and the courts to play a role in keeping politics clean, through employing criminal sanctions against both individual corrupt acts and, in the case of those in positions of authority, against their toleration of systematic abuse. In this short concluding section, something will be said about the possibility that, in relation to the toleration of abuses, action can be taken against MPs as a body rather than against individual MPs in positions of high authority.

What is the legal position of political parties, or parts thereof, when it comes to prosecution? A 'registered party' can be prosecuted under the Political Parties, Elections and Referendums Act 2000, if (say) it enters into a regulated transaction with an unauthorized participant.[355] More broadly, there is the question of the liability of parties as possible unincorporated associations. An unincorporated association exists where:

> two or more persons [are] bound together for one or more common purposes, not being business purposes, by mutual undertakings, each having mutual duties and obligations, in an organisation which has rules which identify in whom control of it and its funds rests and upon what terms and which can be joined or left at will.[356]

In virtue of the Interpretation Act 1978, a 'person' who may be sued or prosecuted for an offence under statute includes 'a body of persons . . . unincorporate' (unless a particular statute embodies a contrary intention).[357] The Labour Party is an unincorporated association, and at least some parts of the Conservative Party (such as the Conservative Party main board,[358] and the Conservative campaign headquarters)

[354] Because there would be no falsity in any document in such a case.

[355] Political Parties, Elections and Referendums Act 2000, s 71L.

[356] *Conservative and Unionist Central Office v Burrell* [1982] 1 WLR 522.

[357] Interpretation Act 1978, Sch 1.

[358] https://www.conservatives.com/Members/Party-Structure-and-Organisation. The board is described here as 'the ultimate decision making body of the Conservative Party', and its membership includes the leader, deputy leader, the treasurer, and the chairman.

are also unincorporated associations, even though the Conservative Party as a whole is not such an association.[359] The most important possibility is that each of the main 'Parliamentary party' groupings within each party amounts to an unincorporated association, and is not just a grouping brought together by the mere fact that each individual was elected to Parliament as a representative of the party. This seems eminently possible, although it has not been tested in law. For example, the '1922 Committee'—the name for the association of backbench Conservative MPs—is an organization with a chairman, vice chairmen, secretaries, and a treasurer. The 1922 Committee thus has the key hallmarks of an unincorporated association.

The courts have found that, at least where strict liability offences are in issue, it may in some circumstances be preferable to prosecute an unincorporated association in its own name, although when the offence in question involves culpability, the right course is more likely to be the prosecution of individual senior officers of the association.[360] Even so, this does not rule out the possibility that the collective, knowing acquiescence by a parliamentary party in, say, corrupt practices, could give rise to a basis for prosecuting that party for assisting or encouraging misconduct in public office by its members.[361] We know that the major parliamentary parties instigated, connived at, and supported such practices, particularly during the rotten Parliament of 2005–2010.[362] Putting aside the existing law, in Chapter 2, I suggested that the offence of misconduct in a public office should be extended to cover organizations, in some circumstances (offence (b)). Principally, this should be possible when gross negligence, in part attributable to senior managers, has led to the commission of individual acts of criminal misconduct by members of the organization. The toleration of expense malpractice, and persistent failures to impose any kind of accounting responsibilities on individual MPs (leading to malpractice), are two grounds on which there would be ample evidence to prosecute the major political parties with an organization-focused version of the misconduct offence such as offence (b).

Returning to the existing law, what should be the approach of the CPS to, let us say, a joint prosecution of both main parliamentary parties for assisting or encouraging misconduct? In the political arena, just as in the commercial arena, a prosecution can be understood as the beginning of a negotiation designed to motivate reform, and not just as the initiation of an adversarial process aimed at proving the guilt of the suspected offender.[363] Imaginatively developed and employed, a statute-based offence of misconduct in public office can be seen in just that light, in relation to UK politics. Consider an analogy with the now well-known process for reaching deferred prosecution agreements (DPAs) with companies, under schedule 17 of the Crime and Courts Act 2013. Under a DPA, the person subject to a prosecution agrees to comply with the terms of an agreement with the prosecution agency, an

359 *Conservative and Unionist Central Office v Burrell* (n 356).
360 *R v RL and JF* [2008] EWCA Crim 370.
361 Contrary to the Serious Crime Act 2007, pt II.
362 See the discussion in section 4.7.
363 For the position in cases of companies see Crown Prosecution Service (2014) para 2.8(ii).

agreement that must be approved by a court. Whilst the DPA is in force, the prosecution is suspended. Amongst other things, a DPA may require the person subject to prosecution (P), '(e) to implement a compliance programme or make changes to an existing compliance programme relating to P's policies', as well as '(d) to disgorge any profits made by P from the alleged offence'. Radical though it might be, thus, one suggestion for dealing with corrupt practices in Parliament is to introduce such a system, when parties are prosecuted for misconduct (or other offences). That would give the parties, and hence Parliament, the opportunity to reform itself, and to restore public trust in its custodianship of the public purse, in order to avoid prosecution.

Should the CPS be trusted with such a prominent role in such a controversial area? It is fair to raise that question, but it must be kept in mind that prosecutors are bound to act in accordance with the public interest, and must not act from political motivation. As the Code for Crown Prosecutors puts it:

> Prosecutors must be fair, independent and objective. They must not let any personal views about the ethnic or national origin, gender, disability, age, religion or belief, political views, sexual orientation, or gender identity of the suspect, victim or any witness influence their decisions. Neither must prosecutors be affected by improper or undue pressure from any source. Prosecutors must always act in the interests of justice and not solely for the purpose of obtaining a conviction.[364]

Should prosecutors breach these norms they will be professionally accountable, in respect of their role responsibilities.

[364] Code for Crown Prosecutors (January 2013) para 2.4.

5

UK Political Corruption and the Role of the Criminal Law

> Those constitutions which consider the common interest are *right* constitutions, judged by the standard of absolute justice. Those constitutions which consider only the personal interest of the rulers are all *wrong* constitutions, or *perversions* of right forms.[1]

5.1 Corruption, Crime, and Reversing Distributive Injustices

In this chapter, I consider what kinds of political corruption are appropriately targeted by the criminal law. That might appear to be a curious question. Surely, in principle, all forms of corruption should be considered for prosecution? How else, someone might ask, can one stop situations of so-called 'dependency' corruption[2] arising in which, in Philip Pettit's words, 'an elite would be likely to commandeer the apparatus of the state for its own ends, thereby destroying the rule of law'?[3] Should anyone be in doubt about the importance of this point, it should be kept in mind that 41 per cent of political donations in Britain were made by just seventy-six people between 2010 and 2014.[4]

What is actually needed is a sophisticated legal approach to political corruption. Politicians—like any other public officials—need to be free from the threat of criminal (or even civil) liability when their conduct *merely* departs from an ideal. Even in cases involving a higher degree of blameworthiness than that, the crude application of the criminal law alone would probably end too frequently in one or other of two unacceptable results. There is the possibility of 'over-achievement', in the

[1] Aristotle, *The Politics*, Bk III, ch 6, at 11 (emphasis in the original).
[2] 'Dependency corruption' is the subordination of one person to another in the political sphere, resulting from the material dependence of the former on the latter: Robert Sparling (2013).
[3] Philip Pettit, *The Common Mind: An Essay on Psychology, Society and Politics* (1996), at 312.
[4] https://www.theguardian.com/politics/2015/jun/14/two-fifths-of-british-political-donations-made-by-just-76-people. It is commonly supposed that this is a special problem for the Conservative party; but in 2014, it was reported that two-fifths of donations to the Liberal Democrats came from just three individuals, all of whom were appointed to the House of Lords by the coalition government between the Conservatives and the Liberal Democrats. See Transparency International (2015a), at 17.

form of excessive punishment, due to an absence of less draconian, but more appropriate remedies. Alternatively, there may be 'under-achievement', due to problems of proof associated with the criminal process, and (again) the lack of sufficiently flexible sanctions, or of alternative ways of preventing or guiding behaviour. I argue that the right approach involves primarily a combination of what I call the non-criminal, public law remedy of 'negation' (in essence, reversing or preventing a gain of some kind), together with specific offences and civil penalties in appropriate regulatory contexts. An important recent focus for such offences and penalties has been election and referendum expenditure.[5] The effect of the creation of a regulatory context for such expenditure had been to shift this field of political activity away (albeit not wholly away) from manipulation through open-ended discretion, towards governance through rules and principles informed by 'ethical universalism'.[6] In such contexts, amongst other things, a dishonest or knowing departure from those rules and principles can appropriately be treated as serious corruption-related criminality. A question raised at the end of the chapter is whether a more comprehensive approach of this kind is needed to govern political 'lobbying'.

Even so, the non-regulatory criminal law, and in particular the offence of misconduct in a public office, should still have a residual role to play as part of this approach to deterring and punishing political corruption. That offence should continue to provide a means of targeting the worst kinds of corruption-related wrongdoing not covered by regulation. It may also appropriately be used as a way of calling to account high-level officials, or their parties, who have tolerated widespread or systematic corruption by those under their control, even if they have not themselves perpetrated it. This approach, as a whole, is broadly similar to the one which currently applies in cases of tax evasion (if one replaces the role of the misconduct offence with the offence of cheating the public revenue). In other words, a serious criminal offence of general application at common law underpins both specific regulatory offences, and a non-criminal system for recovering ill-gotten gains.

Although I will not be drawing on the analogy in detail, there is a further point of comparison between tax evasion and corruption at a theoretical level. Both tax evasion and corruption involve a kind of distributive injustice. The distributive injustice may arise because the tax evader or corrupt person wrongly keeps or acquires more than they should. Corruption cases, however, go beyond this. Corruption may involve denying to others what is their due, even though the person involved in the denial makes or keeps no gain him or herself.[7] So, for example, someone may be denied an honour they were entitled to expect, simply because their politics does not appeal to those in whose gift the honour lies. Further, corruption may clearly involve the bestowal of gains on others, even though the person doing the bestowing gains nothing him or herself. That would be true in a case where, say, planning permissions are granted on a preferential basis to people known to attend church regularly, even though the members of the planning committee pursuing this policy

[5] Political Parties, Elections and Referendums Act 2000. See further section 5.10.
[6] The phrase coined by Alina Mungiu-Pippidi (2015), at 18.
[7] I draw here on an account of justice provided in John Gardner (2013b).

do not benefit themselves. In that regard, abuse of the honours system to confer honours on a corrupt basis illustrates a significant point about distributive justice. It illustrates that distributive injustices can arise even when there are no problems of scarcity involved.[8] In legal terms, the significance of the role of distributive injustice, as an explanation of (part of) the wrong in corruption cases is that it shows why—as in tax evasion cases—a great deal of emphasis is placed on reversing the injustice, or getting as close to that as one can, through what I am calling the process of negation. In many instances, there will be far more compelling reasons to correct any injustice than there will be to punish the unjust (corrupt) person, although the latter may be important too. Moreover, a rigorous insistence on negation may exercise a deterrent effect every bit as effective as the rather less predictable infliction of criminal punishment.

5.2 Political Corruption, Civic Virtue, and Public Goods

What is the wrong of political corruption, against which the criminal (and civil) law should be directed? A full answer to that question might appear to require nothing short of a theory of politics. Unless we know what counts as good—ethical, conscientious, honest—politics, how can we adequately theorize the deterrence and punishment of bad—unethical, cynical, dishonest—politics? Certainly, it is necessary to venture into this territory, at least by setting out the background assumptions I will make about the political structures within which good (as well as bad) politics is pursued. In relation to any society, corruption-based critiques of political governance are shaped by where the governance structures, and—equally importantly—the viewpoint of the critic, lie on a continuum between ('bad'), 'closed access and particularistic exchanges' at one end and ('good'), 'open access and ethical universalism', at the other end.[9] I foreshadowed this issue in Chapter 4.1, when pointing out that it will be always be a contested matter whether some feature of the political-moral landscape is part of the context against which corruption in that society should understood, or whether that feature should itself be regarded as a part of the corruption problem. In that regard, I will take it for granted that UK politics is, and will remain for the foreseeable future, broadly democratic and party-based politics, with (albeit more controversially) an important if residual role for certain Royal prerogatives and historical powers of patronage.

Bearing this in mind, political corruption—as opposed to personal corruption—is in play in the two sets of circumstances: direct political corruption and indirect political corruption. I will consider direct corruption in this section, before turning to indirect corruption in the next section. In Chapter 4.1, I described political corruption as (in)action regarded as improper in context, by a person of moral and political integrity, in virtue of the nature of the conception of the good involved in the distribution of benefit or influence. I indicated that it was convenient to refer

[8] ibid. [9] Mungiu-Pippidi (n 6) 18.

to such (in)action as 'partisan'. Understood in this way, political corruption is not confined to public sector. For example, if a company's human resources manager introduced an employment policy deliberately skewed towards preserving the male or white employee majority that the manager favours, this would (other things being equal) be a form of 'political' corruption.[10] The manager acted in a partisan way, using his position to deploy a distributive policy shaped by a conception of the good that would be rejected as improper by someone of integrity. I will not be further concerned with political corruption cases arising in the private sector. My focus will be corruption in the public sector, where there is a duty on all those in positions of trust to further the public interest or common good, rather than their own conception of the good.

What makes the grant of benefit or influence a manifestation of the common good, the antithesis of corrupt conduct? Those working in the public sector must act in accordance with what John Rawls refers to as 'public' reason. Public reason is reasoning the nature of which is such that it can be justified to all those within a jurisdiction, as free and equal individuals, even when they differ profoundly on profound matters of politics and religion:

> As reasonable and rational, and knowing that they affirm a diversity of reasonable religious and philosophical doctrines [people, including officials] should be ready to explain the basis of their actions ... in terms [they] could reasonably expect that others might endorse as consistent with their freedom and equality.[11]

It is not necessary to go into the deep structure of this argument in order to appreciate its importance in this context.

In essence, Rawls' claim is a republican (bottom-up) claim that the freedom and equality of all those subject to government power must decisively shape the way in which political policies are devised and carried out, and not the other way around. That is to say, to be subject to government power should not amount to finding oneself wholly subjugated to and at the mercy of government.[12] In my capacity as a free and equal citizen, I actually share something in common with officials, which is that I am part of a group constitutive of the state; I am not just one of the objects of state action (the term 'private *citizen*' is in this sense an oxymoron). Further, when state officials take official decisions they represent me, in my capacity as a citizen, and so must act on reasons that apply to me—and to all other citizens—in that capacity: public reasons.[13] When state officials act corruptly, in the sense defined

[10] As pointed out by the Law Commission in its Report on the reform of bribery, duties of trust may bind when ordinary people with integrity would regard them as binding, whatever the private terms on which someone has been permitted to take decisions: see the Law Commission (2008), at paras 3.10 and 3.147.

[11] John Rawls (1993), at 217–18. Rawls in fact suggests that this mode of reasoning is how private citizens should debate with each other, but that seems more contentious and can be left on one side here.

[12] See generally Pettit, *Republicanism: A Theory of Freedom and Government* (1999).

[13] The fact that state officials represent me when they act in an official capacity, means that they do this just as much in cases in which they act to deal with those who are not citizens (such as guest workers, or people in the country illegally), as when they deal with those who are citizens. So, high standards of conduct may apply to state officials when dealing with non-citizens.

above, they betray us all, as citizens, even the citizens who benefit from the corrupt acts.[14] When distributing benefit or influence, public officials must keep faith with the trust placed in them. That means providing benefits or dealing in influence only when the test of public reason is satisfied. I will consider some of the complexities of this demand in section 5.8.

In the UK, the most significant risk of politically corrupt behaviour comes from the influence of party political factors in public life. In Chapter 1, we came across the tendency of parties at Westminster to act in 'groupish' ways that predispose MPs to act corruptly. Here is an example of direct political corruption, involving political party favouritism. In a well-known 1990s scandal, the leader of Westminster Council, Lady Porter, and her fellow Conservative councillors, decided to promote the private purchase of vacant council homes mainly in Westminster wards where the Conservative majority was fragile. The hope was that this would shore up or increase the Conservative vote in those wards, from people grateful to the Conservative Council for the opportunity to buy their home. This hope was pursued by deprioritizing the rights or legitimate expectations of would-be buyers in non-Conservative wards. The influence of party political considerations on the way in which sales of homes were promoted was condemned by the district auditor as 'disgraceful', 'wilful', 'unlawful', 'unauthorised', and 'improper', and the councillors were ordered to pay back the £21 million cost of administering their partisan scheme.[15] There is a strong case for saying that the politicians in question should have been prosecuted for misconduct in public office. In this example, although council tenants were the group intended to benefit from the scheme, there was corruption in the way that the scheme was administered in such a partisan fashion, for the benefit or good of the Conservative Party. As we will see in later sections, however, for some purposes and in some contexts, the use of public money and other resources to support political parties is not improper or partisan, because it passes the test of public benefit.

Here is a Law Commission example of direct political corruption, engaged in by an executive official concerned with the administration of justice:

> In advance of a close run general election, an Ombudsman (W) dismisses a serious complaint, supported by good evidence, against an MP in a marginal seat (Y). W supports the political party Y represents and believes there to be a significant risk that Y will lose the election if W finds Y to have committed a serious breach of professional duty. This belief led the ombudsman to dismiss the complaint.[16]

Again, it is strongly arguable that this kind of political corruption should be open to criminal prosecution and punishment, even though the dismissal of the complaint

[14] This argument has some affinity with Oskar Kurer's argument that corruption is a breach of an 'impartiality' principle, according to which 'a state ought to treat equally those who deserve equally'. See Oskar Kurer (2005), at 223.

[15] See Paul Dimoldenberg (2006); http://www.independent.co.uk/news/uk/dumping-the-poor-nick-cohen-unravels-the-homes-for-votes-scandal-engulfing-dame-shirley-porter-and-1407226.html.

[16] Law Commission (2016a), at para 6.27.

against the MP could also be set aside (negated), and the complaint reinvestigated in an impartial way by someone else.

Direct political corruption is also objectionable when it features in public decision-making, if it threatens or damages certain public goods more generally.[17] Some important public goods are traditionally associated with the prevention of corruption, although they have a broader set of good-making qualities that go beyond this aim. These goods are what might be termed 'Fullerian',[18] such as transparency or accountability. Public officials who are obliged to observe such public goods will—so the Fullerian theory goes—be more likely to behave ethically, even though this cannot be guaranteed. In the case of transparency and accountability, anyone compelled to disclose or to account for their dealings to an impartial third party has an incentive not to engage in ethically questionable conduct. A good example of the force these goods can exert is provided by the fate of the fund formerly available to the British government for 'secret service'.

Edmund Burke's Civil List and Secret Service Money Act 1782 had brought expenditure on the king's household under the control of the Treasury, as part of his programme of economic reform.[19] However, the 1782 Act also made provision for the payment of 'secret service' money by the Home Office: up to £10,000 a year by the time of the abolition of the payments in 1886.[20] It had long been suspected that this money was being used in a partisan way for party political purposes, to benefit the party in government, rather than solely in the national interest.[21] That would make its use a form of political corruption, in the sense described above. Its use was challenged in Parliament on 24 May 1886 by a Mr Rylands,[22] in the following terms:

> We are here as the trustees of the public taxpayer. We are asked to vote a sum of money for a certain purpose, and with regard to every other purpose except the Vote for Secret Service, the House of Commons has in its hands the power of checking any maladministration in the expenditure of the country by any Member of Her Majesty's Government. But, with regard to the Secret Service, the House of Commons has no such control. The Government are practically omnipotent, and they can devote £10,000 or £50,000 to purposes about which we know nothing, and some of them may exercise a corrupt influence in controlling public opinion.[23]

To this, the Chancellor of the Exchequer, Sir William Harcourt replied:

[17] Public goods were discussed in ch 2. They are goods the benefits of which are enjoyed in a largely non-competitive, non-exclusive, and non-excludable (*i.e.* not an individual rights-based) way. Public goods are a wide category including some things that are only of instrumental value, such as road signs or queueing systems, as well as some things that are of intrinsic value, such as the tolerant, civilized, or generous character of a people. For discussion of the importance of the protection of public goods by the criminal law see Jeremy Horder (2016), at ch 3.

[18] After Lon Fuller (1964).

[19] For discussion in a legal context see Jeremy Horder (2017).

[20] Some £1 million now, at the most conservative estimate, as a multiplication of the percentage increase in the RPI.

[21] Robert Harris (2003), at 113.

[22] MP for Burnley, he joined the breakaway Liberal Unionists. He was a former wire manufacturer, and corresponded with Richard Cobden.

[23] HC Deb (24 May 1886) vol 305, at 1847.

There are only two courses really open to Members—they must either do away with Secret Service money altogether, or vote it as it has hitherto been voted. To vote Secret Service money, and then to declare that you must be told how it is spent, is simply an absurdity . . . if the House of Commons does not trust the Secretary of State as to the disposal of the money, the best course is not to vote it . . . What I can tell the House is that I do not think it would be wise or a safe course; if, however, I were to attempt to give any reason for that opinion, I should be violating the rule which I have laid down.[24]

Faced with the prospect of continuing without openness and accountability for the way in which the fund was spent, Parliament voted to do away with Secret Service money.[25]

The simple fact that a public official refuses to disclose their dealings, or refuses to account to another as they are meant to do, does not entail that corruption (be it political or personal) is the explanation for this conduct. An official might seek to hide a transaction because it would reveal incompetence, or might refuse to account to someone because of an intense dislike for that person. In such examples, there may well be misconduct in public office, but not corruption as such. Even so, although they offer no guarantees of ethical behaviour, the public goods of transparency and accountability rightly loom large in the discussion of anti-corruption policy. There is more to this than the Fullerian consideration that the protection and promotion of these goods reduces the scope for, and brings to light, corrupt conduct, alongside other public shortcomings or vices, such as incompetence, idleness, prejudice, and so on. Beyond that there is a sense in which, in liberal democracies influenced by a republican political tradition, to become involved in politics is, above all, to embrace civic virtue and foreswear corruption.[26] Hence, public goods associated with the reduction of corruption must be honoured in all facets of political activity.[27] For that very reason, an organization the *raison d'être* of which is benefiting its own members or associates, such as a criminal organization or a private company, cannot be regarded as a genuine 'political party', however much power or influence it may wield in the political sphere. As we will see, a good deal of regulatory criminal law in the field of political activity concerns the obligation on parties to be transparent and accountable. In imposing such obligations it is, however, easy to overlook the reasons why political parties need to operate in a transparent and accountable way, in order to contrast such reasons with the reasons for companies to operate (to some degree) in such a way.

In the case of companies, measures to ensure transparency and accountability may be required, and enforced if need be through the criminal law,[28] to promote a process value. This value is the public good of efficient markets, wherein it is

[24] ibid 1850. [25] Robert Harris (n 21) 113.

[26] For a useful general discussion see Alan Patten (1996).

[27] See eg Pettit, *The Common Mind: An Essay on Psychology, Society and Politics* (n 3) at 312. There is nothing unique about republican theory in its emphasis on the importance of eradicating corruption in public life. Even so, by placing civic virtue at the forefront of its concerns, republican theory brings into focus important elements crucial to the flourishing of a liberal democracy, such as the need for public officials, as an aspect of their role, to foreswear corruption: see Richard Dagger (2005).

[28] See the discussion in Horder, *Ashworth's Principles of Criminal Law* (n 17) 57.

possible, amongst other things, for consumers to base transactions on reasonably full information. In the political context, such measures are also required on process grounds, to ensure that voters are fully informed about choices, thus promoting a more efficient political 'marketplace'. Beyond that, however, the taking of such measures promotes an important substantive value, the value of policy-formation based entirely on public reason in the political domain.[29] Having said that, it is always important to keep in mind, as indicated just now, that the securing of Fullerian goods does not guarantee political integrity in this sense, even if it does something to promote such integrity. The issue of party finance (a subject to which we will return in section 5.10) provides an example. It might be that, in order to secure political influence over a party, a company with an unassailable market share is quite prepared to make large donations to that party to further its private ends, even at the cost of negative publicity. Let us pursue this point further.

5.3 Political Corruption, Exclusivity, and Inclusivity

> The present system of party funding, whether desirable or not, is lawful and practical, whereas other possible systems, such as funding out of taxation, or mass membership of political parties, are either not provided for by law, or not in practice available to the parties, however much they might wish that they were. This court cannot declare to be corrupt, as a matter of fact, the system of party funding authorised by Parliament and adopted by the Conservative and other parties. That may or may not be an opinion which people may honestly hold. It is not true as a matter of fact that the system is corrupt.[30]

It is well documented that few political parties can now rely for their financial sustainability wholly on mass funding arrangements, with many individual small contributors making up the bulk of finance. Only 1.6 per cent of the UK electorate are members of a political party, and that miniscule figure is a substantial rise on the 0.8 per cent figure that held true as a recently as 2013.[31] It would be possible for political parties to cartelize (as we know that they do with respect to employing their relatives at public expense[32]), by agreeing amongst themselves to use public funds to support their party activities in relation to one or more of their organizational, representational, and governmental functions; and to some extent parties do engage in such behaviour.[33] However, a sense of propriety—sustained by sensitivity to how few people join them—has prevented parties from agreeing to a

[29] The importance of this value is reflected in the modern power of the Electoral Commission to allocate £2 million per annum for eligible parties 'to assist the parties with the development of policies for inclusion in any manifesto': Political Parties, Elections and Referendums Act 2000, s 12.

[30] *Cruddas v Times Newspapers Ltd* [2013] EWHC 2298, para 83 (Tugendhat J).

[31] Richard Keen, Vyara Apostolova, and Lukas Audickas (2017).

[32] See ch 4.

[33] See the discussion of so-called 'Short' money in section 5.8. See also the financing of parties permitted under the Political Parties, Elections and Referendums Act 2000.

headlong rush to turn political parties into state-funded entities.[34] Consequently, the burden of raising finance has increasingly shifted to the efforts and enterprise of party office-holders; but that has led to a different problem of propriety.[35] It has led to ever-increasing reliance on the targeting of a small number of big donors, the historical background to which was considered in Chapter 4.[36] In terms of republican theory, such reliance constitutes a weakness in a political system that no amount of transparency in relation to the donations in question can address, for reasons well explained by Rose-Ackermann:

> [E]ven entirely legal contributions from wealthy interests are a source of concern. The worry is favoritism. Groups that give funds to elected officials expect help in the legislative process. They may also expect special treatment on individual problems in dealing with the bureaucracy or in seeking contracts and concessions. If the interests of such groups or individuals conflict with those of the general public, this undermines democratic values.[37]

In this kind of difficult political terrain, the criminal law is capable of drawing an important line in the sand. Consider this example. Suppose that a political party strikes a deal with an organization (say, a company or union) under which the party agrees to adopt some policies entirely devised by the organization itself, in exchange for very substantial donations to the party. The party is quite open about this bargain, justifying it on the basis that financial stability is essential to the party's future. In accordance with the ideal of a broadly republican, liberal-democratic state, the party's action is a betrayal of politics. It involves turning what should be the public good of policy-formation (based on public reason) into a market-based system where money has become part of the currency of politics. To deter such developments, the party should clearly be obliged to return the money: the public law process of negation, discussed in section 5.9. Should the striking of such a deal by party officials also be regarded as criminal bribery or as misconduct in a public office on their part, in spite of the mitigating factor constituted by their openness? There are strong reasons to think so.

Before we turn to legal analysis, it is worth noting what it is that, morally speaking, makes the deal particularly objectionable. To begin with, the party has clearly been influenced by a conception of the good (its own) at odds with policy formation fully justified by public reason and a concern for the common good. In terms of the understanding of corruption relied on here, this makes the party's action corrupt, even if it accepted no money in exchange for its actions. Even so, the real strength of the objection to the deal should be understood in terms of a distinction between political 'inclusivity' and political 'exclusivity'. What makes the deal corrupt is that

[34] Such a move might eliminate the risk of corruption in relation to fundraising, but it would raise new difficulties. It would provide a perverse incentive to start, or to continue, a political party simply in order to attain or retain state funding for the activities of its members. Difficult questions would also arise about whether the activities or beliefs of a party, or a drop in the level of its support, should ever lead to it having state funding withdrawn, *ex hypothesi*, at the behest of rival parties.

[35] See Jonathan Hopkin (2004), at 631.

[36] See Select Committee on Constitutional Affairs (2006–2007). See also the excellent discussion in K D Ewing and N S Ghaleigh (2007).

[37] Susan Rose-Ackerman (1999), at 133. See also Ewing and Ghaleigh (n 36).

it involves the purchase of a measure of exclusivity, in relation to the influence of a partisan interest on public officials. In so far as the party agrees, in exchange for donations, simply to adopt the policies requested by the organization, that organization has purchased exclusivity in relation to its input in the formation of those particular policies.

As a matter of law, the party officials' conduct (like that of the private organization) may fall within the scope of the law of bribery. If the adoption of the donor's policies was nothing less than an exchange for the donation, we can consider the application of the Bribery Act 2010 (in the following example the party officials are 'R'). Under section 2 of the 2010 Act, it is an offence when a person, 'R':

> requests, agrees to receive or accepts a financial or other advantage intending that, in consequence, a relevant function or activity should be performed improperly (whether by R or another person).

Section 2(6)(b) of the 2010 Act makes it clear that liability will still be incurred when a gift or other advantage is to benefit not R personally, but 'another person' (such as R's party, assuming that a political party can be a 'person' under the 2010 Act). For the purposes of section 3(2) and 3(5) of the 2010 Act, we can probably assume that the party officials are performing a public function, and are in a position of trust in virtue of performing it. The central issue is, of course, whether the agreement to accept the donation is, in the circumstances, an agreement to perform a relevant function—adopting a given policy—'improperly'. In turn, that issue depends on whether, in the circumstances, the adoption of the policy was a breach of a relevant 'expectation', contrary to section 4 of the 2010 Act, about the obligations of trust binding the officials in performing their public function. Section 5 of the 2010 Act makes clear, this is an expectation 'of what [disregarding local custom and practice] a reasonable person in the United Kingdom would expect in relation to the performance of the type of function or activity concerned'. It seems highly likely that a jury would find these tests to be easily satisfied, in a case where a donation to a party has been accepted in exchange for exclusivity, for an agreement to adopt a policy.

To some extent, however, the application of the law of bribery is a matter of happenstance. Suppose the officials adopt the organization's policy simply because the organization has been a large donor to the party in the distant past. In that case, there may not be a connection between the donations and the adoption of the policy of a kind that could sustain a prosecution under the 2010 Act. So, the matter would have to be considered as one of misconduct in public office. The UK constitution is republican to the extent that it rejects exclusivity, and in particular the possibility that ideas should be picked up by political parties simply because someone has paid for that to happen.[38] Republicanism is based on a non-market conception of the rights, duties, and privileges of political citizenship.[39] A republican understanding of the good of policy formation hence rules out gaining access to the ability to determine

[38] By contrast, politics in the United States of America (USA) may involve a much more substantial element of so-called 'cheque book government': see Darrell West (2000).

[39] Pettit, *The Common Mind: An Essay on Psychology, Society and Politics* (n 3) 314.

political policy simply through a process of market exchange. So, the existence of that republican element to the UK's political constitution provides a context against which one can adjudge the party's conduct to be a corrupt practice, in a way it would not be under a fully free-market model for policy-adoption by, or political advancement within, political parties.[40]

Here is a more complex case. Following the UK's general election in 2017, the party with the most seats (but no working majority), the Conservative party, established a working majority in Parliament by striking a 'confidence-and-supply'[41] deal with the Democratic Unionist Party ('the DUP', which had 10 seats), a party based in Northern Ireland. Such agreements involve the securing of a kind of exclusivity, in that one party agrees to surrender part of its political independence to serve the interests of another party. In exchange for their political support, the DUP was promised that an extra £1 billion would be spent in Northern Ireland, chiefly on health, infrastructure, and education. No extra spending, above and beyond normal, was to be dedicated to other regions of the UK. This is an example of what is commonly known as 'pork barrel' politics, in which politicians—in this case, the DUP—use influence or leverage to achieve geographical targeting of benefits through costs dispersed through general taxation.[42] In a common or garden moral sense, 'bribery' is involved here. The Conservative Party has offered a requested financial inducement, in order to persuade the DUP to perform one of its political functions in a way favourable to the Conservative Party; but was criminal bribery, or misconduct in office, involved in the striking of the deal? This seems doubtful. Moreover, criminal prosecution is not the right way in which to address such cases of 'corruption'.

First, as discussed in Chapter 4.1, we should note how this is an example where it is unhelpful to try to equate the wrongdoing (if any) with the improper conferral of 'private' benefit. The financial advantage to the people of Northern Ireland, and the enhanced political importance of the DUP, were both very public kinds of advantage.[43] In relation to the former advantage, is the key issue that the benefiting of a particular region, Northern Ireland, was tainted by impropriety?[44] This is not a simple question to answer. Suppose that the Conservative Party had agreed to give an extra £1 billion to all the UK's devolved regions, as part of its deal with the DUP. Welcome though this might have been to the regions, it can be alleged that this was no more than a way to buy the silence or compliance of the other regions, in relation to the deal struck with the DUP, and does not change the (*ex hypothesi*,

[40] On the free market version see ibid.

[41] On the nature of such agreements see Akash Paun and Ashley Hibben (2017). One party agrees to give the other party support in relation to a range of key issues, including (crucially) opposition motions of no confidence, with support on other matters being dealt with on a case-by-case basis.

[42] Charlie Jeffery (2015).

[43] It would have been a different matter, had the agreement been simply to pour money into the coffers of the DUP itself. That would have been bribery. For a suggestion that something along such lines was contemplated see https://www.thetimes.co.uk/article/damian-green-offered-to-pay-for-adviser-in-secret-dup-deal-p5spbzxfz.

[44] See the distinction between substantive and procedural corruption, discussed in ch 4.1.

corrupt) nature of that deal. Nonetheless, even if the deal was influenced by a conception of the Conservative Party's own good, that does not necessarily make the agreement an improper form of political corruption. As we will see in section 5.6, the promotion of a political party's interests can sometimes serve the public good, even though a party is in some sense a private body. In this instance, the securing of a working majority is a state of affairs constituting a public good (making the formation of a relatively stable government possible), something that can be endorsed by people of moral and political integrity. It is not a state of affairs that is solely in the Conservative Party's own interest. The same conclusion would have been the right one to draw, had the opposition Labour Party won more seats in the election, and then managed to secure a working majority by doing a similar deal with the Scottish Nationalist Party.[45] In effect, one public benefit (increased spending on one of the UK's regions) was promised in exchange for securing another public benefit (the establishment of a working majority in Parliament). So, in the circumstances, it would be wrong to regard the actions of senior officials in the Conservative Party and the DUP, in securing the deal, as criminal bribery or as misconduct in public office.

Having said that, pork barrel politics clearly falls some way short of the ideal. The basis for distributing benefit is particularistic, and thus by its nature open to corruption.[46] In the Northern Ireland example, the distribution was not connected to the more generalist distributive scheme designed to ensure fairness: the 'Barnett' formula for determining levels of spending on the regions.[47] This was, then, an example of process-based impropriety, as indicated in Chapter 4.1. It will be argued in section 5.9 that political corruption in the distribution of benefits is commonly best dealt with through the civil process of 'negation' (the recovery or setting back of the benefit) rather than through criminal proceedings. As we will see, such processes are commonly not court-based but handled by specialized agencies, such as the Honours Forfeiture Committee. In a number of jurisdictions, there are independent corruption commissions capable of making recommendations that benefits bestowed through the political process be negated, on the basis that they were improperly—corruptly—conferred. We consider an example in detail in section 5.5. In the UK, it is unlikely that such a 'quango' would ever be established specifically to address corruption at the highest level. Even if established, it is doubtful whether it would gain the authority and legitimacy required for it to be effective at that level, although the Electoral Commission[48] is an existing body that might be trusted with such a role. More modestly, one solution might be to give a Parliamentary Joint Committee that does have this authority and legitimacy, such as the Joint Committee on Human Rights,[49] the power to order enquiries into cases of alleged political corruption at the

[45] In 2010, the Labour Party sought the support of the DUP, in a bid to form a Government: http://www.irishnews.com/news/2015/09/02/news/hillary-clinton-emails-labour-sought-dup-election-pact-248668/.

[46] See text at n 9 above, and Mungiu-Pippidi (n 6) 18.

[47] 'What is the Barnett Formula?': http://www.bbc.co.uk/news/uk-northern-ireland-38077948.

[48] https://www.electoralcommission.org.uk/. See further section 5.10 below.

[49] http://www.parliament.uk/business/committees/committees-a-z/joint-select/human-rights-committee/.

highest level. The result of the enquiry might be a recommendation for negation of a benefit, or in rare cases, the passing of the Report to the police.

The case of purchasing exclusivity is in some respects, however, the easy case. Much more difficult are cases in which what has been obtained by an individual or organization is 'inclusivity'. Someone obtains political inclusivity when they are personally kept informed or listened to, or have influence, on one or more political issues, but when (putting aside issues raised by, for example, official obligations of secrecy) there are no restrictions on who else may also be informed, listened to, or allowed influence—included—on those issues, whether or not in exchange for payment. In the public sphere, political inclusivity can be a positive virtue when it takes certain forms. To give a simple example, one might consider cabinet government (where decisions emerge from discussions in which all cabinet members are included) to be preferable to 'sofa government', where decisions are reached through more informal consultation only with unofficial advisers.[50] As a form of inclusive political decision-making, cabinet government has certain distinctive features. It is, amongst other things, formalized, regular, and impersonal: based on the holding of a key public office rather than on personal connection. That does not mean that political inclusivity is legitimate only if it is confined in such a way; far from it. However, the formal nature of cabinet government means that it is less prone to give rise to personal corruption, flowing from decision-making unduly influenced by inter-personal dynamics.[51] An example of the latter, discussed in Chapter 4.1, was the corrupt relationship between South Korean President, Park Geun-hye, and her friend and confidante, Choi Soon-sil.[52] Whilst this particular kind of personal favouritism at the highest level of government is relatively uncommon in advanced political systems, other questionable forms of inclusivity—considered below—are more of a threat to clean government in such systems.

Suppose that, at a public meeting, a politician asks for people's experiences concerning the delivery of public services, and a member of the public raises a complaint that the politician then promises to refer to the relevant government department. Few would claim that the politician was improperly influenced in so acting. That is because this example of inclusivity, although involving a private citizen, meets a number of important conditions. The politician's action (a) is ad hoc and 'one-off', (b) is impersonal, in the sense that it is not motivated by a personal or otherwise special connection between the politician and the member of the public, but by the nature of the complaint, (c) involves only a relatively insignificant public commitment, in the form of a referral of the complaint to a public body, (d) is *ex hypothesi* quite open, and (e) is not paid for. When an individual or organization is included in political deliberation or decision-making, a suspicion of corruption may arise when

[50] The Butler Enquiry was critical of former Prime Minister Tony Blair's use of 'informal' procedures for taking decisions, in preference to 'informed collective political judgement' (Cabinet decision-making): Lord Butler (2004), at paras 606–611; http://news.bbc.co.uk/1/hi/uk_politics/3892809.stm.

[51] See the definition of personal corruption in ch 4.1.

[52] http://www.bbc.co.uk/news/world-asia-37971085.

one or more of conditions (a) to (e) are not met. We will return to consideration of these legitimating features in the discussion of political lobbying in section 5.11.

What if business people or unions make political donations in order to meet ministers, and take the opportunity to voice concerns or advice about policy? In such cases, these organizations are paying for inclusivity. A perfectly respectable republican argument can be mounted against any form of payment for inclusivity, for largely the same reasons (given above) for objecting to payment for political exclusivity. However, in the UK, political parties are partially dependent on private funding for their activities. This aspect of UK political culture means that breach of condition (e) in the way that inclusivity is determined does not, in itself, entail that corruption is involved. Moreover, such conduct is substantially mitigated, if not always completely justified, if politicians are also committed to respecting fully the principles of inclusivity: by making sufficient efforts to hear from the widest possible range of people who cannot afford to pay politicians for their time. Breach of condition (e), when including individuals or organizations in political discussion or actions, will only involve corruption in the UK where there is also breach of one or more of the other conditions, (a) to (d).[53] Almost needless to say, to what extent the other conditions must be breached, and how seriously, before corruption is involved and the law—and the criminal law in particular—should provide a remedy, is necessarily a highly contested issue. We return to it in section 5.9.

We should conclude this section with a brief illustration of 'indirect' political corruption, because so far I have been concerned only with direct political corruption. The term 'corruption' can quite properly be applied to political benefits knowingly gained indirectly. Here is an example:

> The Cosmicos Party proposes to lower the voting age from eighteen to sixteen, whereas the Senex Party proposes to raise it to twenty-one. It is public knowledge that young people under the age of 21 have consistently expressed a much higher level of support for the Cosmicos Party than for the Senex party, and that most 18–21 year olds vote for the Cosmicos Party. Each party claims both that its reform is motivated solely by a belief about the age at which people are competent to express political opinions through voting, and that the reform is not connected to a wish to increase or decrease the potential vote share of the Cosmicos Party.

In this example, should the proposal by each, or both, of the parties be regarded as politically corrupt? In other words, is the reform proposal essentially partisan in character, best viewed as furthering party political rather than national interests?

Let us assume that both parties are genuine in their account of their motivations, but that each is also well aware of the effect on voting patterns that the changes in the voting age might have, if their preferred reform came to pass. In such cases, where there is no intention to act in a partisan manner, but a partisan benefit will be a known concomitant of the proposed action, what matters to a judgement on the issue of corruption? What should concern us is whether, and the extent to which, there is an objective justification for the action: whether the action is a proportionate

[53] See further the discussion in section 5.11. See also the discussion of the sale of inclusivity, at different levels, by the Conservative Party, in *Cruddas v Times Newspapers Ltd* (n 30) paras 23–27.

means of meeting a legitimate aim.[54] In that regard, the example just given is sensitive to historic considerations. Today, we might be inclined to say that the Senex Party's proposal has a whiff of corruption about it, whereas that of the Cosmicos Party does not, whatever the direct motivations of each party. That is because we are much more likely to consider that 16-year-olds are competent to vote (an objective justification) than we are to think that people are not competent to vote until they reach the age of twenty-one. A century ago, perhaps we would have reached the opposite conclusion. What is significant is acceptance that it can be right to regard an action as falling within the scope of (indirect) 'corruption', even when someone's motives for engaging in the action cannot be impugned as such.

5.4 Republican Thinking, Political Corruption, and Powers of Patronage

Even if one is prepared to go along with the argument so far, there is further complexity. Societies, including liberal-democratic ones, differ in how thorough-going their commitment is to another dimension to republicanism, alongside the emphasis on civic virtue. This is a commitment to the elimination of very broad discretionary powers vested in the hands of individual public officials, an early controversy over which we considered when discussing the use of press ganging in Chapter 3.9.[55] Consider the practice of Royal patronage. In the relatively anodyne form of, say, a royal seal of approval given to a supplier of some good or service, the practice is widespread around the world and common practice in the UK.[56] In this particular form, such patronage is not corrupt in the sense understood here, so long as the criteria for the award are in a broad sense merit-based (there is no partisan element to any award) and exclude the possibility of personal corruption in the form of nepotism or bribery. Even so, such patronage is obviously anti-republican, not so much because a member of the royal family is involved, but because a significant benefit stands to be distributed only to some, on the basis of a wide discretion in the hands of an individual (and largely unaccountable) public official.

In the UK, there are far more significant and well-known examples of such 'anti-republican' powers. One concerns appointments to the House of Lords. As the UCL Constitution Unit rightly observes:

> The most basic fact is that the pattern of House of Lords appointments lies completely in the hands of the Prime Minister. The Queen appoints to the Lords on the Prime Minister's advice. He has completely free rein over how many appointments are recommended, when, and with what balance between the parties (and independent members).[57]

[54] The obvious analogy here is with indirect discrimination, where an objective justification can support the continuation of a practice that might otherwise be regarded as discriminatory because (say) it is much more likely to favour one gender over another: see the Equality Act 2010.

[55] For this understanding of the fundamental basis for republican thinking see Pettit, *The Common Mind: An Essay on Psychology, Society and Politics* (n 3).

[56] https://www.royalwarrant.org/.

[57] Meg Russell (2015).

I will come on in section 5.9 to consider the way in which an attempt is made, in UK institutional practice, to infuse this particular power of patronage with ethically universalist principles, thus reducing the likelihood that it may produce corrupt outcomes, even if it is by nature a procedure open to corrupt abuse.

Another important example concerns ministerial appointment, another kind of appointment made in the name of the Crown. From 1707 to 1926,[58] the acceptance of a paid Crown appointment entailed resignation of one's seat in Parliament, to avoid a *Crown v Parliament* conflict of loyalty. Someone accepting money from the Crown could hardly be expected impartially to scrutinize its actions in Parliament.[59] The power to appoint ministers is a wide power of patronage lying in the hands of the prime minister. The power may, without fear of significant challenge, be exercised to reward political supporters including (through the House of Lords) influential figures in the business world hitherto without political experience or electoral mandate. To be sure, there are some restraints on the exercise of the power: again, it must not involve any element of personal corruption, such as nepotism, or bribery. However, it is another example of an important power of patronage in the hands of an individual official, the prime minister, respecting the use of which he or she is largely unaccountable in practice. The power is thus anti-republican in nature. No doubt, the argument in favour of the current system is that it would in practical terms be too time-consuming, and potentially highly obstructive to effective government, to make ministerial appointments subject to any kind of significant democratic scrutiny. There are twenty-one cabinet ministers and over 100 ministerial and government appointments combined, and the turnover is high.[60] So, the argument continues, the largely unaccountable power of patronage the prime minister possesses to make such appointments should be accepted, so long as he or she avoids personal corruption in its use. The argument is weak, for two principal reasons.

First, the sheer numbers of new ministerial appointments within the prime minister's gift, and hence the power of patronage itself, have grown significantly in recent years. Amongst other things, that reflects a general decline in successive governments' willingness to rely on senior civil servants to advise them on policy matters. In 1900, members of the House of Commons holding appointments within the prime minister's gift were only 6 per cent of its membership; but the figure had risen to 22 per cent by 2010.[61] Moreover, in 2010, such members also amounted to no less than 39 per cent of the governing party. That brings me to the second reason why the argument in favour of the current patronage system is weak. The number of those holding ministerial appointments who can be paid is limited by statute to 109.[62] However, all those holding such posts (paid or unpaid) are referred to as the

[58] Resignation of Ministers Act 1926.

[59] Mark Sandford (2013), at 4 and 18. However, upon resignation, one was entitled immediately to stand again for Parliament.

[60] https://www.gov.uk/government/news/full-list-of-new-ministerial-and-government-appointments.

[61] http://researchbriefings.parliament.uk/ResearchBriefing/Summary/SN03378; https://whorunsbritain.blogs.lincoln.ac.uk/2013/11/03/the-rise-in-the-payroll-vote/.

[62] Ministerial and Other Salaries Act 1975.

'payroll vote', because by convention they do not vote against the government. If they do, they must resign their position, a significant deterrent. In effect, the payroll vote has become the modern equivalent of the 'secret influence' on Parliament of the Crown through its appointments, so roundly criticized and rejected at the end of the eighteenth century.[63] Someone accepting payment as a government minister can hardly be expected impartially to scrutinize its actions in Parliament. Of such appointments, Charles James Fox said as long ago as 1783:

> Much and gloriously did this house fight and overcome the influence of the crown by purging itself of ministerial dependents ... it would become this house to say [now]—rather than yield to a stretch of prerogative thus unprecedented and alarming—'Withdraw your secret influence. Take back those numerous and tried dependents who so often secured you a majority in parliament ... for God's sake strangle us not ... by an infamous string of bedchamber janissaries!'[64]

The difference now, of course, is that the system of ministerial appointment is being used as a means of providing more cohesive, accountable, and effective leadership to a democratically elected government.[65] So, although it involves partisanship—favouring members of the governing party—the ministerial appointment system is not a corrupt practice, because the partisanship involved has a democratic justification. Even so, to say that the system is not corrupt is not in any sense to commend it as a system, in the way that it is now employed. We can draw on the republican viewpoint to describe powers of patronage as an obverse of duties of transparency and accountability. The existence of such powers is, in other words, what I have described elsewhere as a public 'negative',[66] as contrasted with a public 'good' like transparency or accountability. Whilst the use of such powers is not necessarily corrupt, their possession *tends* to corrupt: a mirror image of the role of Fullerian public goods such as duties of transparency, which tend in the opposite direction (as argued earlier). To counter-balance that tendency, perhaps it would not be unthinkable to set up a ministerial appointment committee, tasked with ensuring that all newly appointed ministers are people likely to act with political integrity, and to adhere to the Ministerial Code.

As this last suggestion indicates, if they cannot simply be abolished, the right approach to practices that tend to corrupt is to infuse them, to a greater or lesser extent, with principles inspired by ethical universalism.[67] These are principles drawn from the public goods of accountability, transparency, and substantial reliance on merit-based criteria for appointment. Once it has become mandatory to follow such principles, to fail to do so for partisan reasons becomes an instance of corruption. In some instances, the sting has to some extent been drawn from powers of patronage by this means. The honours system is perhaps a case in point. In making his

[63] A S Foord (1947).

[64] Commons debate on the influence of the Crown (1783), in William Cobbett (1803), vol xxiv, at 197–225.

[65] See Wolfgang C Müller (2000).

[66] Horder, *Ashworth's Principles of Criminal Law* (n 17) 49–50.

[67] Mungiu-Pippidi (n 6) 18.

recommendations for honours in 1895, Lord Salisbury wrote to the Queen's private secretary:

I am distressed at being obliged to lay so large a list of honours before her Majesty. If she comments on it, pray remind her that this is a Coalition Government; that we have an exceptional number of supporters, and consequently an exceptional number of candidates for honours.[68]

There can be little doubt that such overtly party political use of the honours system would now be regarded not merely as an excessive use of patronage, but as corrupt,[69] an inkling of which is contained in Lord Salisbury's professed 'distress' at the way in which he is using the system to shore up the government. The system is now governed and run by an independent Honours Committee that ensures scrutiny of—and may, in accordance with republican principles, reject—recommendations simply because they come from government.[70] So, the element of 'patronage' in the system has been significantly reduced even if, for some, it is still too dominated by favouritism.[71]

5.5 Patronage and Public Appointments: A Test Case

In the making of public appointments (other than government positions), there is no properly settled understanding of the extent to which largely unaccountable patronage and partisanship may play a continuing role in the way ministers make such appointments.[72] This a troubling matter, because there are some 400 public bodies, and 2,000 appointments are made to them (including reappointments) annually in England and Wales.[73] Such appointments include key posts at the BBC, the Bank of England, NHS trusts, and in many other so-called 'arm's length' bodies. Post 1995 and the Nolan Commission, there has been an independent Centre for Public Appointments,[74] and regard must be had in all appointments to ethically universalist criteria, such as merit and the need for diversity.[75] However, in spite of Nolan's recommendation that public appointments should—in a way similar to the award of honours—be 'governed by the overriding principle of appointment on merit', having regard to the need for 'a balance of skills and backgrounds',[76] Nolan recognized that 'ultimate responsibility for appointments should remain with Ministers'.[77] Perhaps

[68] Cited by Arthur C Benson (1931), at 582. See further E H H Green (1995), at 97.
[69] See eg Sir Hayden Phillips (2004).
[70] https://www.gov.uk/honours/overview. Around 2,000 honours are made each year in the UK.
[71] https://www.theguardian.com/uk-news/2016/dec/31/tories-cronyism-new-year-honours-list-conservative-donors.
[72] https://www.theguardian.com/business/2016/dec/27/government-accused-power-grab-new-public-appointment-rules-bbc-ofsted.
[73] See generally Sir Gerry Grimstone (2016); Cabinet Office (2016).
[74] https://publicappointments.cabinetoffice.gov.uk/.
[75] Michael Pinto-Duschinsky and Lynne Middleton (2013), at 6.
[76] Committee on Standards in Public Life (1995), recommendation 31.
[77] ibid recommendation 33.

predictably, that has led to an increase in the powers of ministers at the expense of an independent element. Today, ministers may themselves choose members of appointment panels, overrule the decisions of any independent panel, dispense with open competition, and appoint people deemed unsuitable by the panel (although they must do so openly).[78] This is objectionable from a republican point of view, notwithstanding the elected status of (most) ministers. It is objectionable simply because it effectively leaves great power of patronage in the hands of an individual minister, and hence leaves in place too much of a public negative, in the form of a built-in temptation to engage in partisan appointment, and hence in corruption.

In that regard, it is instructive to consider an older example from New South Wales of alleged misuse of public office in the making of a public appointment, to test our intuitions about the right approach.[79] The Independent Commission Against Corruption (ICAC) was established in New South Wales in 1988 'in response to growing community concern about the integrity of public administration in NSW'.[80] Section 8 of the Independent Commission Against Corruption Act 1988 defined corruption as, amongst other things:

(a) any conduct of any person (whether or not a public official) that adversely affects, or that could adversely affect, either directly or indirectly, the honest or impartial exercise of official functions by any public official, any group or body of public officials or any public authority, or
(b) any conduct of a public official that constitutes or involves the dishonest or partial exercise of any of his or her official functions, or
(c) any conduct of a public official or former public official that constitutes or involves a breach of public trust ...

Section 9 of the 1988 Act then goes on to qualify this definition by saying that, for the purposes of section 8, conduct will not be regarded as corrupt unless it could constitute or involve a criminal offence, a disciplinary offence, reasonable grounds for dismissing, dispensing with the services of or otherwise terminating the services of a public official, or in the case of conduct of a minister of the Crown or a member of a House of Parliament, a substantial breach of an applicable code of conduct.

In 1991, following an election, the Liberal–National Party, which had introduced the 1988 Act following a campaign alleging corruption in the Labour Party, only just retained power. With Nick Grenier as Premier, the government had forty-nine seats to Labour's forty-six, with four independents. One of the independents generally supported the Liberal–National government, allowing the government to continue (the other three independents also reached an understanding with the government). However, the government's majority was reduced in 1991–1992 by the loss of a seat at a by-election and, more importantly, by the resignation of Liberal MP Tony Metherell from the Liberal party but *not* from Parliament, following his conviction for tax offences. This left Grenier's administration with forty-seven votes, and the

[78] See https://www.theguardian.com/business/2016/dec/27/government-accused-power-grab-new-public-appointment-rules-bbc-ofsted, discussing Cabinet Office (n 73).
[79] Mark Philp (1997).
[80] Independent Commission Against Corruption (2017), overview.

Labour opposition with forty-seven votes, the balance of power lying with the five independent MPs, now including Metherell. In 1992, after a negotiation with the government, Metherell resigned his seat in Parliament. He did so in order to take up, on that very day, a well-paid position in the state's Environmental Protection Agency, after the formal closing date for applications for the position. This meant, of course, that Metherell's safe seat would then be won by someone from the Liberal party.

The Legislative Assembly referred the matter to the ICAC, which investigated. The ICAC found that Grenier was in breach of section 8, having breached 'public trust' – (c) above—in the performance of his public functions. The ICAC also found that section 9 was satisfied, in that Grenier's action was sufficient to give reasonable grounds for dismissing a public servant. However, the ICAC did not find that Grenier had committed any criminal offence, and hence it did not recommend that any action be taken against Grenier, a decision about such action being a matter for the NSW Parliament.[81] The Court of Appeal subsequently quashed the ICAC's finding, on the grounds that section 9 was not satisfied.[82] However, taking its lead from the ICAC, Parliament sought to censure Grenier, in the light of his conduct. In the face of a motion of no confidence that the independent MPs were minded to support, he resigned. It is what Grenier said, in responding to the censure motion, which is of importance here:

> Ultimately, if what was done was against the law, then all honourable members need to understand that it is, for practical purposes, the death of politics in this State ... Under the English common law very serious obligations to act in the public interest are placed on those elected to public office, and yet our highest public officials are at the same time part of a political system which is about what is in many ways a largely private interest in terms of winning or holding a seat ...[83]

In a further response to the case, the ICAC tartly remarked that: 'The whole point of the legislation was to combat a corrupt culture, a culture that regards nothing wrong with things like jobs for the boys ... and accepts corruption as part of the way things are done'.[84] How should these responses be analysed?

We can start by noting that, in one way, Grenier misses the point. Whether or not it is right to describe a political party's interest in a candidate winning a seat as 'private', the process by which seats become vacant, and are filled by someone associated with a particular political party, is covered by the notion of public interest. However, the ICAC's riposte is misleading in different way. It fails clearly to distinguish between personal corruption in the making of appointments (advantaging a friend simply because he is a friend), and political corruption in the making of such appointments: the use of partisan reasoning as a ground for conferring an advantage, when the situation called for reliance on public reason. The latter kind of corruption has been explained in a different way by Dennis F Thompson:

[81] Independent Commission Against Corruption (1992a), at 71.
[82] Mark Philp (n 79) 437.
[83] Speech to the Legislative Assembly (28 April 1992), cited by Philp (n 79) 437.
[84] Independent Commission Against Corruption (1992b), at 3, cited by Philp (n 79) 438–39.

Legislative corruption is *institutional* insofar as the *gain* a member receives is political rather than personal, the service the member provides is procedurally improper, and the *connection* between the gain and the service has a tendency to damage the legislature or the democratic process . . .[85]

Applying this account of corruption, then, the key to understanding the corrupt element in Grenier's action, in making the appointment, is the fact that Grenier sought to instal someone in a post other than in accordance with the (public reason-based) appointment rules established *ex ante*. True enough. Where powers of patronage have been strongly suffused with the principles of ethical universalism, ignoring those principles make the decisions in question corrupt.

However, Grenier's main point, albeit wrongly relied on in this instance, is that even if personal corruption is foresworn, a good deal of the conduct of government is necessarily conducted through the partisan use of powers of patronage, as in the appointment of senior ministers on party political lines. That was a point made at the end of the last section. To attack such practices, in pursuit of an ethically universalist agenda, would—Grenier suggests—be to sound the death knell of 'politics' and to usher in an era of pseudo-technocratic government (and why would anyone be motivated to vote for that?). Perhaps so; but as we will see in section 5.6, there is nothing amiss with a corruption critique founded on the simple failure of public officials to live up to an ideal of public life based purely on public reason. By those standards, even if the post had by law been entirely within Grenier's gift, his use of the appointment to keep his party in power might legitimately be described as 'shoddy', the use of 'dark arts', or indeed as 'corrupt'. That is so, even if such criticism is not meant to imply that there should be a legal remedy available respecting the appointment.

Suppose that Grenier had given Metherell the job simply because he was (*ex hypothesi*) a friend and long-standing political ally. Then, it is the response of the ICAC, cited above, that has greater force than Grenier's complaint. For the abuse of the process of appointment is now clearly a matter of personal corruption, and is not just a matter of (dirty) government politics. In such a case, not only should the appointment be reversed (negation[86]), but there would be a strong case for criminal prosecution for misconduct, as in all cases involving personal corruption. On the actual facts of the case, of course, there was—or so we may perhaps assume—no element of personal corruption involved. Grenier's partisan action was an example of political corruption. Even so, the element of ethical universalism written in to the way in which the particular appointment was meant to be made means that Grenier's improper bestowal of it on Metherell betrayed the applicable values, and hence the

[85] Dennis F Thompson (1995), at 7 (emphasis in the original), cited by Philp (n 79) 439. As Thompson correctly goes on to point out (ibid), of institutional corruption: 'Recognising institutional corruption is not always easy because it is so closely related to conduct that is a perfectly acceptable part of political life'. Something we should notice about Thompson's definition of political corruption is how, through its emphasis on the need for procedural impropriety, it is subtly influenced by a Weberian conception of bureaucratic rationality. See further William D Rubinstein and Patrick von Maravic (2010), at ch 2.

[86] See section 5.9, for a fuller discussion.

public's trust. It could be argued that the fact that it was an example of political corruption, rather than personal corruption, makes reversal of the decision a more important response than resort to criminal prosecution for misconduct. However, such a judgement depends more on the facts of the case than on a clear point of principle. How flagrant was the violation of the rules? Was there an attempt to conceal the incident? Was the incident part of a consistent pattern of abuse? And so on.

5.6 Idealism and Party Politics

One lesson of section 5.5 is that mere failures on the part of public officials to adhere to the ideal, in their conduct and choice of reasons for acting, may fall within the scope of what is properly described as corrupt activity, even though there may be no reason to provide a legal process to remedy them. It is worth briefly exploring this point in more detail, in order to avoid painting a picture of 'corruption' distorted by too exclusive a focus on activity calling for legal remedies in general and for punishment in particular. As a form of critique of corruption, ideal-failure is capable of wide application. It could be perfectly appropriate, for example, to describe as corrupt the conduct of a Chancellor of the Exchequer who invested his or her own income in overseas tax havens, even though he or she is entitled in law to do so. The concept of ideal-failure clearly also informs critiques of the private sector, in terms of corruption. So, it might be alleged that the preference of Chief Executives of public companies for making ever-larger pay awards to themselves, rather than reinvesting in the company, is an example of private sector corruption.[87] In such cases of ideal-failure, 'corruption' can quite properly be used to describe and condemn the social and political conduct or practices, without any necessary implication that the practices should be regarded as unlawful. The potency of any allegation of corruption turns on a combination of the stringency of the ideal, the level of institutional commitment to it, the degree to which someone's conduct betrays or undermines it, and the extent to which rights or legitimate expectations have been prejudiced.

Ideal-failure also has a good deal to do with the fact that party politics commonly features in public perceptions of corruption in politics, whether the public has in mind donations to political parties, or party favouritism in the making of public appointments. What is the ideal implicit in people's thinking when they suggest, as we might put it in the language of Bentham when speaking of the common law,[88] that there is a kind of 'inbred and incurable corruption' about the party influence on politics? Very probably, people have in mind what can be characterized as an old-style republican model of government. Under such a model, the wisest and best suited to govern rise through popular acclaim to take the reins of power, and govern either according to their natural inclination to pursue common good,[89] or

[87] http://www.independent.co.uk/news/business/news/high-pay-for-bosses-hurting-economy-says-senior-bank-of-england-official-a7036246.html. For historical analysis of the understanding of corruption in such terms see Mark Knights (2016).

[88] John Bowring, ed (1838), at 460.

[89] See James A Gardner (2000).

in accordance with a 'greatness of spirit' that grows upon election to public office.[90] As James Madison put it in 1787, the point of the electoral process under republican government is:

> To refine and enlarge the public views by passing them through the medium of a chosen body of citizens, whose wisdom may best discern the true interest of their country and who [through] patriotism and love of justice will be least likely to sacrifice it to temporary or partial considerations.[91]

The domination of politics by political parties can come to be seen as an obstruction to, and not a furtherance of, that ideal. For example, a good deal of the pressure to make the House of Lords an elected—or in some other sense, a more representative—body, rather than one largely comprised of (party) political appointees, reflects this ideal.[92] On the old-style republican account, the need for party loyalty threatens to make politicians perennial shortcomers. Those who wish to govern as representatives of the people must, by and large, obtain positions within or be supported by political parties. Naturally, conceptions of the common good, and a republican commitment to importance of public life, feature in the ideological fabric holding political parties together. However, the competence of a political party to govern is only loosely linked to its fidelity to a conception of the common good (a common good that itself shifts over time, in terms of content and significance). Like any organization, a political party has a life of its own. It may, for example, gain or lose a reputation, and gain or lose the capacity to govern. Most importantly, a political party may also act in a self-interested way. It may seek to raise money (perhaps, from questionable sources, or in questionable ways) in order to survive and prosper.[93] It may seek to cover up wrongdoing by its members, for fear that the publicizing of this wrongdoing will tarnish its reputation. Having gained power at an election, a party might then seek to hold on to that power even when it has lost a sense of direction and has little or no idea of how to further the common good: something that a true old-style republican would never do.[94]

The recognition that parties have self-interest, as well as a commitment to furthering the common good, raises the issue of the connection between political parties and their popular support. Just as defenders of old-style republicanism feared that demagoguery could lead to tyranny and the destruction of civic virtue,[95] more modern republicans fear that political parties might seek to sustain self-interested behaviour, through adopting policies based solely on the popular support those policies enjoy.[96] Once in power, a party that enjoys popular support may enjoy considerable 'wiggle room' to engage in self-interested practices quite far removed from the virtuous pursuit

[90] Bruce James Smith (1985).
[91] The Federalist No 10, in Clinton Rossiter, ed (1961), at 350, cited by Gardner, 'Can Political Parties be Virtuous?' (n 89) 669.
[92] For general discussion of the issue see Russell (n 57).
[93] See generally Keith Ewing (1987); Keith Ewing (2007), at 23–29.
[94] Gardner, 'Can Political Parties be Virtuous?' (n 89) 682.
[95] See generally Mortimer Sellers (1994).
[96] Gardner, 'Can Political Parties be Virtuous?' (n 89) 682.

of the common good. The party may calculate that a certain degree of loss of support, stemming from disenchantment with such practices, is worth the price of, say, staying in power by engaging in such practices. The truth is, as James A Gardner remarks, that:

> Those who act out of self-interest are probably subject to fewer self-imposed constraints than those who seek to do what is objectively right, and this freedom may make them far more effective political agents, if effectiveness is measured in terms of getting what one wants, than their virtuous competitors. This effect, which cuts across political systems, is exacerbated in the case of party politics.[97]

It seems clear that a critique of the tendency of political parties to behave in these kinds of self-interested ways is frequently, if not always, a corruption critique inspired by ideal-failure. Even so, republican political influences are also the ground of duties binding political parties (not) to behave in certain ways, and breach of these obligations may involve wrongdoing serious enough to attract civil or criminal remedies. The principal focus of such duties is fundraising, and the need to avoid falling prey to, or seeking to exercise, certain kinds of influence. I will explore the corruption-based duties binding political parties in ensuing sections.

5.7 Identifying Corruption: Top-down and Bottom-up Perspectives

This brings me to a discussion of the standpoints that shape our assumptions about and our conceptions of corruption. A critique of corruption is substantially influenced in form by whether it is 'top-down' or 'bottom-up'. In a legal context, what this means is that a conception will alter in nature and scope depending on whether the alleged corruption is considered from the perspective of the (non) enforcing authority, or of the citizen facing or demanding enforcement. In Chapter 3, we examined the traditional view of corrupt misconduct, according to which it was a criminally punishable *malum in se* for a public official to engage in personal corruption. This was regarded as a betrayal of the Monarch: the 'top-down' view of misconduct. It was, however, also at one and the same time a republican betrayal of an idealized set of popular principles of natural justice, associated with Magna Carta, enforced in the name of the king on behalf of the people: the 'bottom-up' view of misconduct. However, top-down and bottom-up understandings of corruption may be at variance in a number of situations.

An obvious example is where officials do not, from the top down, regard their conduct as falling within the scope of corruption, either in law or in morality (or both), but the public—or a substantial section thereof—so regards it, from the bottom up; or vice versa. In Chapter 4, I adopted a bottom-up perspective, to make the case for a more far-reaching application of the criminal law to address the use made of public office by MPs for personal benefit. Perhaps less obviously, there is a tendency for

[97] ibid 701.

top-down approaches to corruption to focus on downstream transactions involving private citizens or businesses, and hence on bribery, rather than on upstream features of the political structure that are in themselves corrupt or give rise to transaction-based corruption. An example will serve to illustrate the point:

Following an election, Blueland's state governance structures are now dominated by members of a powerful ethnic or religious group. That group now grants its officials discretion to supplement their salaries by insisting on a premium charge to be paid for access to some state goods and services, but only when it is non-members of the group seeking such access.

In this situation, is it those who pay the premium charge who are guilty of corruption, in the form of bribery, or is it the group that permitted the imposition of the charge to be levied on a partisan basis (and its officials), both, or neither? As Mungiu-Pippidi puts it: 'What is the deviation there, and what should be criminalised'?[98]

In this context, we need to consider the state's responsibility for failing to prevent the perversion or erosion of state-building ideals, or its perpetuation of barriers to the achievement of those ideals. For example, a persistent failure to take steps to prevent the exploitation of UK-linked tax havens,[99] or to prevent the influx of the proceeds of crime into the UK property market, can lead to a judgement that the state is itself to an extent corrupt, if it intends to—or even if it is merely content to—benefit from such laxity, and not just the individuals taking advantage of the (lack of) rules. Understanding corruption from an upstream or top-down perspective, in the example just given, it is those who exploit loopholes who are corrupt. By contrast, understanding corruption from a downstream or bottom-up perspective in this example, the state may be judged as corrupt as those who exploit its rules.

5.8 Partisan Interests and Political Parties

Leading corruption theorist Alina Mungiu-Pippidi says that: 'Everyone', agrees that any corruption involves, 'some undue private profit (for someone) due to abuse of an entrusted public authority'.[100] There a number of reasons to take issue with this claim. To begin with, some abuses of entrusted *private* authority obviously involve corruption, such as the misuse of charitable funds for private purposes, or the making of private profits by an agent supposed to be acting in the interests of a company. I will not be further concerned with such examples. More significantly, in this context, it is doubtful whether corruption in the use of public authority is rightly confined to the making of private 'profits'. Some kinds of political gain are equally to be regarded as corrupt. 'Gerrymandering' (manipulating the boundaries of an electoral constituency so as to favour one party or class) is an example.[101]

The use of public authority to favour political parties, as through gerrymandering, raises another question about Mungiu-Pippidi's definition of corruption that we

[98] Mungiu-Pippidi (n 6) 14. [99] Global Witness (2015).
[100] Mungiu-Pippidi (n 6) 3.
[101] See eg *Vieth v Jubelirer* 541 US 267 (2004). I am grateful to William Walton for this reference.

encountered in Chapter 4.1. Must all gains, in order to count as corrupt, be 'private' gains? That depends on what is meant by a private gain. Consider, for example, the use of public money to promote the cause of a political party. Parties are, in one sense, private bodies.[102] So, in some instances, when an official acts to further the interest of his or her party, he or she acts to further the interests of a private 'person'.[103] This could be regarded as straightforwardly politically corrupt: betraying public trust by acting in accordance with a conception of the good at odds with pursuing the public interest.[104] An example might be where the chancellor of the exchequer authorizes the use of public money to refurbish the gym in a building used exclusively by members of his or her political party. However, public money *is* allocated to political parties, when the purpose is (broadly speaking) Parliamentary business, including the running costs of the office of the leader of the opposition. So-called 'Short' money, running into millions of pounds annually,[105] can be called on by opposition parties who secured either two seats or one seat and more than 150,000 votes at the general election.[106] This need not be a corrupt use of public money, in a state where vibrant political parties play an essential part in the political process; indeed, it will be a reflection of public reason.[107] In this example, thus, entrusted authority is used to make a partly public rather than a wholly private gain, through expenditure on political parties.

As Ewing argues, far from operating purely as private bodies, political parties serve three crucial functions in a democracy, those of organization, representation, and government.[108] They help to organize the shape and character of political debate, by providing a channel through which citizens can influence such debates, and a means by which such debates can lead to an ethical, workable, and affordable political, social, and economic programme.[109] Parties also perform a representative function, by giving a voice and influence to a wide range of groups and sections of society. That, in turn, means that parties tend not to adopt (wholesale) narrow and comprehensive world views. Finally, government is founded on the work of political parties. Voters very largely vote for a candidate's party.[110] They tend not to vote, or not solely, for candidates as individuals.[111] This is perfectly rational voter behaviour, because the better known the parties fielding candidates, the lower the transaction costs involved for voters in working out what individual candidates belonging to those parties are likely to 'stand for'. As James A Gardner aptly puts it:

> The purpose of a pluralist election is to choose a set of representatives, each of whom is committed to some set of policy positions, to engage [if need be] in a final round of negotiation within the legislature concerning the ultimate content of government policy . . . interest group

[102] See eg *Conservative and Unionist Central Office v Burrell* [1981] EWCA Civ 2.
[103] See the discussion in Gardner, 'Can Political Parties be Virtuous?' (n 89).
[104] See ch 4.1. [105] http://www.bbc.co.uk/news/uk-politics-32719087 (13 May 2015).
[106] House of Commons Library (2016).
[107] See Ewing, *The Funding of Political Parties in Britain* (1987), Introduction.
[108] ibid. [109] On this point see also Nancy Rosenblum (2000).
[110] Since the passing of the Representation of the People Act 1969, it has been possible for a candidate to reveal his or her party next to his or her name on the ballot paper: see Vernon Bogdanor (2004), at 726.
[111] See Phillip Jones and John Hudson (1998).

pluralism provides that ballot access conditions should be designed to produce candidates who are committed to advancing the private self-interest of sizable groups of voters.[112]

Hence, one or more parties form the basis of most working governments in democracies. Since the enactment of the Ministers of the Crown Act 1937, it has been recognized in law both that Parliament is comprised of government and opposition, not simply of individual MPs, and that there is a prime minister and cabinet, together with an official 'leader of the opposition'.[113] Accordingly, there is a substantially 'public' dimension, a public interest, to the operation of political parties.[114]

Where does that leave us, in terms of defining political corruption? In broad terms, we may accept Mungiu-Pippidi's claim that, in the political sphere, anti-corruption measures aim 'to constrain particularism and defend the state from being an instrument serving particular private interests rather than the public one ...'.[115] However, the foregoing analysis strengthens the case made in Chapter 4.1 for regarding as no more than a useful rule of thumb, as a marker of corruption, the identification of an interest served as a 'private' interest. The definition of political corruption suggested in Chapter 4.1 (and in section 5.2) was set out in terms of acting in a partisan way: using one's position to act on a conception of the good that could not be endorsed, in the relevant political context, by someone of moral and political integrity. The qualification in this definition relating to political context is an important one. Without contextualization, we cannot distinguish partisan from ethically acceptable public interest motivations in a straightforward way.

Consider a variation on an earlier example:

D, on becoming Chancellor of the Exchequer, orders £5 million of public money to be spent building a hotel and leisure complex to be owned and used solely by members of his or her party.

On the face of it, D's conduct appears to involve the use of state finance for the promotion of a partisan purpose, the interests of his or her party. It would thus seem to amount to a pure case of political corruption by a public official, even if his or her own pockets are not being lined (and so there is no element of personal corruption). However, suppose that D is Chancellor of a one-party state in which all adults are automatically members of the party. In that case, it is arguable that the spending serves the public good in a non-partisan way. The spending will not be a straightforward instance of corruption, simply furthering the party's interests at the public's expense. Perhaps one-party states are politically sub-optimal. That does not, in itself, make one-party states corrupt, even if they have a tendency to become corrupt.

To underline that final point, we should note that just as a one-party state may not necessarily be corrupt, the existence of powerful competing parties in a political system is not guaranteed to act as a bulwark against political corruption. Rival parties may, for example, engage in rent-seeking by explicitly or tacitly agreeing not to challenge each other over the exploitation of certain ways in which public office can

[112] Gardner (n 89) 687. [113] See the discussion in Vernon Bogdanor (2004), at 724.

[114] For this argument, more generally see eg Ingrid van Biezen (2008).

[115] Mungiu-Pippidi (n 6) 18.

be 'milked' for its benefits. The employment of relatives at public expense by MPs across the political spectrum is a case in point, discussed in Chapter 4. Further, the existence of rival political parties opens up greater possibilities for the emergence of distinctive kinds of corruption in politics, such as gerrymandering. To go back to an earlier example, whether or not it is a politically sound policy to encourage the sale of council houses to their residents, what is clear is that a council may not—with a view to boosting votes for the ruling party—promote sales in electorally marginal council wards, whilst doing nothing to encourage such sales in wards much less favourable to that party.[116] That kind of partisan basis for the distribution of benefits is corrupt, and involves misconduct in public office. We must accept that the distinction between public and private interests is a contested one, not least because governance structures may embody an essentially private interest writ large.

5.9 Negation: A Public Law Remedy in Political Corruption Cases

Political corruption may be addressed in a number of ways that do not involve the criminal law. For example, an MP engaged in corrupt or otherwise reprehensible conduct in the course of their duties may face sanctions (such as exclusion from the House of Commons for a period of time), imposed by the Committee on Standards and Privileges.[117] This quasi-regulatory scheme is controversial, because it involves MPs policing their own conduct.[118] However, it is capable of dealing flexibly with, amongst other things, a range of cases in which an MP has behaved with a lack of integrity. A classic case would be the failure to declare a financial interest. It is the failure to declare that is wrong, not (necessarily) having the financial interest itself. Under the MPs' Code of Conduct:

> Members shall fulfil conscientiously the requirements of the House in respect of the registration of interests in the Register of Members' Financial Interests. They shall always be open and frank in drawing attention to any relevant interest in any proceeding of the House or its Committees, and in any communications with Ministers, Members, public officials or public office holders.[119]

Alongside this 'public-institutional' form of discipline is also a 'private-institutional' form of discipline that may be exercised by a political party. For example, an MP may have the whip withdrawn, meaning that he or she is effectively now suspended from the party and sitting as an independent MP unless and until the whip is restored.[120] However, that sanction is used mainly in cases where an MP has defied the leadership on a policy issue, rather than because the MP has behaved inappropriately in some broader way.[121]

[116] See section 5.2. [117] House of Commons (2015), at VI, para 19.
[118] http://www.telegraph.co.uk/news/uknews/12188113/MPs-must-no-longer-police-themselves.html.
[119] House of Commons (2015), at V, para 13.
[120] http://www.parliament.uk/about/mps-and-lords/principal/whips/.
[121] J A Cross (1967).

Alongside the general sanctions regime, however, is a little-recognized public law basis for preventing and deterring corruption. It would be helpful to refer to the public law process or remedy involved as 'negation'. As the name suggests, the central case of this process involves setting back at naught any gains or benefits that have or may have been obtained in a corrupt way or otherwise in circumstances of impropriety. By extension, negation can be understood to include the refusal to reimburse an official such as an MP for an expense incurred, when what is set back or negated is the expectation that reimbursement would be forthcoming. The central case is in issue when a gain or benefit already awarded is withdrawn or claimed back, in the light of circumstances obtaining at the time of, or before, the award or grant. However, the process or remedy of negation goes beyond the central case. It may operate pre-emptively, to prevent a gain or benefit being received, commonly in circumstances where someone has been given an indication that the gain or benefit would or might be received. The process may also operate retrospectively, to deprive someone of a benefit or gain that, even if originally obtained quite properly, should be withdrawn in the light of conduct or circumstances subsequently arising. Negation is related, of course, to developments elsewhere in the civil law. In particular, the failure of the common law to facilitate the recovery of the proceeds of crime led to statutory intervention culminating in the Proceeds of Crime Act 2002. As is well known, under the 2002 Act, it is possible for law enforcement authorities to use civil proceedings to recover property or cash, which is, or represents, property obtained through unlawful conduct. The 2002 Act is, thus, concerned with what I will call 'conduct-based', and not 'ethics-based' negation.

To provide enhanced focus, it would be helpful to divide cases of negation into 'conduct-based' negation, and 'ethics-based' negation, although these are not wholly distinct categories: there is natural and inevitable overlapping. As the name implies, conduct-based negation is in issue principally when the behaviour of a person who has been the recipient of a state good (such as an honour) is such as to justify the withdrawal of that good. In the case of honours, the matter is overseen by the Honours Forfeiture Committee,[122] a committee of the cabinet office. Following a reference from the prime minister, the committee has the power to recommend to the monarch that an honour be rescinded, in the light of the recipient's conduct. The two principal grounds on which it may do this are (a) conviction for a criminal offence, followed by a sentence of three months' imprisonment or more, and (b) instances in which the recipient has been struck off or otherwise disciplined by a relevant professional body, in a matter concerning the award of the honour. Beyond these two instances, the committee may consider other compelling evidence that an honour should be rescinded. Conduct-based negation has been used in corruption cases. An example is the case of *Speechley*,[123] in which a local councillor was stripped of his CBE. He had been sent to prison for 18 months in 2004, having sought to

[122] https://www.gov.uk/honours/having-honours-taken-away-forfeiture.
[123] http://news.bbc.co.uk/1/hi/england/lincolnshire/4221488.stm.

influence the siting of a by-pass without declaring the effect this would have on the value of his own property.

Conduct-based negation may operate pre-emptively. Consider nominations for membership of the House of Lords. The House of Lords Appointments Commission (created in 2000) may block a nomination for membership of the House of Lords,[124] if one of two conditions is satisfied:

(1) the individual is not in good standing in the community in general and with the public regulatory authorities in particular; or

(2) the past conduct of the nominee would reasonably be regarded as bringing the House of Lords into disrepute.[125]

A closely analogous procedure is the procedure for the 'recall' of an MP, in the light of his or her conduct.[126] Under such a procedure, an MP (or, in some US states, a state official) guilty of serious misconduct may have to face a fresh election in his or her constituency, if a sufficient proportion of eligible voters so decide through signing a petition. In England and Wales, the Recall of MPs Act 2015 provides that an MP will become subject to a recall petition (a) if sentenced to a term of imprisonment, (b) if suspended from Parliament for at least ten sitting days, or (c) if convicted of expenses fraud contrary to section 10 of the Parliamentary Standards Act 2009. A kind of negation is involved here, even if the petition does not trigger a by-election. That is because the MP's security of tenure, as an MP for the duration of Parliament that his or her election conferred, becomes defeasible. He or she becomes dependent for the affirmation of that status on the outcome of the petition.

I now turn to ethics-based negation. Ethics-based negation is in issue when a state good or other benefit is denied, rescinded, or must be returned, in the interests of transparency and the maintenance of high standards, irrespective of whether the individual in question is guilty of wrongdoing. There are different examples. A central case example concerns political donations.[127] Under the Political Parties, Elections and Referendums Act 2000, parties are obliged to submit audited accounts to the Commission (quarterly, other than at election times when accounts must be submitted weekly). In May 2014, the ten parties registered in Great Britain reported accepting £14,230,841 in donations between 1 January and 31 March 2014, and the value of outstanding loans to parties at 31 March 2014 was £15,096,219.[128] A donation to a political party must be returned immediately if, amongst other things, the donor is neither an individual on the electoral register, nor a company doing business in the UK.[129] Under section 58 of the 2000 Act, the Electoral Commission may seek a court order requiring the party to forfeit the donation.[130]

[124] The patronage basis of this power was considered in section 5.4.
[125] House of Lords Appointments Commission (2016).
[126] Richard Kelly, Charley Coleman, and Neil Johnston (2014).
[127] To which we return in section 5.10.
[128] Transparency International (2015a), at 17.
[129] Political Parties, Elections and Referendums Act 2000, s 54.
[130] Under s 51 of the 2000 Act, it is an offence knowingly to enter into, or to do an act in furtherance of, any arrangement which facilitates or is likely to facilitate, whether by means of any concealment or disguise or otherwise, the making of donations to a registered party by any person or body other than a permissible donor.

Political parties are themselves placed under a duty by section 56 of the 2000 Act, upon receipt of a donation, to check that the donor meets the conditions set down in section 54. An element of pre-emption is also found in section 54A of the 2000 Act, which requires donors to declare that they meet the conditions for acceptable donors set out in section 54. We consider the criminal penalties created to support this system of negation in section 5.10.

A second example of ethics-based negation is also to be found in the pre-emptive powers of the House of Lords Appointments Commission, alongside their pre-emptive powers in respect of conduct-based negation. Nominations by the prime minister to the House of Lords may be blocked by the House of Lords Appointments Commission, if the nominee fails to confirm:

(a) that they are resident in the UK for tax purposes and accept the requirement to remain so;
(b) that they are not involved in any roles, positions, or activities or have any interests that would conflict with their membership of the House of Lords;
(c) whether or not they have made any donations, loans, or credit arrangements to or with a political party;
(d) whether they have a financial relationship with any senior party member; and
(e) that no close family member has a financial involvement with the party or any senior party member.[131]

The Commission highlights for special treatment the situation in which a nominee has made a donation to a political party. Of this situation, the Committee says:

> Of central concern to the Commission, therefore, is the credibility of individuals who have made significant political donations, loans or credit arrangements. The Commission believes that the best way of addressing this issue is to reach a view on whether or not the individual could have been a credible nominee if he or she had made no financial contribution.[132]

In itself, this statement does not address the issue of what should happen when a perfectly credible nominee has in fact been nominated because of a donation made to a political party. To prevent this happening, the Committee requires the party chairman to issue a certificate affirming, alongside the matters in (a) to (e) above, that 'the recommendation is not associated, directly or indirectly, with any contribution to the party, a political fund or senior party members'.[133]

The Committee has no legal power to call witnesses or order the production of documents that might confirm or undermine the basis for this certificate. Further, by way of contrast with the approach to fraudulent attempts to conceal donations to political parties by ineligible donors, it is not a criminal offence for a party chairman knowingly to issue a false certificate. A cynic might suggest that system either lacks

[131] House of Lords Appointments Commission (2016); http://www.telegraph.co.uk/news/politics/11826722/Revealed-Seven-peerages-blocked-after-failing-vetting-process.html.
[132] http://lordsappointments.independent.gov.uk/vetting-for-propriety.aspx.
[133] http://lordsappointments.independent.gov.uk/vetting-for-propriety.aspx.

bite, or is too little too late. Transparency International has reported that the total value of donations (from 2001 to November 2014) from members of the House of Lords totalled £39 million, and that eleven individuals who were nominated as peers collectively donated £14 million before they were ennobled.[134] An authoritative academic study has affirmed the significant role that donations have played in recent years in the path to ennoblement.[135]

A final example of negation involves a mixture of conduct-based and ethics-based elements, and concerns MPs' expenses. MPs' expenses are now governed by a code of practice set out by the Independent Parliamentary Standards Authority (IPSA).[136] Under the current version of the Code (more generous than previous versions), MPs may only claim 'for expenditure for parliamentary purposes'.[137] This can be referred to as the 'basic rule'. On a pre-emptive basis, the IPSA may refuse to reimburse an MP for an expense incurred, if the incurring of that expense breaches the basic rule, or is otherwise in breach of the 'Fundamental Principles'.[138] Prior to 2017, amongst these fundamental principles, the IPSA indicated that:

> 3. MPs must not exploit the system for personal financial advantage, nor to confer an undue advantage on a political organisation …
>
> 11. The system should prohibit MPs from entering into arrangements which might appear to create a conflict of interests in the use of public resources.[139]

Fearful of being perceived as overbearing, the IPSA no longer includes these principles amongst the fundamental principles by which MPs must abide. Instead, their place has been taken in the Code by principles binding on the IPSA instead (presumably, to increase the legitimacy of the IPSA in the eyes of MPs, as opposed to the public at large).[140] Even so, in terms of the analytical structure set out above, Principle 3 provided a conduct-based reason for refusing to reimburse an expense, whilst Principle 11 provided an ethics-based reason for doing so.

MPs' expenses may also be dealt with through an application of the central case of negation (explained above): the return of a financial advantage received corruptly or in circumstances of impropriety. Section 26 of the Constitutional Reform and Governance Act 2010 (CRGA 2010) created the position of compliance officer (CO) for IPSA. Under section 9A of the Parliamentary Standards Act 2009, the CO may investigate expense claims paid.[141] In a case where the CO finds that the

[134] Transparency International (2015a), at 17.

[135] Andrew Mell, Simon Radford, and Seth Alexander Thévoz (2015).

[136] Independent Parliamentary Standards Authority (2017b).

[137] Independent Parliamentary Standards Authority, *The Scheme of MPs' Business Costs and Expenses 2017–18* (n 136) 6. Previous versions of the Code had restricted claims to 'unavoidable costs where they are incurred wholly, exclusively, and necessarily in the performance of their parliamentary functions': see eg Independent Parliamentary Standards Authority (2015), at 10.

[138] Independent Parliamentary Standards Authority, *The Scheme of MPs' Business Costs and Expenses 2017–18* (n 136) 6.

[139] Independent Parliamentary Standards Authority, *The MPs' Scheme of Business Costs and Expenses* (n 137) 10.

[140] Independent Parliamentary Standards Authority, *The Scheme of MPs' Business Costs and Expenses 2017–18* (n 136) 6.

[141] In 2015, a procedure for investigation was agreed: Compliance Officer for the Independent Parliamentary Standards Authority, *The MPs' Scheme of Business Costs and Expenses* (n 137).

amount in question should not have been paid, the CO may reach an agreement with the MP in question that the amount should be repaid. In the absence of a satisfactory agreement of this kind, under Schedule 4 of the 2009 Act (introduced by the CRGA 2010) the CO may impose a 'repayment direction' requiring the MP to repay the amount in question. A failure to comply with this direction may lead to the amount being deducted from the MP's salary, and an additional financial penalty being imposed on the MP by the CO. In determining whether an expense claimed must be repaid, the CO will have regard to the basic rule (set out above) and to the fundamental principles set down by the IPSA.

So far, I have sought only to explain certain existing practices in terms of negation, but there is clearly potential for the remedy to be applied more widely. One suggestion, made in Chapter 4.5, was that when a former minister has taken a job or other remunerative position, in breach of the Ministerial Code, he or she should be required to account to the public purse for any profit made (or the financial equivalent of other benefits received). Another possibility relevant here is that, when a political party accepts money or other benefits in exchange for the provision of inclusivity (and, a fortiori, of exclusivity), in breach of certain conditions designed to ensure propriety, it can be fixed with a similar liability to account. Such conditions were mentioned in section 5.3, and will be discussed further in section 5.11.

Negation is arguably the most important legal resource for countering political, as opposed to personal, corruption, although—as in the cases of expense claims and some conflict of interest cases—it may also be applied in cases of personal corruption. A noticeable feature of negation in English law is that it is generally not a court-based or litigious process. The process is more regulatory in nature, handled by specialized or expert bodies. In seeking to deal with political corruption, a decision to go beyond negation, decided on by a specialized quasi-regulatory body, and make available criminal punishment administered through the criminal courts, is potentially one of momentous importance. When is this appropriate?

5.10 Political Financing: Regulation and Duties to Promote Public Goods

In Chapter 2, I made the argument for the retention of a (moderately) flexible offence of misconduct in a public office. A key constitutional function played by this offence is to serve as a means by which prosecutors and courts can apply some independent deterrent to the corrupt activities of MPs. However, the offence of misconduct in a public office cannot be expected satisfactorily to provide a sophisticated set of disincentives fit for a nuanced and wide-ranging anti-corruption agenda, without the support of specifically targeted regulatory offences.[142] In turn, such offences would be likely to operate in a haphazard manner, liable to the kind over

[142] Any more than the offence of public nuisance could do the same for an environmental strategy without the support of regulatory offences under the Environmental Protection Act 1990.

and under-achievement described in section 5.1, without the support of the public law remedy of negation described in the preceding section.

So far as regulatory offences are concerned, an important foray into the regulation of political activity came (alongside the regulation of MPs' expenses) in the form of regulation of party fundraising.[143] The Report of the Neill Committee in 2007–2008[144] led to the passing of the Political Parties, Elections and Referendums Act 2000 (2000 Act). The 2000 Act set up a regulatory body, the Electoral Commission,[145] with a remit broad enough to make possible a coherent approach to management of the broader electoral context in which party-funding takes place.[146] As is commonly the case in relation to regulated activity, a good deal of the work of the Commission is pre-emptive. It is aimed at monitoring and securing compliance on the part of those subject to the rules by, for instance, issuing guidance on standing for election, managing a political party, and running elections.[147] Even so, under the Political Parties, Elections and Referendums (Civil Sanctions) Order 2000, the Commission can impose civil penalties (up to a maximum of £20,000) for breach of the applicable rules.

The Liberal Democrat Party was fined the maximum civil penalty of £20,000 for committing an offence contrary to section 84(1)(b) of the 2000 Act (culpable failure to provide a proper accounting return),[148] in relation to irregularities concerning its General Election spending in 2015. 'Systematic' failings were uncovered in relation to its returns: 307 payments totalling £184,676 were missing from the Liberal Democrats' spending return without a reasonable excuse, and invoices supporting 122 out of the 307 payments were missing from the return.[149] Subsequently, the Conservative and Unionist Society has also faced sanctions for accounting failures in respect of its election spending.[150] The Electoral Commission found a contravention relating to the treasurer's obligations under section 41 of the 2000 Act.[151] The Commission reported that, in no less than three instances in 2014, in relation to three by-elections, the registered treasurer failed to ensure that the Party's accounting records were sufficient in the relevant respects.[152]

[143] Political Parties Elections and Referendums Act 2000.

[144] Committee on Standards in Public Life (2008).

[145] http://www.electoralcommission.org.uk/.

[146] Justin Fisher (2001).

[147] http://www.electoralcommission.org.uk/.

[148] 'The treasurer of a registered party commits an offence if, without reasonable excuse, he—

(a) fails to comply with the requirements of subsection (1) or (2) in relation to any return or report to which that subsection applies;
(b) delivers a return which does not comply with the requirements of section 80(3) or (4); or
(c) fails to comply with the requirements of subsection (3) in relation to a return under that subsection.'

[149] http://www.electoralcommission.org.uk/i-am-a/journalist/electoral-commission-media-centre/news-releases-donations/electoral-commission-calls-for-stronger-powers-to-sanction-political-parties,-as-liberal-democrats-are-fined-maximum-penalty.

[150] See generally Electoral Commission (2017).

[151] Section 41 states that: 'The treasurer of a registered party must ensure that accounting records are kept with respect to the party which are sufficient to show and explain the party's transactions'.

[152] Electoral Commission (n 150) 4.

The Commission's activities are also supported by no fewer than 98 regulatory criminal offences.[153] For example, in the Conservative Party case, the Electoral Commission found that the treasurer had failed to make complete statements of its campaign spending in the 2015 general election, and failed to include all invoices and receipts relating to campaign spending (as required by section 80(3) of the 2000 Act). Such failures are made criminal by section 80(4)(b) of the 2000 Act, if engaged in without reasonable excuse. The party was fined a total of £70,000, including penalties for the contraventions mentioned above.[154] With some of the more serious offences under the 2000 Act—especially those involving subjective fault—the Electoral Commission cannot itself sanction the treasurer or the party, and must refer the matter to the police. In the Liberal Democrat Party case, as well as imposing a penalty for breach of section 84(1)(b), the Commission referred to the police the question of whether, contrary to section 83(3) of the 2000 Act, the Liberal Democrat Party treasurer had committed a more serious offence. This is the offence of knowingly or recklessly making a false declaration concerning the return when it is made, given his or her obligation under section 83(2) to declare that to the best of his or her knowledge and belief it is a complete and correct return.[155] In the Conservative Party case, the Commission also referred the party's treasurer to the police for investigation into whether this offence had been committed.[156]

I shall try to set the scheme in context. I said in section 5.2 that the analysis of corruption in this chapter would be culturally relative in that, amongst other things, I would take for granted a political background in which a relatively small number of widely supported parties compete for power in a democratic system. In that regard, first, the legislation seeks to bureaucratize party politics, in the interests of financial transparency. It does this in order to facilitate the coercion of parties into behaving in a transparent way, in relation to their financing. So, sections 22 and 24 respectively require parties and their office-holders to be registered, if they are to field candidates at elections.[157] Once registered, under sections 41 and 42, parties become subject to obligations to keep accounting records and to produce annual statements of accounts. By virtue of section 47, a failure to produce accounts as required, or a production of them other than in the form required, is made a criminal offence committed by the party treasurer, unless there is a reasonable excuse for the failure in question.[158] Section 46 places an obligation on the Electoral

[153] A small number of these are re-enactments of older provisions, but most are new to the criminal calendar.

[154] For a contextual examination of this case see https://www.theguardian.com/news/2017/mar/23/conservative-election-scandal-victory-2015-expenses.

[155] The offence carries a maximum sentence of one year's imprisonment, at trial on indictment. In relation to the EU Referendum, the Commission has also fined a campaigner £4,000 for failing to include details about himself in a political advertisement in the *Metro* newspaper on 22 June 2016 (the day before the referendum), contrary to section 126(8).

[156] Electoral Commission (n 150) 4.

[157] It is, of course, possible to stand as an independent, and thus avoid the rules governing party registration.

[158] The 'reasonable excuse' defence was introduced into what was formerly a strict liability offence by the Political Parties and Elections Act 2009.

Commission to make the statement of accounts open to public inspection as soon as reasonably practicable.

It may seem obvious but is worth highlighting that, alongside this system aimed at increasing financial transparency in relation to party political activity, is a commitment to the other 'Fullerian' public good of accountability, in the form of what might be called 'bureaucratic' accountability.[159] It is to the independent Electoral Commission, and only hence to the public, that registered parties must account in a specified form for their money-raising and spending. It would have been possible simply to insist that political parties make their accounts available to the public, leaving as matters for public and media criticism any defects or inadequacies in the manner and form in which those accounts were presented by the parties. Clearly, however, this kind of 'direct' accountability threatens the goal of transparency. Quite apart from the risk that the parties will present accounts in a misleading way designed to cast their activities in the best light, it would become much more difficult to compare the accounts of different parties with one another for the purposes of critical analysis. One of the advantages of the bureaucratization of election fundraising is that it is capable of producing new forms of accountability-based wrongdoing. A party's right to present accounts in the way it chooses has been transformed into a duty to present them in a form that serves a public good, breach of the duty being the new species of wrong.

Securing the transparent and accountable operation of political parties does not, in itself, prevent 'cheque-book' government in a broad sense.[160] The 2000 Act says little about this issue.[161] One result of the 2000 Act may be that party funding will become dominated by a smaller number of wealthy donors who meet two key informal criteria: (a) they are not themselves concerned with public exposure about their status as donors, and (b) the party in question equally has no concerns on that score. Neither of these two key criteria is necessarily connected to the goal of securing cleaner politics. Having said that, there are some substantive restrictions on parties' financial activities, inspired by a republican conception of politics. First, there is a ban in section 54 on keeping or using anonymous donations, or donations from overseas, in relation to which there may in some instances be greater difficulties in checking the financial probity of the donor than would be the case in the UK.[162] Secondly, in section 79 and schedule 9, there is an attempt to prevent election campaigns involving a financial 'arms race', in the form of overall restrictions on what may be spent on an election campaign.[163] Nonetheless, political parties are in important respects private organizations, and are likely to remain largely

[159] On Fullerian public goods see section 5.2.

[160] In a narrow sense—exchanging policy agreements for donations—such conduct is criminal: see section 5.3.

[161] http://www.electoralcommission.org.uk/__data/assets/pdf_file/0014/102263/to-donations-rp.pdf.

[162] In speaking of 'donations' I include loans, which are covered by the 2000 Act. In the USA, the Federal Election Commission makes it possible to search for politicians' financial backers online, where both names and amounts given are provided: http://www.fec.gov/disclosurep/pnational.do.

[163] See further Ministry of Justice (2008); Committee on Standards in Public Life (2011).

self-sustaining financially.[164] It follows that, as a political philosophy, republicanism is always liable to make its influence felt in UK politics in a relatively uneven and patchy way.

As is the case with many regulatory schemes, the large number of offences created by the 2000 Act is principally designed to coerce those subject to regulation into assisting the regulatory body to perform its function: here, securing the financial transparency and accountability of political parties. To that end, as in other such schemes, the offences fall into different categories. First, there are content-independent obligations, obligations common to regulatory schemes irrespective of their subject matter. Typical examples are the obligation not to engage either in conduct liable in general to frustrate the goals of the legislation, or in conduct that, in particular, interferes or obstructs the regulatory body in the performance of its duty to secure these goals.[165] An example in this context can be found in section 148(1), which creates the offence of altering, suppressing, concealing or destroying relevant documents, with an intention of falsifying the documents or of evading any of the provisions of the 2000 Act. Another example is the offence contrary to paragraph 17(4) of Schedule 7: knowingly giving a compliance officer false information relevant to his or her enquiry. A different kind of example is illustrated by section 146(6), which makes it an offence intentionally to obstruct a person lawfully exercising a right to enter premises at a reasonable time, to inspect documents, or make copies of records.

Secondly, there are content-dependent obligations (more specific to the legislative context and purposes) not to engage in conduct that is liable to frustrate the goals of the legislation. Examples are making a false declaration about the value of property,[166] incurring campaign expenditure without authority,[167] or facilitating the making of donations by impermissible donors.[168] Alongside these types of offence are numerous provisions creating positive obligations, breach of which is made a criminal offence. Some 44 out of the 98 offences created by the 2000 Act involve a 'failure' to do some particular act, or to assist the Commission to perform its function in some respect. This makes the imposition of positive obligations the major plank of the offence structure, whether in relation to content-dependent or content-independent offences.[169] It would be pointless to go through many of the numerous examples, but typical is the offence under section 65(3) of failing to deliver donation reports to the Commission within the time limits, or the offence under section 65(4) of failing to comply with the requirements for recording donations in the donations report.

No one could accuse Parliament of having failed to make full use of the criminal law, in seeking to promote transparency and accountability in respect of the

164 See the discussion in section 5.3.

165 For further discussion see Jeremy Horder (2015).

166 Section73(8).

167 Section75(2).

168 Section 61(1).

169 We should note that, under the 2000 Act, such offences are normally made subject to a 'reasonable excuse' defence, or a defence that all due diligence was exercised and all reasonable steps taken to avoid committing the offence.

raising and spending of party finance.[170] So, the question now is what role, if any, is left for the offence of misconduct in public office in this field? To begin with, no offence created by the 2000 Act imposes a maximum sentence longer than one year. It follows that it may be desirable to use the misconduct offence to deal with, for example, planned and systematic evasion of a party's obligations that went undetected over a long period of time. Beyond such cases, there are situations in which use of the misconduct offence may be appropriate, targeting culpable failures by those high up in an organization to prevent systematic corruption. Under the 2000 Act, a considerable number of the offences understandably focus on the activities of the treasurer of a Party.[171] He or she is specifically mentioned as the person who commits the offence (or through whose action the offence is committed) in nine of the offences, and very many more will, in effect, be committed by the treasurer if they are committed at all. There is even a largely 'status-based' offence that can be committed by a treasurer created by section 71L(6):

A person commits an offence if—

(a) he is the treasurer of a registered party,
(b) the party benefits from or falls to benefit in consequence of a connected transaction to which any of the parties is not an authorised participant, and
(c) he knew or ought reasonably to have known of the matters mentioned in paragraph (b).[172]

However, what remains obscured by the legislation is the relationship between the treasurer and the party leader, even though, if a treasurer resigns or is yet to be appointed, it is the party leader who is regarded as the treasurer, for the purposes of the 2000 Act.[173]

In most UK parties, the treasurer would be appointed by the party leader. Even before the passing of the 2000 Act, a split had emerged between the person—probably a paid employee—treated in official documents as the treasurer, for the purposes of compliance, and what we can call the 'Treasurer' (with a capital 'T'), a more grandiose or well-known figure who acts unpaid as principal fundraiser, and sometimes as a donor.[174] The reward for performing the latter role is likely to be nomination for a peerage.[175] It seems obvious that the way in which the treasurer (with a little 't') performs or fails to perform his or her duties under the 2000 Act may be swayed, perhaps unduly, by the conduct, either individually or in concert, of the Treasurer and the party leader. That being so, the offence of misconduct may play a legitimate role in deterring the latter from any high-level connivance at failures to ensure that the treasurer (with a little 't') follows both the letter and spirit of the 2000 Act.

170 For praise of the 2000 Act more generally see Justin Fisher (2001).

171 The Electoral Commission provides a specific guide to being a party treasurer: Electoral Commission (2016).

172 See also s 24(8): being a registered treasurer, having been convicted of an offence within the last five years.

173 Electoral Commission (n 171) 3.

174 See the discussion in Seth Alexander Thévoz (2016), at 4.

175 ibid 6–7, focusing on the fate of Conservative Party Treasurers.

To conclude this section, we should also consider the possibility that political parties themselves could be prosecuted for such high-level connivance, or even active encouragement, of evasion of the requirements of the 2000 Act. In such cases, offence (b)—the organizational offence—as set out in Chapter 2.1, would be engaged. The legal position of parties was considered in Chapter 4.13, and the analysis will not be repeated here. Suffice to say that if and when a party (or a section thereof such as a parliamentary group) can be considered to be an unincorporated association, then that body could be subject to prosecution under offence (b). In appropriate circumstances, such as where there is a shared decision to ignore or overlook legal requirements, such a body may have the fault element for a criminal offence such as misconduct; but offence (b), as set out in Chapter 2, also contemplates organizational liability based on gross negligence, so long as the conduct of senior managers played a significant part in that.

5.11 Corruption and the Lobbying Industry

Even within a modern bureaucratic state, wrongdoing may be hard to disentangle from legitimate but (perhaps) unwelcome practices that border on corruption. The activity of 'lobbying'—seeking to influence officials in relation to an agenda that would benefit from legislative or political support—provides a good example of this problem. A study by the Joseph Rowntree Foundation Trust in 2006 found that, whilst 67 per cent of people surveyed thought that large companies had a significant amount of influence on government policy, only 27 per cent thought that they should have such influence.[176] Similarly, Transparency International has found that 59 per cent of respondents considered that the UK's government was 'entirely' or 'to a large extent' run by a few big entities acting in their own best interests, while an additional 31 per cent thought that this was 'somewhat' the case.[177] By contrast, some influential MPs have taken the view that there is too little opportunity for them to be influenced by lobbying, rather than too much. In 2005–2006, the House of Commons Select Committee on Modernisation suggested that Parliament should 'revise its procedures so that it is easier for ... lobby groups, representative organisations and other stakeholders to influence Parliament's consideration of Bills'.[178]

Looked at from the top-down, lobbying may be conducive to the public good of policy formation, in so far as it ensures that officials are properly informed when they take decisions. From the bottom up, there may seem correspondingly to be importance in a citizen's liberty to engage in lobbying. The House of Commons has in the past staunchly defended the practice of lobbying, albeit in the language of rights rather than liberties:

[176] Joseph Rowntree Reform Trust (2006), cited by Philip Pavin (2007), at 6.

[177] Transparency International (2015a), at 12.

[178] Select Committee on the Modernisation of the House of Commons (2006), at 3, cited by Pavin (n 176) 5.

It is the right of any citizen to lobby his Member of Parliament, and if he considers that his case can be better advanced with professional assistance he has every right to avail himself of that assistance.[179]

Nonetheless, particular controversy surrounds the reference at the end here to professional or commercial lobbying: the use of professionals to try to influence Government, Parliament, the devolved legislatures or administrations, regional or local government or other public bodies on any matter within their competence. A study in 2007 estimated that the business of lobbying in the UK was worth about £1.9 billion, and employed 4,000 people.[180]

The toleration of commercial lobbying is controversial as a form of inclusivity,[181] in republican terms. It is liable to skew input into official decision-making in favour of those who can afford to engage in it. Unchecked toleration of commercial lobbying opens the door to elitist government involving, at its worst, too many important 'influence cards' being held by an unrepresentative combination of those represented by or constituting powerful lobbying groups, direct donors to political parties (as we saw earlier), and politicians and civil servants beholden to one or both of these groups. Permitting the purchase of inclusivity risks enhancing and entrenching inequality of political influence amongst citizens.[182] A study by the respected Hansard Society and the Electoral Commission found that only 23 per cent of the public felt that they had a say in the way that the country is run.[183] Further, the practice of lobbying is attended with a number of corruption risks. In pursuit of inclusivity for their clients, lobbying organizations may be tempted to offer inducements to public officials,[184] although such conduct risks falling foul of bribery legislation. Beyond conduct amounting to bribery, in the debates and legislative initiatives taken in this field, there has been a disproportionate focus on private sector lobbyists, and too little attention paid to the public officials who deal with them. For that reason, in Chapter 4.5, I considered an enhanced regime of criminal offences to govern illegitimate dealings with lobbyists engaged in by politicians.

Parliament took faltering steps towards regulation of private sector lobbying in the Transparency of Lobbying, Non-Party Campaigning and Trade Union Administration Act 2014 (the 2014 Act). The preamble describes the relevant part of the 2014 Act as an Act:

to make provision for establishing and maintaining a register of persons carrying on the business of consultant lobbying and to require those persons to be entered into the register.

Under section 2 of the 2014 Act, 'consultant lobbying' is engaged in when a VAT registered[185] person in the course of business, and in exchange for payment,

[179] Select Committee on Members' Interests (1984), HC 408, at para 3, cited by Pavin (n 176) 5.
[180] Pavin (n 176) 10. [181] Inclusivity is discussed in section 5.3.
[182] See generally Martin Gilens (2012). [183] Hansard Society (2006), at 3.
[184] See eg https://www.theguardian.com/commentisfree/2014/oct/14/yacht-cannes-selling-homes-local-government-officials-mipim.
[185] A business with a VAT taxable turnover over £85,000.

personally communicates orally or in written form with a minister of the Crown or a permanent secretary, regarding any proposed legislative or policy activity,[186] or regarding the award of any contract, grant, or licence. Section 1 of the 2014 Act prohibits engagement in consultant lobbying by anyone who is not registered with the Registrar of Consultant Lobbyists (created by section 3 of the 2014 Act), whose task it is to keep the published register up to date and monitor compliance with obligations under the 2014 Act. Under section 4 of the 2014 Act, lobbyists must provide information for the register concerning: the individual, partnership or company name and address, the names of the directors and secretary, and a statement of whether they have undertaken to comply with a code of conduct on lobbying.[187] Crucially, by virtue of section 5 of the 2014 Act, lobbyists must also provide certain client information: the name of the person on whose behalf lobbying was done, or was paid to be done. Section 12 of the 2014 Act creates the offences of unregistered lobbying, and of engaging in lobbying whilst the lobbyist's entry in the register is inaccurate or incomplete and the lobbyist has failed—when required to do so—to provide information enabling the inaccuracy or omission to be rectified. The Registrar has the power to issue, and has issued,[188] civil penalties to lobbyists in breach of section 12. However, as noted in Chapter 4.5, MPs or ministers who knowingly engage with unregistered or improperly registered lobbyists are not covered by the section 12 offence, although in some instances they might be found to have assisted or encouraged its commission.

From the start, the provisions concerning lobbying in the 2014 Act have been subject to trenchant criticism, focused on their narrowness and their exiguous nature.[189] The 2014 Act has nothing like the comprehensiveness or transformative effect of the regime introduced to govern political fundraising by the Political Parties, Elections and Referendums Act 2000.[190] By making it clear that only lobbying of ministers of the Crown and permanent secretaries is covered, section 2(3) of the 2014 Act in effect excludes a vast swath of lobbying of MPs and lower-level civil servants and others whose advice to ministers may be highly influential.[191] On the supply side, at the time that the Bill went through Parliament, the Government anticipated that over 700 firms would register, but at the end of August 2016 only 136 had done so.[192] By confining its provisions to 'consultant'

[186] Although, bizarrely, this does not explicitly extend to lobbying aimed at keeping the law or policy exactly the way it is.

[187] For example, the Chartered Institute of Public Relations has produced such a code: Chartered Institute of Public Relations (2015).

[188] http://registrarofconsultantlobbyists.org.uk/wp-content/uploads/2016/03/20160330-Press-Release-on-issuing-of-Advocate-Civil-Penalty-Notice-Final.pdf.

[189] Transparency International (2015b). See also House of Commons Select Committee on Public Administration (2009).

[190] Ironically, Part 2 of the 2014 strengthens the 2000 Act still further, by bringing third-party campaigning on behalf of candidates within its regime.

[191] A provision in the 2014 Act to extend its application to 'special advisers' has never been brought into force.

[192] Hansard Vol 774 (9 September 2016) (Lord Brooke).

lobbyists, the architects of the 2014 Act intentionally excluded in-house lobbyists (for example, employees of a pharmaceutical company), and hence covered no more than an estimated 4 per cent of all lobbyists.[193] This is significant, not least because 80 per cent of the most frequent lobbyists are from FTSE 100 companies. Further, in terms of information that must be disclosed, in adopting a 'name, rank and serial number only' approach to lobbying, the 2014 Act imposes no meaningful requirements respecting questions of the greatest importance: how much is being spent by clients, to what end, and to lobby which officials? As Transparency International has observed:

1. All lobbyists in the UK may keep any information about whom they have lobbied and on what issues they have lobbied concealed from the public.
2. In-house lobbyists do not have to register any details, regardless of whom they lobby.
3. There is no requirement for lobbyists to report their expenditure on lobbying, including gifts and hospitality to public officials.
4. There is no obligation on lobbyists to publish how they have used secondments or advisers placed within government to influence policy.[194]

The minimalism of the 2014 Act, in this respect, has had a correspondingly negative effect on voluntary codes of conduct, which confine themselves to meeting the demands of the 2014 Act, with no 'gold plating'. For example, the code of conduct adopted by Chartered Institute of Public Relations starts well enough, by saying:

> Professional lobbyists respect the public's right to know about lobbying activity – the Chartered Institute of Public Relations believes good professional conduct requires lobbying to be carried out in plain view.[195]

However, when the code then goes on to spell out what this involves, we find nothing added beyond the requirements of the 2014 Act:

> This means that professional lobbyists should be willing to publicly identify themselves and disclose the interests on whose behalf they lobby, as well as disclosing their clients.[196]

Chari, Murphy, and Hogan conducted a study in 2007 dividing jurisdictions into 'relatively lowly regulated', 'medium regulated' and 'relatively highly regulated' regimes for the control of lobbying.[197] In relatively lowly regulated regimes, there are rules on individual registration, but few details need be given. Typically, there are also no rules requiring disclosure of individual spending, or of employer spending. In such regimes, restrictions on public officials engaging in lobbying are also weak. So far as professional lobbyists are concerned, it seems clear that the 2014 Act falls into this 'relatively lowly regulated' category, especially when the details just discussed are put alongside the weak constraints on politicians revolving out, discussed in

[193] See generally Transparency International (2015a).
[194] Transparency International (2015a), at 3; http://www.theguardian.com/politics/2014/mar/12/lobbying-10-ways-corprations-influence-government.
[195] Chartered Institute of Public Relations (2015), at 7.
[196] ibid.
[197] Raj Chari, Garry Murphy, and John Hogan (2007), at 427.

Chapter 4.5. In medium regulated regimes, registered lobbyists must state the subject matter of the lobbying, the relevant bill, and the government institution being lobbied. There will also be regulations on individual spending disclosures, such as rules requiring political contributions to be disclosed. The UK's Codes of Conduct for ministers and MPs do require the reporting of gifts and financial support, and as we saw in section 5.10, there is an obligation to record the details of a donor to an election campaign. So, in these respects at least, the UK is at least a medium regulated regime. However, medium regulated regimes do nothing about free consultancy provided by lobbyists close to particular political parties (that is certainly true of the 2014 Act, which is focused on lobbying in exchange for payment), and do not require lobbyists' employers to compile spending reports. In relatively highly regulated regimes:

(a) details of the subject matter, and the institution are required for the register;
(b) the lobbyist must state the name of all employers;
(c) the lobbyist must file a spending report, and report his or her own salary;
(d) all people on whom money was spent must be identified, and all campaign spending accounted for; and
(e) the state agency conducts mandatory reviews and audits.

Some of the supply-side defects of the 2014 Act, in terms of openness, were addressed in the Lobbying (Transparency) Bill 2016–2017 (the 2016–2017 Bill), sponsored by Lord Brooke of Alverthorpe, which had its third reading in December 2016.[198] Clause 2(2) extends the definition of 'lobbyist' to include in-house lobbyists. Clause 2(3) extends the scope of those lobbied, respecting whom lobbying activity must be reported, to all 'public officials', including those working for executive agencies (clause 2(5)). Clause 5 of the Bill requires that the names of those actually doing the lobbying are declared, along with any public post that they have held in the last decade 'to guard against perceptions of privileged access and cronyism'.[199] Clause 5 also requires that the lobbyist make public the names of the persons being lobbied, and the subject matter of the lobbying, whilst clause 6 makes it compulsory for a lobbyist to disclose an estimate of how much money has been spent on the lobbying activity. However, the original proposal to include a statutory lobbying code was dropped, in favour of continuing the present system under which industries devise their own codes voluntarily. Were the Bill to become law, the UK would move towards being a relatively highly regulated regime, in Chari, Murphy, and Hogan's terms.[200]

In discussing inclusivity in section 5.3, I noted a number of features that could make the practice of lobbying perfectly legitimate, although the absence of any

[198] http://services.parliament.uk/bills/2016-17/lobbyingtransparency.html.

[199] Hansard Vol 774 (9 September 2016) (Lord Brooke). In this important respect, the Bill captures a dimension to the regulation of lobbying overlooked by Chari, Murphy, and Hogan, in their analysis of relatively highly regulated regimes: see Chari, Murphy, and Hogan (n 197).

[200] Chari, Murphy, and Hogan (n 197) 427.

individual feature would not necessarily make the inclusivity in question illegitimate. The features relevant here are that the influence on a public official was: (a) ad hoc and 'one-off', (b) impersonal, in the sense that it was not motivated by a personal or otherwise special connection between the politician and the member of the public, but motivated instead by the merits of the request, (c) involved only a relatively insignificant public commitment, and (d) was quite openly made.[201] Clause 5 of the 2016–2017 Bill addresses (d), and hence does something to address (b), by ensuring that the public will at least have the basis for discovering the nature of any connection between the lobbyist (and their clients) and the person lobbied. A failure to disclose such information, in the absence of a due diligence defence, would be an offence under clause 12. The openness requirements of clause 5 also do something to address issues that arise when lobbying falls outside (a) and (c). In key sectors of an economy that have undergone substantial privatization,[202] the scale, cost, and nature of the services to be provided by the private sector mean that, in practice, only a few providers nationwide (or even worldwide) will be capable of meeting the state's demands: an oligopoly is created. So, it will inevitably be largely the same small group of private sector providers bidding—on a repeat basis—for immensely valuable contracts, the reliable delivery of which is a matter of national and international significance. In such circumstances, it is in the interests of would-be contractors to form stable long-term relationships with key public officials in the relevant departments, as well as to lobby MPs and have MPs lobbying on their behalf. In a well-known example, British Airports Authority executives met Department of Transport officials 117 times between 2002 and 2007, including twenty-four meetings with the Secretary of State for Transport.[203] It is, thus, especially important to know who has been in contact with public officials, in such circumstances, how much they have spent in securing such contact, and the subject matter of the contact; but is that enough?

It is arguable that there should be reporting of any and all contact between public officials and would-be contractors, or their representatives, in relation to any public service contract, or in relation to legislative or policy change that may affect such contracts, worth more than a certain amount or concerning certain kinds of service to be delivered (such as defence, health, correctional services, and transport). Further, the burden of disclosure in this respect should be on the public official, as much or more than it is on the contractor or lobbyist. In the second reading debate of the 2016–2017 Bill, Lord Norton had suggested an amendment as follows:

> A Minister of the Crown, at the time of making a statement relating to [any clause 2 legislative, policy or contractual matter involving a public official] shall publish details of any oral or written communication received in respect of that matter by the Minister of the Crown, or civil servants within the Minister's Department, or a special adviser.[204]

201 Condition (e) was that the lobbying was undertaken without payment.

202 Such as defence contracting, transport, banking, healthcare, nuclear power, or correctional services.

203 http://webarchive.nationalarchives.gov.uk/20081107073126/http://www.dft.gov.uk/foi/responses/2007/july2007/aviationmeetings/aviationmeetings.

204 Hansard Vol 774 (9 September 2016).

This would have been a welcome addition to the Bill but even so, it is ambiguous on a crucial point. When so much is at stake, would-be contractors and their lobbyists have reasons to approach MPs, and in particular shadow ministers, long before the latter have the opportunity to form part of a government. It should be made explicit that details of communications to be disclosed must go beyond those received by a minister in his or her capacity as such, and should extend historically to any communications engaged in by him or her in relation to the issue in question whilst he or she was an MP.

Select Bibliography

Alesina, Alberto and Giuliano, Paola (2013): 'Family Ties', IZA Discussion Paper No 7376 https://www.econstor.eu/bitstream/10419/80709/1/745840558.pdf.

Allen, Nicholas and Birch, Sarah, *Ethics and Integrity in British Politics* (Cambridge University Press, 2015).

Aristotle, *The Politics*, Ernest Barker, ed (Clarendon Press, 1946).

Archbold, W, *Criminal Pleading, Evidence and Practice* (Sweet & Maxwell, 2014).

Ashworth, Andrew, 'The Elasticity of Mens Rea' in Colin Tapper (ed), *Crime, Proof and Punishment* (Butterworths, 1981) 45–77.

Ashworth, Andrew, 'Testing Fidelity to Legal Values: Official Involvement in Criminal Justice' in S C Shute and A P Simester, *Criminal Law Theory: Doctrines of the General Part* (Oxford University Press, 2002) ch 13.

Ashworth, Andrew, 'Ignorance of the Criminal Law, and Duties to Avoid it' (2011) 74 Modern LR 1.

Ashworth, W J, 'Practical Objectivity: The Excise, State and Production in Eighteenth Century England' (2004) 18 Social Epistemology 181.

Australian Government, *Lobbying Code of Conduct* (Department of the Prime Minister and Cabinet, 2013).

Baugh, Daniel A, *British Naval Administration in the Age of Walpole* (Princeton, 1965).

Beetham, David, *Bureaucracy* edn(2nd edn, Open University Press, 1996).

Benson, Arthur C (ed), *The Letters of Queen Victoria*, 3rd Series, Vol II (John Murray, 1931).

Bentham, Jeremy, 'Observations on Mr Secretary Peel's House of Commons Speech, 21 March 1825' *The Pamphleteer*, vol xxv (A J Valpy) 405.

Baker, W J, *The History of the Marconi Company* 1874–1965 (Routledge, 1998).

Besley, Timothy and Larcinese, Valentino, 'Working or Shirking? Expenses and Attendance in the UK Parliament' (2011) 146 Public Choice 291.

Big Brother Watch, *NHS Breaches of Data Protection Law* (2011), https://www.bigbrotherwatch.org.uk/files/NHS_Breaches_Data_Protection.pdf.

Bingham, Lord, Memorandum for the Joint Committee on Parliamentary Privilege, *Parliamentary Privilege: First Report* (1999) HC 214-III http://www.publications.parliament.uk/pa/jt199899/jtselect/jtpriv/43/4302.htm.

Birkenhead, Lord, *Famous Trials* (Hutchinson, 1926).

Blackstone, Sir William, *Commentaries on the Laws of England* (Clarendon Press, 1765).

Bogart, Dan, 'Turnpike Trusts and the Transportation Revolution in 18th Century England' (2005) 42 Explorations in Economic History 479.

Bogdanor, Vernon, 'The Constitution and the Party System in the Twentieth Century' (2004) 57 Parliamentary Affairs 717.

Bolen, Cheryl, 'The Great Georgian Gambling Epidemic' (2006) http://www.cherylbolen.com/gambling.htm.

Bowring, John (ed), *The Works of Jeremy Bentham Part IV* (William Tait, 1838).

Braggion, Fabio and Moore, Lyndon, 'The Economic Benefits of Political Connections in Late Victorian Britain' (2013) 73 The Journal of Economic History 142.

Breihan, John R, 'William Pitt and the Commission on Fees 1785–1801' (1984) 27 Historical Journal 59.

Brewer, John, *The Sinews of Power: War, Money and the English State, 1688–1783* (Century Hutchinson, 1988).

Broad, John, 'Cattle Plague in Eighteenth Century England' (1983) 31 Agricultural History Review 104.

Brooke, John, *The House of Commons 1754–1790* (Oxford University Press, 1964).

Brudnick, Ida, *Members' Representational Allowance: History and Usage* (Congressional Research Service 7-5700, 2017) https://fas.org/sgp/crs/misc/R40962.pdf.

Burtt, Shelley, 'Ideas of Corruption in Eighteenth Century England' in William C Heffernan and John Kleinig (eds), *Private and Public Corruption* (Rowman & Littlefield, 2004).

Butler, Lord, *Review of Intelligence on Weapons of Mass Destruction* HC898 (TSO, 2004).

Cabinet Office, *Governance Code on Public Appointments* (Cabinet Office, 2016).

Capp, Bernard, *Cromwell's Navy: The Fleet and the English Revolution, 1648–1660* (Oxford University Press, 1989).

Chan Smith, David, *Sir Edward Coke and the Reformation of the Laws: Religion, Politics and Jurisprudence 1578–1616* (Cambridge University Press, 2014).

Chari, Raj, Murphy, Gary and Hogan, John, 'Regulating Lobbyists: A Comparative Analysis of the United States, Canada, Germany and the European Union' (2007) 78 The Political Quarterly 422.

Chartered Institute of Public Relations, *Professional Lobbying: Introducing the UK Lobbying Register* (2015) https://www.cipr.co.uk/content/policy-resources/policy/lobbying

Chesterton, G K, *The Autobiography of GK Chesterton* (Sheed & Ward, 1943).

Civil Service, Civil Service Code (2010) https://www.gov.uk/government/publications/civil-service-code.

Cobbett, William, *A Parliamentary History of England* (E Bagshaw, 1803).

Coffee, John C Jr, 'Modern Mail Fraud: The Restoration of the Public/Private Distinction' (1997–98) 35 Am Crim L Rev 427.

College of Policing, *Code of Ethics* (College of Policing, 2014).

Colley, Linda, *Britons: Forging the Nation 1707–1837* (Yale University Press, 1992).

Commissioners of Public Accounts, 6th Report, *Commons Journal*, xxxv (1780–82).

Committee on Standards in Public Life, *First Report* (HMSO, 1995).

Committee on Standards in Public Life, *The Funding of Political Parties in the United Kingdom*, Cm 4057 (TSO, 2008).

Committee on Standards in Public Life, *MPs' Expenses and Allowances: Supporting Parliament, Safeguarding the Taxpayer*, 12th Report Cm 7724 (TSO, 2009).

Committee on Standards in Public Life, *Political Party Finance: Ending the Big Donor Culture*, 13th Report Cm 8208 (TSO, 2011).

Compliance Officer for the Independent Parliamentary Standards Authority, *Procedures and Guidance for the Compliance Officer for IPSA* (2014) https://www.gov.uk/government/uploads/system/uploads/attachment_data/file/372970/CSPL_response_to_IPSA_compliance_officer_consultation_Final.pdf.

Covington & Burling LLP, 'China Amends Criminal Law: Impact on Anti-Bribery Enforcement' (2015) https://www.cov.com/en/offices/-/media/1aa92ed9de6e4c918788 5a705b9c6977.ashx.

Craig, Paul, *Administrative Law* (6th edn, Sweet & Maxwell, 2008).

Craig, Paul, 'Public Law, Political Theory and Legal Theory' [2000] Public Law 211.

Cross, J A, 'Withdrawal of the Conservative Party Whip' (1967) 21 Parliamentary Affairs 166.

Crown Prosecution Service, *The Code for Crown Prosecutors* (2013) https://www.cps.gov.uk/sites/default/files/documents/publications/code_2013_accessible_english.pdf.

Crown Prosecution Service, 'Deferred Prosecution Agreements: Code of Practice' (2014) https://www.cps.gov.uk/sites/default/files/documents/publications/dpa_cop.pdf.

Dagger, Richard, 'Autonomy, Domination, and the Republican Challenge to Liberalism' (2005) http://scholarship.richmond.edu/cgi/viewcontent.cgi?article=1145&context=polisci-faculty-publications.

Dimoldenberg, Paul, *The Westminster Whistle-blowers: Shirley Porter, Homes for Votes and Scandal in Britain's Rottenest Borough* (Politico's Publishing, 2006).

Doig, Alan, 'Conflicts of Interest of Elected Officials: The Experience of the United Kingdom Committee on Standards in Public Life' (2006) https://www.coe.int/t/dg1/legalcooperation/economiccrime/cybercrime/cy%20activity%20Interface2006/143%20_2006_-if-rep%20alan%20doig.pdf.

Duff, R A, *Answering for Crime: Responsibility and Liability in the Criminal Law* (Hart Publishing, 2007).

Dworkin, Ronald, *Law's Empire* (Fontana, 1986).

Dyzenhaus, David, 'The Politics of Deference: Judicial Review and Democracy' in Michael Taggart (ed), *The Province of Administrative Law* (Hart Publishing, 1997) 279–302.

Eastwood, David, *Government and Community in the English Provinces 1700–1870* (Palgrave MacMillan, 1987).

Electoral Commission, *Challenging Elections in the UK* (Electoral Commission, 2012).

Electoral Commission, *Introduction to Being a Party Treasurer* (2016) http://www.electoralcommission.org.uk/__data/assets/pdf_file/0013/102262/intro-party-treasurer-rp.pdf.

Electoral Commission, 'Investigation in respect of the Conservative and Unionist Party campaign spending returns for the 2014 European Parliamentary Election, and 2015 UK Parliamentary General Election, and in respect of the 2014 parliamentary by-elections in Clacton, Newark and Rochester and Strood' (Electoral Commission, 2017).

Erskine May, *Parliamentary Practice* (23rd edn, LexisNexis, 2004).

Ewing, Keith, *The Funding of Political Parties in Britain* (Cambridge University Press, 1987).

Ewing, Keith, *The Cost of Democracy: Party Funding in Modern British Politics* (Hart Publishing, 2007).

Ewing, K D and Ghaleigh, N S, 'The Cost of Giving and Receiving: Donations to Political Parties in the United Kingdom' (2007) 6 Election Law Journal 56.

Feinberg, Joel, *Harm to Others* (Oxford University Press, 1984).

Feinberg, Joel, *Offense to Others* (Oxford University Press, 1985).

Feinberg, Joel, *Harm to Self* (Oxford University Press, 1986).

Ferejohn, J, 'Incumbent Performance and Electoral Control' (1986) 50 Public Choice 5.

Financial Action Task Force, 'Politically Exposed Persons' (2013) http://www.fatf-gafi.org/media/fatf/documents/recommendations/Guidance-PEP-Rec12-22.pdf.

Fisher, Justin, 'The Political Parties, Elections and Referendums Act 2000' (2001) 38 Representation 11.

Flinders, Matthew and Mathews, Felicity, 'Think Again: Patronage, Governance and the Smarter State' (2010) 38 Policy & Politics 639.

Foord, A S, 'The Waning of the Influence of the Crown' (1947) 62 English Historical Review 484.

Forsyth, Chris, 'Of Fig Leaves and Fairy Tales: The *Ultra Vires* Doctrine, the Sovereignty of Parliament and Judicial Review' [1996] CLJ 122.

Fox, Henry, Lord Holland, 'Memoir' in Countess of Ilchester and Lord Stavordale, *Life and Letters of Lord Lennox* (2nd edn, John Murray, 1902).

Fox-Decent, Evan, *Sovereignty's Promise: The State as Fiduciary* (Oxford University Press, 2011).

Fuller, Lon, *The Morality of Law* (Revised edn, Yale University Press, 1964)

Gainsborough, Martin, 'Keeping Up Appearances: MPs' Expenses and the Hidden Dimensions of Rule in Britain Today', School of Sociology, Politics and International Studies, University of Bristol Working Paper No 03-11 (2011) www.bristol.ac.uk/spais/research/workingpapers/wpspaisfiles/gainsborough03-11.pdf.

Gardiner, Samuel R (ed), *The Constitutional Documents of the Puritan Revolution 1625–1660* (Oxford University Press, 1906).

Gardner, James A, 'Can Political Parties be Virtuous?' (2000) 100 Columbia Law Review 667.

Gardner, John, 'Justification under Authority' (2010) 23 Canadian Journal of Law and Jurisprudence 71.

Gardner, John, 'Douglas Husak, Overcriminalisation: The Limits of the Criminal Law' *Notre Dame Philosophical Reviews* 03.08.2011 https://ndpr.nd.edu/news/overcriminalization-the-limits-of-the-criminal-law/.

Gardner, John, 'Criminals in Uniform' in R A Duff, Lindsay Farmer, S E Marshall, Massimo Renzo, and Victor Tadros (eds), *The Constitution of the Criminal Law* (Oxford University Press, 2013a) ch 6.

Gardner, John, 'Finnis on Justice' in John Keown and Robert P George (eds), *Reason, Morality, and Law: The Philosophy of John Finnis* (Oxford University Press, 2013b) ch 10.

Gateshead Council, Councillors' Code of Conduct (2017) http://www.gateshead.gov.uk/Council%20and%20Democracy/Councillors-and-committees/Councillors-Code-of-Conduct.aspx.

Gay, Oonagh, *Parliamentary Privilege: Current Issues* (Parliament and Constitution Centre, 2013).

Gay, Oonagh, and Tomlinson, Hugh, 'Freedom of Speech' in Alexander Horne, Gavin Drewry, and Dawn Oliver, *Parliament and the Law* (Hart Publishing, 2013), ch 2.

Gilens, Martin, *Affluence & Influence: Economic Inequality and Political Power in America* (Princeton University Press, 2012).

Gilje, Paul A, *Free Trade and Sailors' Rights in the War of 1812* (Cambridge University Press, 2013).

Gisborne, Reverend Thomas, *An Enquiry into the Duties of Men in the Higher and Middle Classes of Society in Great Britain* (B & H White, 1794).

Goldie, Mark, 'The Unacknowledged Republic: Officeholding in Early Modern England' in Tim Harris, *The Politics of the Excluded c 1500–1850* (Palgrave 2001) ch 6.

Global Witness (2015) https://www.globalwitness.org/en-gb/blog/uk-must-get-tough-tax-havens-its-anti-corruption-efforts-work/.

Goodman, Godfrey, *The Fall of Man of the Corruption of Nature* (Felix Kyngston, 1616).

Greaves, C S, *Russell on Crime, vol II* (3rd edn, Saunders & Benning, 1843).

Green, E H H, *The Crisis of Conservatism: The Politics, Economics and Ideology of the British Conservative Party 1880–1914* (Routledge, 1995).

Green, Stuart P, *Lying, Cheating and Stealing: A Moral Theory of White Collar Crime* (Oxford University Press, 2006).

Griffith, J A G, *The Politics of the Judiciary* (5th edn, Fontana Press, 2010).

Grimstone, Gerry, *Better Public Appointments: A Review of the Public Appointments Process* (Cabinet Office, 2016).

Guide to Judicial Conduct https://www.judiciary.gov.uk/wp-content/uploads/JCO/Documents/Guidance/judicial_conduct_2013.pdf.

Hale, Sir Matthew, *The History of the Pleas of the Crown* (Nutt and Gosling, 1736).

Hansard Society, *Audit of Engagement* (Hansard Society, 2006).
Harris, Robert, *Political Corruption In and Beyond the Nation State* (Routledge, 2003).
Hawkins, Angus, *Victorian Political Culture: Habits of Heart and Mind* (Oxford University Press, 2015).
Hawkins, Sir William, *A Treatise of the Pleas of the Crown*, 8th Edition by John Curwood (Sweet & Maxwell Stevens, 1824).
Hay, Douglas, 'Dread of the Crown Office: the English Magistracy and King's Bench, 1740–1800' in Norma Landau (ed), *Law, Crime and English Society, 1660–1830* (Cambridge University Press, 2002) ch 2.
Hayton, D W, *The House of Commons 1690–1715* (Cambridge University Press, 2002).
Helland, Leif and Sørensen, Rune, 'Persistent Rent Extraction' (2012) 153 Public Choice 205.
Her Majesty's Revenue and Customs, *Guidance: Annual Tax on Enveloped Dwellings* (2014) https://www.gov.uk/guidance/annual-tax-on-enveloped-dwellings-the-basics.
Heuwiser, Raphael (2015), 'MP Expenses and their Assessment in the Media: Towards a More Informed Analysis' http://blog.politics.ox.ac.uk/mp-expenses-and-their-assessment-in-the-media-towards-a-more-informed-analysis/.
High Pay Centre, 'The Revolving Door and the Corporate Colonisation of UK Politics' (High Pay Centre, 2015).
Hindle, Steve, *The State and Social Change in Early Modern England c 1550–1640* (Palgrave, 2000).
Hirst, F, Murray, G, and Hammond, J L, *Liberalism and the Empire* (R Brimley Johnson, 1900).
Holdsworth, William, *A History of English Law* (Methuen, 1938).
Home Office (2003), Home Office Circular 051/2003: *National Recruitment Standards: Eligibility Criteria for Police Recruitment and Consistent Recruitment Practices* https://www.gov.uk/government/publications/national-recruitment-standards-eligibility-criteria-for-police-recruitment-and-consistent-recruitment-practices.
Hopkin, Jonathan, 'The Problem with Party Finance' (2004) 10 Party Politics 627.
Hoppit, Julian, 'Patterns of Parliamentary Legislation 1660–1800' (1996) 39 Historical Journal 116.
Horder, Jeremy, *Provocation and Responsibility* (Oxford University Press, 1992).
Horder, Jeremy, *Homicide and the Politics of Law Reform* (Oxford University Press, 2012).
Horder, Jeremy, 'Excusing Information-Provision Crimes in the Bureaucratic State' (2015) 68 Current Legal Problems 197.
Horder, Jeremy, *Ashworth's Principles of Criminal Law* (8th edn, Oxford University Press, 2016).
Horder, Jeremy, '*R v Bembridge* (1783)' in Philip Handler, Henry Mares, and Ian Williams (eds), *Landmark Cases in Criminal Law* (Hart Publishing, 2017) ch 5.
House of Commons Committee on Standards, *Patrick Mercer*, 11th Report of 2013–14 (HC 1225) http://www.publications.parliament.uk/pa/cm201314/cmselect/cmstandards/1225/122503.htm#a2
House of Commons, *The Green Book: A Guide to Members' Allowances* (House of Commons, London 2009).
House of Commons, *Administration Annual Accounts 2014–15* (HC 274) http://www.parliament.uk/documents/commons-expenditure/Admin%20Annual%20Accounts/Administration_Annual_Accounts_2014_15.pdf.
House of Commons, *The Code of Conduct* (HC 1076, 2015).
House of Commons Library, 'Inflation: The Value of the Pound 1750–2011' (Research Paper 12/31 (29 May 2012)) http://researchbriefings.parliament.uk/ResearchBriefing/Summary/RP12-31.

House of Commons Library (2016), 'Short Money' http://researchbriefings.parliament.uk/ResearchBriefing/Summary/SN01663.

House of Commons Members Estimate Committee, *Review of Past ACA Payments: First Report of 2009–10* (HC 348, 2010).

House of Commons Select Committee on Public Administration (2009), *Lobbying: Access and influence in Whitehall: First Report of Session 2008–09* http://www.publications.parliament.uk/pa/cm200809/cmselect/cmpubadm/36/36i.pdf.

House of Commons Select Committee on Public Administration (2016–17), *Managing Ministers' and Officials' Conflicts of Interest: Time for Clearer Values, Principles and Action* https://www.publications.parliament.uk/pa/cm201617/cmselect/cmpubadm/252/25203.htm.

House of Commons Select Committee on Public Administration and Constitutional Affairs, 'The Advisory Committee on Business Appointments' (HC 977, 2016).

House of Commons Standards and Privileges Committee (2010–11), *Mr Denis MacShane* http://www.publications.parliament.uk/pa/cm201011/cmselect/cmstnprv/527/52703.htm.

House of Lords, 'Guide to Financial Support for Members' (2013) https://www.parliament.uk/documents/lords-information-office/2013/Guide-to-Financial-Support-For-Members-2013.pdf.

House of Lords Appointments Commission (2016) http://lordsappointments.independent.gov.uk/vetting-for-propriety.aspx.

House of Lords Committee for Privileges and Conduct (2013–14), 'The Conduct of Lord Hanningfield' http://www.publications.parliament.uk/pa/ld201314/ldselect/ldpriv/181/18103.htm#a2.

Ilbert, Courtney, *The Mechanics of Law-Making* (Columbia University Press, 1913).

Independent Commission Against Corruption, *Report on Investigation into the Metherell Resignation and Appointment* (ICAC, 1992a).

Independent Commission Against Corruption, *Second Report on the Investigation into the Metherell Resignation and Appointment* (ICAC, 1992b).

Independent Commission Against Corruption (2017) https://www.icac.nsw.gov.au.

Independent Parliamentary Standards Authority, *Annual Report and Accounts*, HC 318 (TSO, 2013a).

Independent Parliamentary Standards Authority, *MPs' Pay and Pensions: A New Package* (IPSA, 2013b).

Independent Parliamentary Standards Authority, *The MPs' Scheme of Business Costs and Expenses* (HMSO, 2015).

Independent Parliamentary Standards Authority, *IPSA's First Parliament 2010–2015: Regulation, Support and Remuneration* (IPSA, 2016a).

Independent Parliamentary Standards Authority, *Review of the MPs' Scheme of Business Costs and Expenses and IPSA's Publication Policy: A Consultation* (HMSO, 2016b).

Independent Parliamentary Standards Authority, *Review of the Scheme of MPs' Business Costs and Expenses and IPSA's Publication Policy: Consultation Report and Equality Impact Assessment* (HMSO, 2017a).

Independent Parliamentary Standards Authority, *The Scheme of MPs' Business Costs and Expenses 2017–18* HC 1024 edn(9th edn, HMS0, 2017b).

Jaffe, Louis J, 'Suits Against Governments and Officers: Sovereign Immunity' (1963) 77 Harvard Law Review 1.

Jaffe, Louis J, and Henderson, Edith, 'Judicial Review and the Rule of Law: Historical Origins' (1956) 72 LQR 345.

Jay, Stuart, *Most Humble Servants: The Advisory Role of Early Judges* (Yale University Press, 1997).

Jeffrey, Charlie, 'The Pork Barrel Election' (2015) http://blogs.lse.ac.uk/politicsandpolicy/the-pork-barrel-election/.

Jenkins, T A, *Parliament, Party and Politics in Victorian Britain* (Manchester University Press, 1996).

Johnson, Jeremy, 'Observations on Behalf of the House of Lords Authorities' (13 July 2016) http://www.parliament.uk/documents/lords-information-office/2016/91881-Treas-Lord-Hanningfield-Observations.pdf.

Johnson, Paul, *Making the Market: Victorian Origins of Corporate Capitalism* (Cambridge University Press, 2010).

Johnson, Victor L, 'Internal Reform or External Taxation: Britain's Fiscal Choice, 1763' (1954) 98 Proceedings of the American Philosophical Society 31.

Joint Practitioners Advisory Group, *Governance and Accountability for Local Councils: A Practitioners' Guide* (2010) www.nalc.gov.uk/Latest_News/Governance_and_Accountability_2010.aspx.

Joint Select Committee on Parliamentary Privilege (1998–99), *First Report* HL Paper 43/HC214-1 http://www.publications.parliament.uk/pa/jt199899/jtselect/jtpriv/43/4306.htm.

Joint Select Committee on Parliamentary Privilege (2013–14), *Parliamentary Privilege* http://www.publications.parliament.uk/pa/jt201314/jtselect/jtprivi/30/3004.htm.

Jones, Phillip and Hudson, John, 'The Role of Political Parties: An Analysis Based on Transaction Costs' (1998) 94 Public Choice 175.

Joseph Rowntree Reform Trust, *State of the Nation Poll* (Joseph Rowntree Reform Trust, 2006) http://www.jrrt.org.uk/publications/state-nation-2014.

Judiciary of England and Wales, *Guide to Judicial Conduct* (March 2013) https://www.judiciary.gov.uk/about-the-judiciary/the-judiciary-the-government-and-the-constitution/how-the-judiciary-is-governed/guide-to-judicial-conduct/.

Jupp, Peter, *The Governing of Britain 1688–1848* (Routledge, 2006).

Kamenka, Eugene and Tay, Alice, 'Beyond Bourgeois Individualism; the Contemporary Crisis in Law and Legal Ideology' in Eugene Kamenka and R S Neale, *Feudalism, Capitalism and Beyond* (Edward Arnold, 1975) 126–44.

Kaufmann, D and Vincente, P C, 'Legal Corruption' (2011) 23 Economics and Politics 195.

Kaul, Inge, Grunberg, Isabelle, and Stern, Mark S (eds), *Global Public Goods: International Co-operation in the 21st Century* (Oxford University Press, 1999).

Keen, Richard, Apostolova, Vyara, and Audickas, Lucas (2017), 'Political Parties' http://researchbriefings.parliament.uk/ResearchBriefing/Summary/SN05125.

Kelly, Richard, Coleman, Charley, and Johnston, Neil, *Recall Elections* (House of Commons Library, 2014).

Kelly, Richard, and Hamlyn, Matthew, 'The Law and Conduct of Members of Parliament' in Alexander Horne, Gavin Drewry and Dawn Oliver, *Parliament and the Law* (Hart Publishing, 2013) ch 4.

Kelso, Alexandra, 'Parliament on its Knees: MPs' Expenses and the Crisis of Transparency at Westminster' (2009) 80 Political Quarterly 329.

Kleinig, John, 'Re-thinking Noble Cause Corruption' (2002) 4 International Journal of Police Science and Management 287.

Knights, Mark (2016), 'Old Corruption: What British History Can Tell Us about Corruption Today' http://www.transparency.org.uk/publications/old-corruption-what-british-history-can-tell-us-about-corruption-today/#.Wl8eV65l_IU.

Kramnick, Isaac, 'Corruption in Eighteenth-Century British and American Political Discourse' in Richard K Matthews (ed), *Virtue, Corruption and Self-Interest* (Lehigh University Press, 1994) 59–82.

Kurer, Oskar, 'Corruption: An Alternative Approach to Its Definition and Measurement' (2005) 53 Political Studies 222.

Landau, Norma, 'The Trading Justices' Trade' in Norma Landau (ed), *Law, Crime and English Society 1660–1830* (Cambridge University Press, 2002) 46–70.

Lankester, Tim, 'Conflict of Interest: A Historical and Comparative Perspective (2007) https://www.oecd.org/site/adboecdanti-corruptioninitiative/39368062.pdf.

Larcinese, Valentino and Sircar, Indraneel, 'Crime and Punishment the British Way: Accountability Channels Following the MPs' Expenses Scandal' Political Science and Political Economy Working Paper No 9 of 2012 http://www.lse.ac.uk/government/research/resgroups/PSPE/pdf/PSPE_WP9_12.pdf.

Law Commission, *Reforming Bribery: Consultation Paper No 185* (TSO, 2007).

Law Commission, *Reforming Bribery*, Law Com No 313 (TSO, 2008).

Law Commission, *Criminal Law in Regulatory Contexts: Consultation Paper No 195* (TSO, 2010).

Law Commission, *Misconduct in Public Office Issues Paper 1: The Current Law* (TSO, 2016a).

Law Commission, *Reforming Misconduct in Public Office: Law Commission Consultation Paper No 229* (Law Commission, 2016B).

Lawrence Smyth, Liam, 'Privilege, Exclusive Cognisance and the Law' in Alexander Horne, Gavin Drewry, and Dawn Oliver, *Parliament and the Law* (Hart Publishing, 2013) ch 1.

Legg, Sir Thomas, *Assisted Cost Allowance Review: Report to the Members Estimate Committee* (2010) http://www.publications.parliament.uk/pa/cm200910/cmselect/cmmemest/348/app1.pdf.

Lemmings, David, *Law and Government in England during the Long Eighteenth Century* (Palgrave MacMillan, 2011).

Liebenstein, Harvey, 'Allocative Efficiency vs X-Efficiency' (1966) 56 American Economic Review 392.

Lilburne, John and Overton, Richard, *The Out-cryes of Oppressed Commons* 1646 (Eebo Editions, 2010).

Lind, Charles, *Essays on Several Subjects* (J & F Rivington, 1769).

Lipscombe, Sally and Horne, Alexander, 'Parliamentary Privilege' in Alexander Horne, Gavin Drewry, and Dawn Oliver, *Parliament and the Law* (Hart Publishing, 2013) ch 3.

Lock, F P, *Edmund Burke 1730–1784, vol 1* (Oxford University Press, 2008).

Locke, John, *Second Treatise on Civil Government (1690)* in Ernest Barker and Gerard Hopkins (eds), *Social Contract; Essays by Locke, Hume and Rousseau* (Oxford University Press, 1948).

Lord, Nicholas, *Regulating Corporate Bribery in International Business: Anti-corruption in the UK and Germany* (Ashgate Publishing, 2014).

MacIntyre, Alasdair, *After Virtue: A Study in Moral Philosophy* (University of Notre Dame Press, 1981).

Maitland, F W, 'The Shadows and Silences of Real Life' in H A L Fisher (ed), *The Collected Papers of Frederick William Maitland* (Cambridge University Press, 1911) 467–79.

Marshall, T H, *Citizenship and Social Class & Other Essays* (Cambridge University Press, 1950).

Martí, José Luis and Pettit, Philip, *A Political Philosophy in Public Life: Civic Republicanism in Zapatero's Spain* (Princeton University Press, 2010).

Marx, Karl, *Capital: A Critique of Political Economy*, (reprint, Cosimo Classics, 2007).

McBain, Graham, 'Modernising the Common Law Offence of Misconduct in a Public or Judicial Office' (2014) 7 Journal of Politics and Law 46.
McDonald, Andrew, 'Farewell to the Golden Goodbyes and Backroom Deals' (2013) http://parliamentarystandards.org.uk/sites/ipsablog/Lists/Posts/Post.aspx?ID=21.
McGowen, Randall, 'Making the "Bloody Code"? Forgery Legislation in Eighteenth-Century England' in Norma Landau (ed), *Law, Crime and English Society 1660–1830* (Cambridge University Press, 2002) 117–38.
Mell, Andrew, Radford, Simon, and Thévoz, Seth Alexander, 'Is There a Market for Peerages? Can Donations Buy You a British Peerage? A Study in the Link Between Party Political Funding and Peerage Nominations' 2005–14 (March 2015) http://www.economics.ox.ac.uk/materials/papers/13888/paper744.pdf.
Mill, John Stuart, *On Liberty* (2nd edn, John W Parker and Son, 1859).
Ministerial Code (Cabinet Office, 2016).
Ministry of Defence, *The Government's Response to the Report of Enquiry into National Recognition of Our Armed Forces* (Ministry of Defence, October 2008).
Ministry of Justice, *Party Finance and Expenditure in the United Kingdom*, CM7329 (Ministry of Justice, 2008).
Müller, Wolfgang C, 'Political Parties in Parliamentary Democracies: Making Delegation and Accountability Work' (2000) 37 European Journal of Political Research 309.
Mungiu-Pippidi, Alina, *The Quest for Good Governance* (Cambridge University Press, 2015).
Murphy, Phillip, *Party Politics and Decolonization: The Conservative Party and British Colonial Policy in Tropical Africa 1951–1964* (Oxford University Press, 1995).
Nagel, Thomas, *Mortal Questions* (Cambridge University Press, 1979).
Nenner, Howard, 'Loyalty and the Law: The Meaning of Trust and the Right of Resistance in Seventeenth Century England' (2009) 48 Journal of British Studies 859.
Newgate Calendar (Knapp and Baldwin, 1824).
Norman, Jesse, *Edmund Burke* (William Collins, 2013).
Nye, J S, 'Corruption and Political Development: A Cost-Benefit Analysis' (1967) 61 American Political Science Review 417.
Office of the Leader of the House of Commons, *Audit and Assurance of MPs' Allowances* (Cm 7460, 2008).
Office of the Leader of the House of Commons, *Parliamentary Privilege* (Cm 8318, 2012).
Oglethorpe, James, *The Sailor's Advocate* (Henry Whitridge, 1728).
Ogus, Anthony, 'Regulatory Law: Some Lessons from the Past' (1992) 12 Legal Studies 1.
Oliver, Dawn, 'Psychological Constitutionalism' (2010) 69 Cambridge Law Journal 639.
Olken, Benjamin A and Pande, Rohini, *Corruption in Developing Countries* (National Bureau of Economic Research, 2011).
Organisation for Economic Co-operation and Development (2006), 'The OECD Fights Corruption' https://www.oecd.org/daf/anti-bribery/anti-briberyconvention/37418910.pdf.
Ormerod, David, 'Cheating the Public Revenue' [1998] Crim LR 627.
Parliamentary Commissioner for Standards, *Commissioner's Information Note* (2015) https://www.parliament.uk/documents/pcfs/New%20Website%20Documents/PCS-information-Note.pdf.
Parker, Henry, *Observations upon some of his Majesties late Answers and Expresses* 1642 (Anne Arbor, 2005–2010).
Parsons, Simon, 'Misconduct in a Public Office: Should it still be Prosecuted?' (2012) 76 JCL 179.
Patten, Alan, 'The Republican Critique of Liberalism' (1996) 26 British Journal of Political Science 25.

Paun, Akash and Hibben, Ashley, *Supplying Confidence: How Confidence and Supply Agreements between Minority Governments and Smaller Parties Work* (Institute for Government, 2017).

Pavin, Philip, 'Friend or Foe? Lobbying in British Democracy: A Discussion Paper' (Hansard Society, 2007).

Pettit, Philip, *The Common Mind: An Essay on Psychology, Society and Politics* (Oxford University Press, 1996).

Pettit, Philip, *Republicanism: A Theory of Freedom and Government* (Oxford University Press, 1999).

Pettit, Philip, *On the People's Terms: A Republican Theory and Model of Democracy* (Cambridge University Press, 2012).

Pettit, Philip, 'Criminalisation in Republican Theory' in R A Duff, Lindsay Farmer, S E Marshall, Massimo Renzo, and Victor Tadros (eds), *Criminalisation: The Political Morality of the Criminal Law* (Oxford University Press, 2014) ch 5.

Phillips, Sir Hayden, *Review of the Honours System* (Cabinet Office, 2004).

Philp, Mark, 'Defining Political Corruption' (1997) XLV Political Studies 436–462.

Pinto-Duschinsky, Michael and Middleton, Lynne, *Reforming Public Appointments* (Policy Exchange, 2013).

Pitler, Robert M, 'The Fruit of the "Poisonous Tree" Revisited and Shepardized' (1968) 56 California Law Review 579.

Platt, D C M, 'The Commercial and Industrial Interests of Ministers of the Crown' (1961) 9 Political Studies 268.

Porter, Roy, *English Society in the Eighteenth Century* (Rev edn, Penguin, 1991).

Postema, Gerald J, *Bentham and the Common Law Tradition* (Clarendon Press, 1986).

Rawls, John, *Political Liberalism* (Columbia University Press, 1993).

Raz, Joseph, *The Morality of Freedom* (Oxford University Press, 1986).

Raz, Joseph, 'Autonomy, Toleration and the Harm Principle' in Ruth Gavinson (ed), *Issues In Contemporary Legal Philosophy* (Clarendon Press, 1987) 313–39.

Raz, Joseph, *Ethics in the Public Domain* (Clarendon Press, 1994).

Raz, Joseph, 'Authority, Law and Morality' in Joseph Raz, *Ethics in the Public Domain* (Clarendon Press, 1995) ch 10.

Rigby, Richard, *Authentic Memoirs, and a Sketch of the Real Character, of the Late Right Honourable Richard Rigby* (Debrett, 1788).

Rogers, Nicholas, 'Liberty Road: Opposition to Impressment in Britain during the American War of Independence' in Colin Howell and Richard Twomey (eds), *Jack Tar in History* (Acadiensis Press, 1991) 55–75.

Rogers, Nicholas, 'Impressment and the Law and Eighteenth Century Britain' in Norma Landau (ed), *Law, Crime and English Society, 1660–1830* (Cambridge University Press, 2002) ch 4.

Rose-Ackerman, Susan, *Corruption and Government* (Cambridge University Press, 1999).

Rosenberg, Joshua, 'How Pinochet Tainted Hoffmann's Brilliant Career' *Law Society Gazette* (23 April 2009) https://www.lawgazette.co.uk/analysis/how-pinochet-tainted-hoffmanns-brilliant-career-/50436.article.

Rosenblum, Nancy, 'Political Parties as Membership Groups' (2000) 100 Columbia Law Review 813.

Rossiter, Clinton (ed), *The Federalist Papers* (The New American Library, 1961).

Rubinstein, W B, 'The Victorian Middle Classes: Wealth, Occupation, and Geography' (1977) 30 The Economic History Review 602.

Rubinstein, William D, and von Maravic, Patrick, 'Max Weber, Bureaucracy, and Corruption' in Gjalt de Graaf, Patrick von Maravic, and Pieter Wagenaar (eds), *The Good Cause: Theoretical Perspectives on Corruption* (Budrich, 2010) 21–35.

Rules of the House of Representatives (114th Congress, 2015) https://rules.house.gov/sites/republicans.rules.house.gov/files/114/PDF/House-Rules-114.pdf.

Russell, Meg, *Reform of the House of Lords: Lessons from Overseas* (Oxford University Press, 2000).

Russell, Meg, 'The Truth about House of Lords Appointments' https://constitution-unit.com/2015/07/29/the-truth-about-house-of-lords-appointments/.

Ryan, Alan, 'Utilitarianism and Bureaucracy: the Views of JS Mill' in Gillian Sutherland (ed), *Studies in the Growth of Nineteenth Century Government* (Routledge & Kegan Paul, 1972) 33–62.

Sandford, Mark, 'Resignation from the House of Commons: A House of Commons Background Paper' (House of Commons Library, 18 July 2013).

Saunders, John, 'Parliamentary Privilege and the Criminal Law' [2017] Crim LR 521.

Schofield, Philip and Harris, Jonathan (eds), *'Legislator of the World': Writings on Codification, Law and Education* (Clarendon Press, 1998).

Seaward, Paul, 'Sleaze, Old Corruption and Parliamentary Reform: An Historical Perspective on the Current Crisis' (2010) 81 Political Quarterly 39.

Searle, John, 'How to Derive "Ought" from "Is"' (1964) 73 The Philosophical Review 43.

Select Committee on Constitutional Affairs, *First Report: The Funding of Political Parties in the UK* http://www.publications.parliament.uk/pa/cm200607/cmselect/cmconst/163/16305.htm#n84.

Select Committee on Members' Interests, *First Report* HC 408 (HMSO, 1984).

Select Committee on Modernisation of the House of Commons, *The Legislative Process, First Report of Session 2005–06*, HC1097 (TSO, 2006).

Sellers, Mortimer, *American Republicanism: Roman Ideology in the United States* (The MacMillan Press, 1994).

Shapiro, Susan, 'Collaring the Crime, Not the Criminal: Reconsidering the Concept of White-Collar Crime' (1990) 55 American Sociological Review 346–365.

Simester, A P and Von Hirsch, Andreas, *Crimes, Harms and Wrongs: On the Principles of Criminalisation* (Hart Publishing, 2011).

Simons, Kenneth W, 'The Crime/Tort Distinction: Legal Doctrine and Normative Perspectives' (2008) 17 Widener Law Journal 719.

Simpson, Thomas W, 'The Impossibility of Republican Freedom' (2017) 45 Philosophy and Public Affairs 27.

Skinner, Quentin, *The Foundations of Modern Political Thought, vol 1, The Renaissance* (Cambridge University Press, 1978).

Smith, Bruce James, *Politics and Remembrance: Republican Themes in Machiavelli, Burke and Tocqueville* (Princeton University Press, 1985).

Sparling, Robert, 'Political Corruption and the Concept of Dependence in Republican Thought' (2013) 41 Political Theory 618.

Spencer, John, 'Policemen Behaving Badly: The Abuse of Misconduct in Office' (2010) 69 Camb LJ 423.

St John, Henry, Viscount Bolingbroke, *A Dissertation upon Parties, vol II* (1794).

Standards and Privileges Committee, *Third Report, Mr Derek Conway MP* (2009) www.publications.parliament.uk/pa/cm200809/cmselect/cmstnprv/207/20702.htm.

Stephen, Sir James, *Digest of the Criminal Law* (4th edn, MacMillan and Co, 1887).

Sunderland, David, 'A Monument to Defective Administration? The London Commissions of Sewers in the Early Nineteenth Century' (1999) 26 Urban History 349.
Sutherland, Edwin, 'White-Collar Criminality' (1940) 5 American Sociological Review 1.
Sutherland, Lucy and Binney, J, ' Henry Fox as Paymaster General of the Forces' (1955) 70 English Historical Review 229.
Tadros, Victor, *The Ends of Harm: The Moral Foundations of Criminal Law* (Oxford University Press, 2011).
Tadros, Victor, 'Fair Labelling and Social Solidarity' in Lucia Zedner and Julian V Roberts (eds), *Principles and Values in Criminal Law and Justice: Essays in Honour of Andrew Ashworth* (Oxford University Press, 2012) ch 5.
Teachout, Zephyr, 'The Anti-Corruption Principle' (2009) 94 Cornell Law Review 340.
Thévoz, Seth Alexander, ' "Every Treasurer of the Party has Gone to the Lords, and I Hope I Don't Set a Precedent by Being the First Who Doesn't": Conservative Party Treasurers and Peerages, 1986–2016' (Gwilym Gibbon Centre Working Paper, 2016) http://ggcpp.nuff.ox.ac.uk/wp-content/uploads/2016/09/Every-Treasurer-of-the-Party-has-Gone-to-the-Lords.pdf.
Thomas, Mr Justice, *Judicial Ethics in Australia* (2nd edn, LexisNexisAustralia, 1997).
Thompson, Dennis F, *Ethics in Congress: From Individual to Institutional Corruption* (The Brookings Institution, 1995).
Todd, Geoffrey, 'Some Aspects of Joint Stock Companies 1844–1900' (1932) 4 The Economic History Review 46.
Toulmin-Smith, Joshua, *Self-Government and Centralisation* (John Chapman, 1851).
TRACE International, 'The High Cost of Small Bribes' (2015) https://www.traceinternational.org/Uploads/PublicationFiles/TheHighCostofSmallBribes2015.pdf.
Transparency International, *Corruption in the UK Part 1: National Opinion Survey* (Transparency International, 2010).
Transparency International, 'Corruption in the UK; Overview and Policy Recommendations' (2011) http://www.transparency.org.uk/publications/corruption-in-the-uk-overview-policy-recommendations/#.Wl8q0a5l_IU.
Transparency International, *Fixing the Revolving Door between Government and Business: Policy Paper Series Number Two* (2012) http://www.transparency.org.uk/publications/policy-paper-series-2-fixing-the-revolving-door-between-government-business/#.Wl8ri65l_IU.
Transparency International, *Global Corruption Barometer 2013* www.transparency.org/gcb2013.
Transparency International, *Lifting the Lid on Lobbying: the Hidden Exercise of Power and Influence in the UK* (2015a) http://www.transparency.org.uk/publications/liftthelid/#.Wl8sx65l_IU.
Transparency International, *Accountable Influence: Bringing Lobbying out of the Shadows* (2015b) http://www.transparency.org.uk/publications/accountable-influence-bringing-lobbying-out-of-the-shadows/#.Wl8tJa5l_IU.
Transparency International, 'What is Corruption?' (2016) https://www.transparency.org/what-is-corruption/#define.
Trenchard, John and Gordon, Thomas, *Cato's Letters* (Liberty Fund, 1995).
Trevelyan, Sir George, *The Early History of Charles James Fox* (Harper, 1880).
United Nations, *Manual on Anti-Corruption Policy* (2001) http://www.unodc.org/pdf/crime/gpacpublications/manual.pdf.
United States House of Representatives (2008) https://ethics.house.gov/staff-rights-and-duties/nepotism.

Van Biezen, Ingrid, 'State Intervention in Party Politics: The Public Funding and Regulation of Political Parties' (2008) 16 European Review 337.
Vermeule, Adrian, 'Contra *Nemo Iudex in Sua Causa*: The Limits of Impartiality' (2012) 122 Yale Law Journal 384.
Walter, John, *Crowds and Popular Politics in Early Modern England* (Manchester University Press, 2006).
Wasik, Martin, 'Computer Misuse and Misconduct in Public Office' (2008) 22 International Review of Law Computers & Technology 135.
Weber, Max, *The Theory of Social and Economic Organisation* (Henderson, S M, and Parsons, Talcot, *trans*, Oxford University Press, 1947).
Wert, Sarah, and Salovey, Peter, 'A Social Comparison Account of Gossip' (2004) 8 Review of General Psychology 122.
West, Darrell, *Checkbook Democracy* (Northeastern University Press, 2000).
Wilks-Heeg, Stuart, 'Revolving Door Politics and Corruption' in David Whyte (ed), *How Corrupt is Britain?* (Pluto Press, 2015) ch 10.
Williams, Martin, *Parliament Ltd: A Journey to the Dark Heart of British Politics* (Hodder and Stoughton, 2016).
Williams, S G, 'Indeterminacy and the Rule of Law' (2004) 24 OJLS 539.
Williams, Terence F, 'Neglect of Duty and Breach of Trust: Ancient Offences in the Modern Battle Against Impunity in the Public Service' (2010) 13 Journal of Money Laundering Control 336.
Winnett, Robert and Rayner, Gordon, *No Expenses Spared* (Transworld, 2009).
World Bank, 'The Fight against Corruption: A World Bank Perspective' (2015) http://investpost.org/options/the-fight-against-corruption-a-world-bank/.
Yeung, Karen, 'Can We Employ Design-based Regulation While Avoiding the *Brave New World*?' (2011) 3 Law, Innovation and Technology 1.

Index